G000124900

SPEAKING TRUTHS TO POWER

CLARENDON STUDIES IN CRIMINOLOGY

Published under the auspices of the Institute of Criminology, University of Cambridge; the Mannheim Centre, London School of Economics; and the Centre for Criminology, University of Oxford.

General Editor: Robert Reiner
(London School of Economics)

Editors: Manuel Eisner, Alison Liebling, and Per-Olof Wikström
(University of Cambridge)

Jill Peay and Tim Newburn
(London School of Economics)

Ian Loader, Julian Roberts, and Lucia Zedner
(University of Oxford)

RECENT TITLES IN THIS SERIES:

Prisoners, Solitude, and Time
Ian O'Donnell

Criminal Careers in Transition: The Social
Context of Desistance from Crime
Stephen Farrall, Ben Hunter, Gilly Sharpe, and Adam Calverley

Hate Crime and Restorative Justice: Exploring
Causes, Repairing Harms
Mark Austin Walters

Policing the Waterfront: Networks, Partnerships,
and the Governance of Port Security
Russell Brewer

Traces of Terror: Counter-Terrorism Law, Policing, and Race
Victoria Sentas

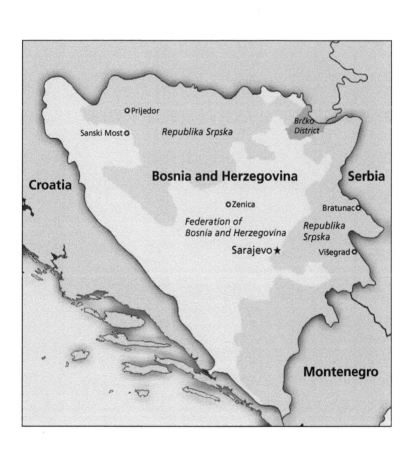

Prijedor

Sanski Most

Republika Srpska

Brčko
District

Bosnia and Herzegovina

Serbia

Croatia

Zenica

Bratunac

Federation of
Bosnia and Herzegovina

Republika
Srpska

Sarajevo ★

Višegrad

Montenegro

Speaking Truths to Power

Policy Ethnography and Police
Reform in Bosnia and Herzegovina

JARRETT BLAUSTEIN

OXFORD
UNIVERSITY PRESS

Great Clarendon Street, Oxford, OX2 6DP,
United Kingdom

Oxford University Press is a department of the University of Oxford.
It furthers the University's objective of excellence in research, scholarship,
and education by publishing worldwide. Oxford is a registered trade mark of
Oxford University Press in the UK and in certain other countries

© Jarrett Blaustein 2015

The moral rights of the author have been asserted

First Edition published in 2015
Impression: 1

Published in the United States of America by Oxford University Press
198 Madison Avenue, New York, NY 10016, United States of America

British Library Cataloguing in Publication Data
Data available

Library of Congress Control Number: 2015931224

ISBN 978–0–19–872329–5

Printed and bound by
CPI Group (UK) Ltd, Croydon, CR0 4YY

Cover Image: © Orhan Cam / shutterstock.com

General Editor's Introduction

Clarendon Studies in Criminology aims to provide a forum for outstanding empirical and theoretical work in all aspects of criminology and criminal justice, broadly understood. The Editors welcome submissions from established scholars, as well as excellent PhD work. The *Series* was inaugurated in 1994, with Roger Hood as its first General Editor, following discussions between Oxford University Press and three criminology centres. It is edited under the auspices of these three centres: the Cambridge Institute of Criminology, the Mannheim Centre for Criminology at the London School of Economics, and the Centre for Criminology at the University of Oxford. Each supplies members of the Editorial Board and, in turn, the Series Editor.

Speaking Truths to Power: Policy Ethnography and Police Reform in Bosnia and Herzegovina by Dr Jarrett Blaustein is an important, highly innovative and illuminating addition to our understanding of contemporary developments in policing and police reform in societies hopefully embarked upon transition from totalitarian to democratic polities, and/or recovering from civil wars. It is based on a period of intense ethnographic fieldwork in Bosnia and Herzegovina. Its empirical heart consists of two case studies, a 'Safer Communities' project, and an attempt to establish 'community policing' in Sarajevo Canton. The community policing venture was based on a Swiss prototype which was itself modelled on what were regarded as the 'best practices' of community policing in Western Europe and the United States. Conducting detailed and sustained ethnographic research on controversial issues like policing in the context of emerging democracies is itself a significant achievement. The case studies are meticulously carried out and reported, providing fascinating insights into both policy-making and attempts to implement it in practice.

Dr Blaustein's achievement is not only this important ethnography in a hard to research environment. It is embedded in an analytic framework that contributes greatly to several expanding and contentious issues not only in policing but in international

development and democratic reform more generally. The core theoretical issue that threads throughout the book is posed clearly
thus: 'How and why do international development workers and
rank-and-file police officers in developing and transitional states
mediate the global convergence of discourse, policies, and practice
relating to crime control and security?'

The key methodological and conceptual tools used to analyse
this are signalled in the book's title: *policy ethnography* and *glocal*. On the one hand, in recent decades the dominant governmental and corporate institutions of the global 'North' have sought to
'liberalize' and 'democratize' emerging political economies in the
global 'South'. Sometimes this has been by coercive means under
a would-be legitimating banner of humanitarian intervention. But
more fundamentally a panoply of soft or at any rate softer power
tools, economic and cultural, have been deployed. A pivotal aspect
of this has been policing and security reform agendas. On the other
hand, the success of these imported models has been questioned
across the spectrum, from those who champion them but complain
of resistance and mishandling by local agents, to critical scholars
and activists who see the models themselves as vehicles for Western
power, displacing local with metropolitan values and knowledge.

Dr Blaustein sees both these perspectives as flawed analyti-
cally and normatively. His lucid yet sophisticated and penetrating
critical review of the literature on democratization and international policing reform qualifies both the top-down optimism of
the policy entrepreneurs, and also the fatalistic pessimism of some
critical theories, by emphasizing the mediating role of local agents,
modifying imported models to local values and needs with varying
degrees of success. The concept of policy transfer, on which there
is a burgeoning criminal justice literature, is reworked as policy
translation, a dialectical process in which meanings are both lost
and found, but never straightforwardly transferred. The polarity
of local and global is similarly supplanted by the idea of the 'glocal' (initiated by Bauman and others), which in the policing field
means 'the idea that glocal policing is crafted through continuous
dialogues between the global and the local'.

These theoretical insights are derived from the empirical case
studies as well as by critical analysis of existing literature. The ethnographic fieldwork suggests that 'while it is accurate to describe
the global structures that give rise to police capacity development
projects as asymmetrical or ideologically-loaded, the institutional

composition of the policy translation networks that facilitate policy convergence is also diverse. This means that the efforts of the so-called architects of global liberal governance to promote the glocalization of policing in weak states are mediated by the actions and interpretations of a diverse array of participants who activate key nodes within these networks' (p. 209). For example, 'The first case study of the Safer Communities project found that international development workers may feel compelled to align their work with what they perceive to be the interests of powerful donors. It also accounted for their attempts to modify policy meaning and content in ways that were thought might resonate with the interests and the understandings of this international audience. Despite the evident effects of this governmentality, the habitus of my colleagues from the Safer Communities project remained primarily responsive to an institutionalized ethos for capacity development. Furthermore, the habitus was interpreted differently by members of the Safer Communities team meaning that their individual backgrounds and experiences shaped their actions and interactions within this contact zone. The cumulative effect of their contributions to the policy translation process was to mitigate the effects of securitization by identifying creative solutions for retaining a local focus for the project. Their reflexive awareness and abilities supported them to this effect and it also allowed them to limit the risk that the project would contribute to harmful or contextually inappropriate outputs' (p. 210).

The overall conclusions from the theoretical and empirical analyses suggest some hope of moving towards democratization, given the observed capacity of local agents to translate global policies into local conditions in some circumstances, although the playing field is far from level and loaded against them. 'It is evident that international development workers and police practitioners can use their agency to support democratically responsive policing in countries like BiH but one must not ignore the elite characterization of the policy translation processes that structure the contours of glocal policing in these contexts' (p. 212). At the same time, 'Northern' criminologists are exhorted to facilitate this 'glocalization'. 'Speaking truths to power describes an agenda for promoting discursive empowerment and representation through criminological research and engagement', eschewing both the imposition of one-size-fits-all models and the pessimistic fatalism that nothing can be done (p. 213).

Dr Blaustein's monograph is an important contribution to several crucial areas of contemporary debate: globalization and democratization of policing most centrally, but beyond this the understanding of policing policy development and implementation in general. Along the way it adds much to specific concerns such as police culture, community policing, and democratic policing. It is a most welcome and valuable addition to the Clarendon Studies in Criminology series.

Robert Reiner
London School of Economics
January 2015

Preface and Acknowledgements

This book has been adapted from a doctoral thesis completed at the School of Law at the University of Edinburgh (2009–2013). The research was funded by a generous studentship awarded by the University of Edinburgh.

I've had many friends ask me, 'what made you decide to complete a PhD on the topic of police reform in Bosnia?' My typical and admittedly lackadaisical response is, 'it seemed like the thing to do at the time'. In preparing this section, I have finally taken the time to reflect on this question and come up with a better response. The idea for the research which forms the basis of this book was born out of my desire to use the theoretical and methodological frameworks that I was first introduced to as a taught postgraduate criminology student at the University of Edinburgh to explore the complex, post-conflict security environments that I learned about as an undergraduate student of international relations at the University of St Andrews. It was my undergraduate lecturer Michael Boyle who first sparked my interest in conflict and security. Had it not been for his stimulating lectures, dutiful supervision, and candid advice about the pros and cons of pursuing a career in academia, I doubt very much that I would have developed the curiosity or the confidence to undertake this research.

Numerous individuals at the University of Edinburgh have subsequently influenced the ideas put forth in this work. I am indebted first and foremost to Andy Aitchison and Alistair Henry who co-supervised my PhD. Andy and Alistair took a genuine interest in my research and my development as a scholar. I am forever indebted to them for their guidance, their friendship, and their ability to 'crack the whip' as was sometimes necessary.

Lesley McAra and Richard Sparks sat on my first year review panel. Their feedback helped me to recognize the value of researching criminal justice policy transfers from an interpretivist perspective at an early stage of the project. Lesley's comments and our subsequent chats have also helped me to appreciate the limitations of deterministic representations of policymaking processes while

Richard's suggestion that I 'keep a field journal' and to treat my experiences and reflections as data played no small part in inspiring the epistemological position of this book. As a postgraduate at the University of Edinburgh, Richard Jones, Susan McVie, and Anna Souhami were also influential in shaping a number of theoretical and methodological ideas that appear in this book, while the research activities of Jo Shaw, Igor Stiks, and their colleagues from the Europeanisation of Citizenship in the Successor States of the Former Yugoslavia (CITSEE) project enabled me to develop my contextual and historical knowledge of Bosnia and Herzegovina and the Western Balkans during the first year of my PhD.

In the second year of the PhD, I was assured by Richard Sparks that my viva would be a memorable experience. Neither of us anticipated at the time that he would act as my internal examiner. Richard was correct in his assurance and my viva, which he conducted with Trevor Jones in March of 2013, proved to be both rigorous and rewarding. It was Richard and Trevor along with my supervisors, Andy and Alistair, who encouraged me to write this book soon after completing the PhD. The book I have produced bears a reasonable resemblance to the thesis, however, it was my subsequent conversations with Richard that have prompted me to explore the wider relevance of policy translation and policy ethnography to the transnational study of criminal justice policymaking and the global governance of crime. Richard's invitation to present my research at the final session of an ESRC seminar series on 'Crime Control and Devolution: Policy-Making and Expert Knowledge in a Multi-Tiered Democracy' also prompted me to conceive of the idea of 'speaking *truths* to power', which I have since selected as the title for this book. Finally, I owe an enormous debt of gratitude to my friends Louise Brangan and Diarmaid Harkin for providing me with detailed, constructive feedback on previous drafts of this manuscript. I look forward to returning the favour someday.

Beyond the 'Auld Reekie', many friends and colleagues have influenced this work. In the first instance I would like to thank my colleagues from the Department of Law and Criminology at Aberystwyth University. I am fortunate enough to have been assigned the one-and-only Richard Ireland as my mentor in the Department. If you are not familiar with Richard's work, you should be. Richard is a well-respected legal historian who has written extensively about the history of crime and punishment in

England and Wales. He has also been known to blame his cat for errors or omissions in his work. More importantly, he is a kind and patient mentor who has helped me to grow as both a scholar and a colleague in the Department. His feedback on the introductory chapter was invaluable as were his insights into the process of writing a book. Richard's modesty and selflessness are a source of inspiration in the increasingly competitive and individualistic world of academia. His expressed belief that writing is a deeply personal endeavour resonated with my own experience of completing a PhD so I have decided to retain the use of the first person throughout this book. Like Richard, I believe that any interpretation, be it historical or ethnographic, is to some degree autobiographical.

I am also fortunate enough to have benefited from the friendship and mentorship of my 'boss' at Aberystwyth, Alan Clarke. The fact that I am not permitted to refer to him as my 'boss' is a testament to his egalitarian outlook and supportive disposition. I am grateful for Alan's ongoing advice and encouragement throughout the writing process and, more specifically, for his comments on a previous version of Chapter 6 and sections of Chapter 2. My colleague Sarah Wydall joined the Department at the same time as I did and our regular conversations about methodology and epistemology have helped me to refine the idea of 'speaking truths to power'. My colleagues Kate Williams and John Williams were my first contacts in the Department and I continue to benefit from their advice and support on a daily basis. Finally, I owe thanks to Chris Harding for commenting on a previous draft of Chapter 6 and for initiating the tradition of Friday afternoon visits to the Ship and Castle. Our pub visits have prompted stimulating discussions about a wide range of matters ranging from the changing nature of academia as a profession to the Pinkertons. Finally, I would like to thank Claudia Hillebrand and Milja Kurki from the Department of International Politics for taking an interest in my work.

Outside of Aberystwyth, I'd like to thank Sarah Armstrong, Ben Bowling, Irma Deljkić, Graham Ellison, Alice Hills, Megan O'Neill, Liam O'Shea, Nathan Pino, Barry Ryan, James Sheptycki, Justice Tankebe and numerous anonymous reviewers for their feedback and advice. There is no space to detail their individual contributions so I hope it suffices to state that many of these individuals have graciously taken the time to meet or correspond with me to discuss my ideas and many have shared their experiences of publishing monographs. On more than one occasion, these colleagues have helped me to access their work in times of need so I hope that this book will make for a worthy contribution to their respective fields of study.

My policy ethnography and field work with the Sarajevo Canton Police would not have been possible without the gracious support of my former colleagues from the Safer Communities team at UNDP in Bosnia and Herzegovina. Their names must be withheld to preserve their anonymity but the 'local development worker' as an archetypical agent of change deserves to be recognized for their efforts to improve the quality of life in countries like Bosnia and Herzegovina amidst challenging and, at times, structurally unjust circumstances. I would also like to thank the Ministry of the Interior for Sarajevo Canton, the Sarajevo Canton Police, the Swiss Agency for Development and Cooperation, and their staffs for affording me access and insights into their worlds. Finally, I am forever indebted to my friend Adnan Fazlić for helping out as an occasional research assistant and interpreter 'in the field'.

I am grateful to Lucy Alexander and the OUP team along with the Clarendon Studies in Criminology editors for their advice, feedback, and assistance throughout the publication process. The author and Oxford University Press would like to thank the following publishers for permission to reproduce material for which they hold copyright: Taylor & Francis for sections of Chapter 5 which appeared in *Policing & Society* as 'The space between: negotiating the contours of security governance via 'Safer Communities' in Bosnia and Herzegovina' 24/1 (2014) 44–62. I would also like to thank Taylor & Francis for allowing me to reproduce sections of Chapter 6 which have been published as 'Community Policing from the "Bottom-Up" in Sarajevo Canton' (Online First in 2014) 1–21. Sections of Chapters 2, 5, and 7 have been adapted from my chapter 'Reflexivity and Participatory Policy Ethnography: Situating the Self in a Transnational Criminology of Harm Production', in: Lumsden, K. and A., Winters (eds) *Reflexivity in Criminological Research* (2014).

On a personal level, I am forever indebted to my wife Laura, our parents, and our extended families, all of whom have supported me emotionally (and at times, financially) while I completed my PhD. Laura knows more about police reform in Bosnia and Herzegovina than any non-specialist ever should. Her love and companionship has been a continuous source of inspiration and so I dedicate this book to her.

In light of these contributions, it seems appropriate for me to conclude with the usual disclaimer. Unlike my colleague Richard Ireland, I do not own a cat so I must take full responsibility for any errors, omissions, or flawed interpretations contained in this book. I do not expect that everybody who reads it will agree with my analysis or support my vision for a global civic criminology which rejects the idea that there is a single, critical truth that is waiting to be revealed and disseminated. I will, however, be very pleased if it stimulates a critical and constructive dialogue about the aims, means, and implications of criminological engagement in transnational fields.

Hvala vam.
Jarrett Blaustein
January 2015

Table of Contents

List of Figures and Tables

Figures

Tables

List of Abbreviations

AVPP	UN Armed Violence Prevention Programme
BiH	Bosnia and Herzegovina
CBP	Community-based Policing
CCTV	Closed-circuit Television
CP	Community Policing
CPO	Community Police Officer
CSF	Citizen Security Forum
CSP	Community Safety Partnership
CSS	Centre for Security Studies (Sarajevo)
DFID	Department for International Development (UK)
ECPN	European Crime Prevention Network
EFUS	European Forum for Urban Security
ESPAD	European School Survey Project on Alcohol and Other Drugs
EU	European Union
EUFOR	European Union Stabilisation Force in Bosnia and Herzegovina
EUPM	European Union Police Mission
FBiH	Federation of Bosnia and Herzegovina
ICG	International Conflict Group
ICITAP	International Criminal Investigation Training Assistance Program
ILO	International Liaison Officer
INTERPOL	International Criminal Police Organization
IPTF	United Nations International Police Task Force
MUP KS	Ministry of the Interior, Sarajevo Canton
MZ	'Mesne Zajednice'(local neighbourhood centre)
NCJRS	National Criminal Justice Reference Service
NGO	Non-governmental Organization
NIT	National Implementation Team
OECD	Organisation for Economic Co-operation and Development
OHR	Office of the High Representative in Bosnia and Herzegovina

OSCE	Organization for Security and Cooperation in Europe
PIC	Peace Implementation Council
PRC	Police Restructuring Commission
RBM	Results-based Management
RDB	Resor Državne Bezbednosti (secret police in SFRY)
RPZ	Rad Policije u Zajednici (Bosnian word for 'community policing')
RS	Republika Srpska
RSC	Regional Security Complex
SACBiH	Small Arms Control and Reduction Project in Bosnia and Herzegovina
SALW	Small Arms and Light Weapons
SARA	'Scanning, Analysis, Response, Assessment'
SBS	State Border Service
SDC	Swiss Agency for Development and Cooperation
SFRY	Socialist Federal Republic of Yugoslavia
SIPA	State Investigation and Protection Agency
SSAJP	DFID Safety, Security and Access to Justice Programme
SSR	Security Sector Reform
UN	United Nations
UN CIVPOL	International Civilian Police
UNDP	United Nations Development Programme
UNFPA	United Nations Population Fund
UNMBiH	United Nations Mission in Bosnia and Herzegovina
UNSC	United Nations Security Council

1

Introduction

When I first arrived in Sarajevo, Bosnia and Herzegovina (BiH) in 2010, I noticed the phrase 'Fuck the Police!!!' graffitied on the side of a shed in what looked like a peaceful residential neighbourhood named Grbavica (see Figure 1.1). The meaning of this phrase appeared to be self-evident and one can reasonably assume that it carries strong cross-cultural resonance. What intrigued me about this tag was that the 'artist' decided to make this proclamation in English, the 'international language' of Sarajevo, rather than translate it into a 'local language': Bosnian, Croatian, or Serbian. Perhaps this decision reflected the individual's contempt for the upwardly-responsive nature of the governance of security and, indeed, governance in general. In other words, maybe the intended audience was not the local police but, rather, representatives of the international community who have been present in the country since 1996. Or perhaps the 'artist' assumed that 'local' police officers would be able to decipher the message and take offence, despite their limited knowledge of the English language. A more mundane explanation might be that an individual with an appreciation for American gangsta rap from the late 1980s[1] and a desire to impress their friends created the tag on a whim, possibly after consuming a few too many shots of 'rakija'.[2]

The point is this: I wasn't there so I lack the ability to meaningfully interpret the circumstances or the decision-making process that resulted in the tag's creation. Tempting as it is to discuss the tag as a sign of disaffection and resistance to the perceived structural injustices of police development assistance programmes being implemented throughout the developing world, the absence of ethnographic detail obscures the complex interplay between the individual, cultural, and structural factors that prompted an

---

[1] The song 'Fuck tha Police' was released by the hip hop group N.W.A. in 1988.
[2] Rakija refers to local brandy which is widely available in South East Europe.

Figure 1.1 'Fuck the Police!!!' (2010)

individual, or perhaps even a group of individuals, to scribe 'Fuck the Police!!!' on the side of a shed in Sarajevo. Accordingly, the first aim of this book is to initiate a new direction in ethnographic research on a particular aspect of transnational policing: police development assistance. The second aim is to initiate a critical and reflexive dialogue about the purpose and potential implications of 'Northern' criminological engagement with transnational policy communities.[3]

---

[3] The distinction between 'Northern' and 'Southern' criminologists emphasizes the development status of their countries of full-time employment. It is not strictly geographic. For example, criminologists working at world-class universities in Australia or New Zealand might be classed as 'Northern' insofar as they can be said to represent what Connell (2007) identifies as the 'metropole' (as opposed to the 'periphery'). Distinguishing between 'Northern'/'Southern' or 'metropolitan'/'peripheral' criminology is admittedly overly simplistic (see Aas 2012) and there is reason to consider how different aspects of a researcher's biography and identity shape their understandings, dictate the resources available to them (which, for example, may determine their ability to engage with relevant international networks), and, thus, influence global discourses about crime, policing, and security. The underlying assumption, however, is that 'Northern' criminologists have access to resources that are not available to 'Southern' criminologists and this enhances their relative discursive influence within the field.

The concepts of 'policy ethnography' (Yanow 1997), 'interactive globalisation' (Cain 2000), and 'policy translation' (Lendvai and Stubbs 2009) provide the methodological and conceptual tools that I use to illuminate the capacity of seemingly disempowered reformers and practitioners to structure the mentalities and practices of local policing through their involvement in active, transnational police development assistance projects. Policy ethnography is a methodology which recognizes that the administrative spaces through which policies are formulated and take on meaning can be studied empirically as important and contested sites of power (Mosse 2005; Shore and Wright 1997; Yanow 1997). The concept is drawn from the field of policy anthropology which 'provides a new avenue for studying the localization of global processes in the contemporary world' by seeking to access, interpret, and ultimately reconstruct the 'contested political' character of these spaces using 'multi-site ethnographies' and discourse analysis (Shore and Wright 1997: 15).

The concept of 'interactive globalisation' (Cain 2000), elsewhere referred to as 'glocalisation', describes the idea that the global increasingly influences the local but that the local inevitably exerts a mediating influence upon the convergent pressures generated by the global. By extension, the term 'glocal policing', at least as it is used in this book, accounts for the sociological fact that in countries around the world (including advanced liberal democracies), a constant interplay between global and local influences have come to structure both the governance and provision of what Reiner (2010: 5) describes as 'the set of activities aimed at preserving the security of a particular social order, or social order in general'. In other words, all policing is now 'glocal' because the orders it seeks to secure, the social conflicts it must respond to, and the means by which they are addressed are, to varying degrees, structured by supranational influences. As discussed in the following chapter, however, this is not the same as arguing that all policing is global.

The concept of 'policy translation' (Lendvai and Stubbs 2009), as opposed to 'policy transfer' (Dolowitz and Marsh 1996), highlights the potential utility of employing a policy ethnography approach to study institutional dynamics of convergence, modification, and resistance associated with interactive globalization. Simply, the concept of 'policy translation' recognizes that '...a series of interesting, and sometimes even surprising disturbances can occur in the spaces between the "creation", the "transmission" and the "interpretation" or "reception" of policy meanings' (Lendvai and Stubbs 2007: 4). Situating one's self within these spaces enables a researcher to actively interpret the 'glocal' interactions that ascribe form and meaning to certain policies. The empirical content of this book consists of case studies of two different police reform projects that were actively being pursued in BiH at the time of my fieldwork in 2011. It is impossible for a researcher to embed themselves throughout the entire policy translation process so they must work to generate detailed 'snapshots' of key moments or stages. For policy translation researchers, the sampling approach that is used to identify and access these 'snapshots' is generally one of convenience and opportunity. Accordingly, my case studies focus on different stages of distinct, albeit mutually-aware community-oriented policing projects. Participatory methods were used to generate the first case study which considers how members of the United Nations Development Programme's (UNDP) 'Safer Communities' project in BiH shaped the contours of an 'off-the-shelf model' for governing local security. Non-participatory methods,[4] including observation and ethnographic interviewing, were used for the second case study which considers how local community police officers (henceforth 'RPZ officers') were working to implement, or impede upon the implementation of, a community policing project developed by a Swiss organization in BiH.

I discuss my methodology at greater length in Chapter 4 but it is worth initially stating that BiH was selected as the context for this research because the country was identified as a paradigmatic example of a transitional, post-conflict society that is governed by an internationally-driven process of liberal state-building. The country is a former constituent republic of the Socialist Federal Republic of Yugoslavia (SFRY) which is bordered by Croatia to the north and west, Serbia to the east, and Montenegro to the South. It is a multi-ethnic country in the sense that it features significant populations of Bosniaks (Bosnian Muslims), Bosnian Croats, and Bosnian Serbs as well as smaller Jewish, Roma, and Chinese

---

[4] I recognize that my status as a researcher employing ethnographic methods rendered me a 'participant' in the sense that my presence, interactions, and interpretations structured the field. By presenting this distinction between 'participatory' and 'non-participatory' methods, my emphasis is on one's ability or inability to assume aspects of the role of informants.

populations. The last census taken in 1991 indicates that none of these populations formed an absolute majority. In April 1992, BiH declared its independence from the SFRY. During the three years which followed, the country experienced a particularly brutal interethnic conflict that prompted the international community to intervene and broker the Dayton Peace Agreement in December 1995. The Dayton Peace Agreement marked an end to the Bosnian War but its constitutional prescriptions have been criticized for establishing fragmented and dysfunctional political institutions (McMahon and Western 2009), creating dependency on the international community (Belloni 2001), and establishing the country as an international protectorate (Chandler 1999; Knaus and Martin 2003). It prescribed a weak central government that is based in the country's political capital of Sarajevo, two entity-level governments (Federation of Bosnia and Herzegovina and Republika Srpska) and the Brčko District. The entity-level government of the Republika Srpska (RS) is highly centralized and 'is vested with all state functions and powers which are not expressly granted to the central Government of Bosnia and Herzegovina' while that of the Federation of Bosnia and Herzegovina (FBiH) is subdivided into ten administrative cantons, each with its own governing institutions.[5]

The country is also historically significant with respect to the development of the Western police reform literature. It was in part due to the work of the United Nations International Police Task Force (IPTF) following the Bosnian War (1992–1995) that the mantra of 'democratic policing' emerged as what is today a universal prescription for pursuing police reforms in transitional and developing countries around the world (see Bayley 2006: 7–8). Since 1996, international police reforms have played an important role in enabling the transposition of a particular variant of liberal order through security governance at the national and sub-national levels. This order was primarily constructed to reflect the interests of BiH's primary supranational architect and benefactor since 2003: the European Union (EU). It has been less responsive to the interests or the needs of BiH citizens or of constitutionally

---

[5] See 'Bosnia Herzegovina'. Division of Powers. European Union Committee of the Regions, n.d. Web. 08 Apr 2014. Available: <https://portal.cor.europa.eu/divisionpowers/countries/Potential-Candidates/BAH/Pages/default.aspx> [Accessed 6 June 2014].

established governing institutions, which as the 2014 protests associated with the seemingly short-lived 'Bosnian Spring' indicate, are themselves perceived to be ill-responsive by BiH citizens.

Throughout this book, reference is made to Brodeur's (1983; 2010) distinction between 'high' and 'low' policing. High policing refers to state-level policing designed to 'protect national security' while 'low policing' describes 'everyday policing performed by uniformed agents and detectives' (Brodeur 2010: 224). One effect of the political fragmentation produced by the Dayton Peace Agreement is that the governance of low policing in BiH is decentralized. Each canton in FBiH has its own police while RS has one centralized police organization that is accountable to the entity-level government. This means that the implementation of local policing reforms has not been uniform and a significant degree of internal variation exists in terms of police capabilities and practices (ICG 2005). The fragmented political structures also mean that the high policing capacities of the BiH state were initially rather limited. As of 2012, the state-level agency that deals with issues relating to organized crime and terrorism is the State Investigation and Protection Agency (SIPA) which forms part of the state's Ministry of Security.[6]

In addition to the various policing agencies and state, entity, and cantonal governmental institutions that are formally charged with governing security in BiH, other security nodes can be identified in relation to the various international actors and institutions involved with policing reforms since the late 1990s. These actors primarily populate nodes involved with what Wood and Shearing (2006: 115) describe as the 'governance of governance' meaning that they are not formal participants in legislative processes and nor do they actively contribute to the provision of policing.[7] Rather, their role involves influencing these processes from a distance by lending their policy expertise, resources, and

---

[6] At the state level, there also exists the BiH Border Guards (previously the State Border Service) that was officially activated in June 2000.

[7] A possible exception is the Integrated Police Unit of the European Union Force ALTHEA (EUFOR) which is mandated to 'conduct operations in support of BiH Law Enforcement Authorities, as well as in cooperation with other International actors or even autonomously'. See 'IPU—Integrated Police Unit'.

influence to various initiatives that relate to the local governance of security. They also play an important role in facilitating policy transfers that seek to 'democratize' the police in BiH
and improve its institutional capacities.[8] Examples of particularly influential nodal actors in BiH include major multi-lateral
supranational institutions like the European Commission,
the European Union Police Mission (EUPM), the Office of the
High Representative in BiH (OHR) and the Organization for
Security and Cooperation in Europe (OSCE). Also important
are: multi-lateral international development organizations like
UNDP, international non-governmental organizations such as
the Saferworld Group; and bilateral development organizations
like the UK's Department for International Development (DFID)
and the Swiss Agency for Development and Cooperation (SDC).
Collectively, these organizations have contributed to the development and implementation of grass-roots community policing
reform initiatives in BiH and have been described as important
activators of liberal governmentality in the country (Ryan 2011;
see Chapter 2).

The EU is chief amongst the supranational architects of
state-building and police reform processes in BiH (Buzan and
Wæver 2003). Although the EUPM concluded in June 2012,
the EU continues to play an indirect role in dictating the agenda
for police reform in BiH. This agenda is implemented by proxy
through the work of the EU's Special Representative to BiH, the
OHR, and various international organizations including (to name
but a few) the OSCE, UNDP, and the SDC. Since 2004, these agencies have worked to implement an upwardly-responsive policing
agenda designed to align the governance and provision of public policing in BiH with the EU's interest in securing its periphery and eventually preparing BiH for accession to the EU (Juncos
2007). It remains questionable whether this aspiration has actually been realized empirically in relation to the policy outputs and
outcomes generated by different police reform projects. Doubts
about transferability, impact, and sustainability are particularly
evident from a handful of community policing initiatives that have

Available: <http://www.euforbih.org/index.php?option=com_content&view=art
icle&id=626:ipu&catid=187&Itemid=87> [Accessed: 30 July 2012].

[8] A more detailed critique of democracy promotion in the sphere of policing is
provided in Chapter 2.

been introduced in BiH since 2003 (see, for example, Deljkić and Lučić-Ćatić 2011).[9]

The case studies presented in this book speak to the complexities of transnational policing networks and the police reform projects they generate. They also highlight the transformational capacities of structurally disempowered actors and institutions who occupied key sites of power within these networks. My argument is that the mentalities, the practices, and the 'habituses' (Bourdieu 1968)[10] which collectively constitute police development assistance programmes are shaped by translational processes which have been largely overlooked by macro-structural critiques of global policing (Bowling and Sheptycki 2012) and international police reform projects (Ellison and Pino 2012; Ryan 2011).[11] These translational processes enable different policy actors to participate in the 'crafting of transnational policing' (Goldsmith and Sheptycki 2007) by imparting their preferences and designs upon local policing institutions. However, one cannot simply assume that the policy outputs which result from policy translation processes structure policy outcomes in predictable ways. Rather, the outcomes and the outputs they generate inevitably come to reflect the culturally and historically structured interests and understandings of actors involved with different stages of the policy translation process. This means that the conceptual and programmatic features of 'Western'-inspired community policing models are 'simultaneously lost and *discovered* in translation' (paraphrasing Melossi, Sozzo, and Sparks, 2011: 1 original emphasis). This

---

[9] These are examined in greater detail in Chapter 3.

[10] By habitus, I refer to the structured mentalities and dispositions that shape the practices and perceptions of individuals. This simplified definition of habitus draws from definitions by Elias (2000) and Bourdieu (1968; 1977). It is intended to emphasize the idea that habitus is shaped by the continuous interplay between structure and agency and between objective and subjective forces. The idea is that these seemingly diametrically opposed concepts are in practice mutually reinforcing and a key determinant of power. Both Elias (2000) and Bourdieu (1977) dismiss objectivist, structural theories which present habitus as 'a vague notion that mechanically replicates social structures' (quoting Wacquant 2011: 82) and subjective, constructivist theories of habitus (see Sartre 2003) which overstate the case for the rational free will of individuals while overlooking the important role that social structures play in shaping their mentalities and expectations of what it means to be rational and what it means to be free. The implication is that both Elias (2000) and Bourdieu (1977) treat habitus as mutable.

[11] These works are reviewed in Chapter 2.

view is consistent with aspects of Hills's (2012*a*: 92) work on police reform in Nigeria in which she concludes that a 'globalising security culture' does not exist because the work of 'globalising security structures', including the United Nations, are mediated by 'elite decision makers in an intermediary state ... [who] construct, exercise, and validate adaptive forms of security knowledge that are best described as hybrid'. Whereas Hills's research focuses on the transformative agency of politicians and senior police managers, this book is concerned with that of the international development worker and the local rank-and-file police officer.

Chapter 2 begins by reviewing the relationship between global liberal governance and police development assistance as a driver of police capacity-building commonly pursued in developing and transitional countries. Key critical themes that are touched upon in this trans-disciplinary review include: the relationship between development and security discourses since the collapse of the Soviet Union; the relationship between global policing and global liberal governance; their impact on 'glocal' order in developing and transitional countries; the transnational networks that foster this ordering process; the relationship between 'democratic policing' and legitimate policing; the political disempowerment which is argued to result from police capacity-building projects; and the possibility that this particular variant of transnational policing power may generate harms in recipient societies. The chapter concludes by considering the idea of 'speaking truth to power' (Scraton 2011) and its centrality to the development of what Bowling (2011: 374) identifies as a 'transnational criminology of harm production' that seeks to 'document the harms produced by global crime control practices'.

In Chapter 3, I relate these themes to the police reform process in BiH. The discussion in Chapter 2 and the account of the police reform process in BiH in Chapter 3 indicate that the international community's role in governing security in BiH has, at times, undermined the prospect of establishing 'democratically responsive' police institutions in weak and structurally dependent societies. In a paper published with Aitchison, I have previously argued that a key determinant of whether a police service is democratically responsive involves the qualified[12] question of

---

[12] Aitchison and I identify these qualifiers as equity and a minimum level of service delivery (see Aitchison and Blaustein 2013: 500).

whether its governance and activities are primarily responsive to the interests of its demos (see Aitchison and Blaustein 2013). It is in relation to Andrew Kuper's (2006: 103–4) work on global democracy that we identified 'responsiveness' as *the* key determinant of democratic governance. Kuper's work identifies two dimensions to democratic responsiveness: horizontal and vertical. Aitchison and I summarize both forms of responsiveness in the excerpt below:

Vertical responsiveness describes a situation in which the 'reasonable contestations' of citizens generate a 'proper response' from those in positions of authority. This is not a case of simple acquiescence to the demands of a majority, or a particularly vocal minority, and responses may vary from explanation through to policy change (Kuper 2006: 104). Horizontal responsiveness captures the checks and balances between political actors and institutions. The fact that a range of authorities are interdependent encourages them to build consensus and operate together (Kuper 2006: 103). Kuper aims to sketch out a structural arrangement whereby the aspirations of deliberative theorists might be realised. (Aitchison and Blaustein 2013: 498)

Kuper's (2006) work indicates that responsiveness accounts for something more than acquiescence with a generally expressed will. In other words, responsiveness must exist as a deliberative process because 'no individual actor can claim perfect knowledge [so] constellations of "knowers" are forced into mutual responsiveness' (quoting Aitchison and Blaustein 2013: 498).

Chapter 4 elaborates on the concept of 'policy translation' and reviews the methodology used to generate ethnographic data for this research. Specifically, it discusses the possibility of studying this phenomenon using participatory and non-participatory ethnographic methods.

Chapter 5 introduces UNDP's Safer Communities project in BiH by reviewing the institutional context and organizational culture at UNDP as well as the origins of the project before presenting my interpretive analysis of this 'contact zone'. My analysis which follows indicates that the nodal positioning of the project afforded members of the Safer Communities team meaningful opportunities to shape the policy discourses surrounding community safety and community policing reform in BiH and, thus, opportunities to promote policy prescriptions and support project activities that reflected UNDP's capacity development ethos more than the security-driven agenda of supranational donors which is the focus of Chapter 2.

Chapter 6 reflects on the implementation phase of the SDC community policing project in Sarajevo Canton. It begins by contextualizing the SDC's involvement with police reform activities in Sarajevo and details the specific community policing model prescribed for transplant in this context. It contrasts the experiences of two different community policing units working to implement the model in order to consider the degree to which it resonated with local cultural and contextual understandings of police work. The theme of translation is illustrated throughout the chapter in relation to the observed capacity of rank-and-file police officers to use their agency and discretion to potentially enhance or negate its resonance.

Chapter 7 concludes by summarizing my key findings as they relate to my three main research questions. The first question is: how do international development workers and rank-and-file police officers operating in developing and transitional states translate the expectations of external, global bodies into local policing policy and practice? The second question relates to whether the translational abilities of international development workers and rank-and-file police officers might support democratically responsive policing outcomes in countries like BiH. The third question considers how future Northern criminological engagement with transnational policy communities might foster a better transnational politics of crime and security.

To summarize, my argument in response to the first question is that global cultural and structural inequalities which privilege international interests over the needs of local policy recipients are not deterministic of the work of international reformers or rank-and-file police officers. Imbalances do exist but so do opportunities for motivated and reflexively aware policymakers and practitioners to mitigate the potential consequences of their work and improve its resonance with local circumstances. With respect to the second question, my case studies indicate that the policy translation process itself may be used to foster greater deliberation between diverse groups of stakeholders involved with different stages of a reform. Additionally, the case studies suggest that scholars and reformers should not be too quick to dismiss the deliberative credentials of certain community-oriented policing models and the mentalities which accompany them.

In response to the final question, my argument is that Northern criminologists who decide to insert themselves in transnational fields have a responsibility to use their research to 'speak *truths to power*' rather than a single 'truth' (see also Blaustein 2014a). Epistemologically, the researcher who speaks truths to power attempts to do so by assuming the role of what Kvale (1996: 3–4) labels the 'traveller' (as opposed to that of the 'miner'). In other words, they must use their research to '[ask] questions that lead [participants] to tell their own stories of their lived world, and [converse] with them in the original Latin meaning of conversation as 'wandering together with' (Kvale 1996: 4). The researcher's reflexive awareness thus compels them to reject the belief that 'knowledge is waiting in the [participant's] interior to be unconverted, uncontaminated by the miner' (Kvale 1996: 3).

Embracing this perspective is necessary for confronting what Aas (2011: 410) identifies as the 'duality' of transnational criminological engagement: 'its democratic potential and hegemonic undertones'. It therefore provides a resource for actualizing Loader and Sparks's (2010) vision for a 'civic criminology' at the global level by fostering conditions that are conducive to what Dryzek (2006) describes as 'transnational discursive democracy', a variant of deliberative democracy. In Dryzek's words (2006: 27):

> ...deliberation occurs whenever participants are amenable to changing their minds as a result of reflection induced by non-coercive communication. Deliberation only becomes deliberative democracy to the degree that it provides opportunities for participation by all those affected by a decision.

With this in mind, the long-term aim of a global civic criminology is to make a modest contribution to the development of a better transnational politics of crime by identifying and supporting opportunities for seemingly disempowered stakeholders, notably Southern scholars, policymakers, and practitioners, to participate in the deliberative processes through which transnational criminology and transnational policing as fields of scholarship, policy, and practice are crafted. In cases where the prospects for encouraging direct or indirect participation are limited, a global civic criminology can benefit from Dryzek's (2010) advocacy of discursive representation within transnational networks of governance. In other words, if it is not viable for all relevant stakeholders to exercise their political agency within a particular policy node, deliberative democracy may still be said to exist within a network of governance to the degree that it accommodates a plurality of discourses which relate to the particular issue. The idea of discursive representation is grounded in a recognition of both the practical limitations of fostering political participation in many sites of governance as well as a normative belief that 'there are times when it may be more important for the quality of deliberation that all relevant discourses get represented, rather than that all individuals get represented' (Dryzek 2010: 44).[13]

For researchers with modest ambitions and limited resources, policy ethnography and the conceptual framework of policy translation may be used to support this critical-yet-constructive agenda. For those with loftier aspirations and better resources, a future aim might be to identify, develop, and evaluate innovative methods for either improving participation or systematically activating a diverse array of under-represented discourses within transnational networks of crime control governance. Even in the absence of meaningful opportunities for improving direct or indirect participation within these sites of power, Northern criminologists may nonetheless be able to use their influence and resources to enhance discursive representation. Doing so is essential for promoting balanced and legitimate policy deliberations which account for the interests and understandings of global and local stakeholders when it comes to the global governance of crime and security.

---

[13] Dryzek (2010: 31) defines a discourse as 'a set of concepts, categories and ideas that will always feature particular assumptions, judgements, contentions, dispositions, intentions, and capabilities'.

2

Police Capacity Building

The term 'glocalization' is helpful for conceptualizing the phenomenon of 'globalization' as 'interactive rather than hegemonic' (paraphrasing Cain 2000: 252). Giddens (1990: 64) describes globalization as '...the intensification of worldwide social relations which link distant localities in such a way that local happenings are shaped by events occurring many miles away and vice versa'. Implicit in this description is the idea that globalization represents a two-way process. The global increasingly structures the local but the local invariably mediates the structuring effects of the global. This emphasis on two-way interaction is also central to Bauman's (2013: 2) description of glocalization as 'local repair workshops servicing and recycling the output of global factories of problems'. Indeed, the quote from Bauman illuminates the possibility that the local may be prompted to act in response to 'problems' generated by globalization.[1]

By extension, the phenomenon of 'glocal policing' is described by Bowling (2010: 111; paraphrasing Cain 2000: 251) as policing that is 'indigenous but globally aware'. Glocal policing has been theorized as a sub-category of 'global policing' by Bowling and Sheptycki (2012: 8) who define the latter as '...the capacity to use coercive and surveillant powers around the world in ways that pass right through national boundaries unaffected by them'. This description of global policing implies the existence of global structural hegemonies and, contra to Cain's (2000: 252) description of the interactive nature of globalization, it seemingly understates the

---

[1] Chapter 1 of Ellison and Pino's (2012) *Globalization, Police Reform and Development* provides an excellent review of the structural problems generated by 'neoliberal globalisation' and the destabilizing effect that these have on countries in the developing world. They write, 'uneven development can promote global risks involving ecological hazards, financial instability, and technological change' (Ellison and Pino 2012: 13).

regularity of balanced interactions occurring between the global and the local when it comes to the use of 'coercive and surveillant powers'. In order to reconcile the interactive nature of glocal policing with the hegemonic quality of global policing, it is necessary to revisit Brodeur's (1983; 2010) distinction between 'high' and 'low policing'. Specifically, it is necessary to consider that opportunities for 'glocal' interaction may be limited in relation to transnational high policing activities that have limited visibility or are of direct strategic significance to powerful international interests who may be tempted to draw from their coercive authority in the absence of legitimate authority for the purpose of pursuing their security aims. By contrast, a growing body of research on police development assistance projects in developing and transitional states which I review in this chapter illustrates that opportunities for interaction do exist in relation to the transnational policy communities that seek to develop the capacities of low policing in these contexts.

My aim is therefore to illuminate the relationship between global liberal governance, glocal policing, and police capacity building projects. The chapter begins by discussing how the emergence of 'global liberal governance' and the normative convergence of 'development' and 'security' agendas in the age of globalization (Duffield 1999; 2007) have precipitated a series of international interventions used to transpose liberal orders upon and within weak and unstable countries. Liberal state-building accounts for one specific method of intervention that has been applied to BiH since 1996. This intervention has been characterized as asymmetrical and coercive in relation to its governing structures which are primarily responsive to supranational interests rather than the needs of local citizens. Similar criticisms have also been levelled at the international development community which plays an indirect role in supporting BiH's liberal 'transformation' by promoting what are marketed as 'bottom-up' reforms. By the late 1990s, police reform emerged as an attractive 'market' for international development agencies who embraced the logic that development and security were mutually dependent aims.[2]

---

[2] Western involvement in police reform projects in developing countries predates the paradigm of global liberal governance but the convergence of development and security discourses in the 1990s has rendered police development an attractive market (see Ellison and Sinclair 2013).

Following this review, I proceed to examine established critiques of the international community's attempts to promote 'democratic policing' in developing and transitional societies. It considers the relationship between global policing and police development assistance and proceeds to deconstruct the concept of 'democratic policing' by distinguishing it from the idea of 'legitimate policing'. This is followed by a review of two influential templates for promoting 'democratic policing' from the 'bottom-up' in the developing world: community policing and community safety partnerships (CSPs). A further review of the work of Ellison and Pino (2012) and Ryan (2011) suggest that these initiatives are invariably tainted by coercive and asymmetrical power structures thereby constituting mechanisms of global liberal governmentality. The implication is that international police development assistance projects aspire to control rather than empower their intended recipients. In some instances, the literature suggests that the outputs generated by transnational policing agents who share a collective world view (Bowling and Sheptycki 2012) may even be harmful or 'iatrogenic' for host countries (Cohen 1988a; also Bowling 2011). I conclude the chapter by arguing that these critiques and Bowling's advocacy of a 'transnational criminology of harm production' establish an important future direction pursuing empirical research on international police reform projects as mechanisms for expanding glocal policing power.

Global Liberal Governance and Governmentality

I first turn to the discipline of international relations and field of critical security studies in order to contextualize the convergence of development and security discourses in the 1990s. Mark Duffield (1999) attributes this convergence to the demise of 'Third Worldism' and the subsequent collapse of the bipolar international system beginning in the 1980s. As a result of this important shift in the ideological power structure of the international system, characterized by the advent of what Fukuyama (1992) would enthusiastically and prematurely describe as 'the end of history', Duffield (1999: 30) argues that 'development', be it economic, political, or social, emerged as an important strategy for consolidating liberal power and securing the preservation of liberal peace as prescribed by 'networks of global liberal governance'. In other words, the ideal of liberal peace developed in tandem with the assumption that the causes of international conflict are inherently linked to underdevelopment rather than global structural inequalities. Development has since been embraced by representatives of the international community as a strategy for not only reducing the risk of conflict in underdeveloped states, but also as a mechanism for preserving the integrity of the emergent liberal status quo (Duffield 1999:112).

In relation to this envisioned global liberal order, Duffield (2007) argues that a broadened definition of security has been embraced by both international policy circles and by prominent academics working in the field of international relations (for example, Doyle 1983; 2011). This broadened definition has emphasized the idea that threats to international security are no longer limited to conventional military conflict between sovereign states but now also include threats to 'human security' (Kaldor 2007). Duffield (2007: 112) writes that the idea of human security implies 'a more diffuse and multiform threat associated with alienation, breakdown and insurgency emanating from the nominal populations of Southern states'. For powerful international actors of the global North, facilitating the development of weak states through financial assistance represents an appealing strategy for regulating the risk of underdevelopment leading to conflict. Managing this risk is thought to be important due to the assumption that localized conflicts can produce a ripple effect and threaten regional and global stability.[3]

Before I expand on Duffield's (2007) discussion of global liberal governance, it is worth accounting for the various actors that collectively shape the contours of global liberal order and security. Rather than associating global governance with a single state hegemon, Buzan and Wæver (2003) argue that prescriptions for global liberal order are constructed through negotiated geo-political processes involving an array of 'regional security complexes' (henceforth 'RSC'). Examples of RSCs include the United States and the EU. Buzan and Wæver (2003: 491) define

---

[3] Dryzek (2006: Chapter 1) argues that a similar doctrine of 'prevention and pre-emption' also underpins the popularization of a 'counter-terror discourse' which emerged in the aftermath of the 9/11 attacks. His analysis thus suggests that global liberal governance cannot be reduced to a single hegemonic discourse but, rather, exists as the product of the continuous interactions between several influential discourses (e.g. 'market liberalism', 'globalization', 'neoconservatism', and 'human rights' to name a few).

RSCs as 'set[s] of [political] units' whose security interests 'are so interlinked that their security problems cannot be reasonably analysed or resolved apart from one another'. They are said to shape the contours of global governance by using their regional influence to structure the international community's response to specific issues or disruptions that affect their spheres of influence. This analysis is consistent with Bowling and Sheptycki's (2012: 23) discussion of the polycentric power structures that shape the contours of global policing and Andreas and Nadelmann's (2008: 21) claim that 'global prohibition regimes' are shaped by various actors that include governments 'able to exert hegemonic influence in a particular issue area' and 'transnational moral entrepreneurs' with self-interested motives for promoting and advancing particular definitions for liberal order.

The degree of influence enjoyed by these actors varies between different geopolitical contexts. For example, a regional security hegemon like the European Union plays a relatively greater role in shaping the agenda for regional security in proximate regions while the United States or China appear to enjoy greater hegemonic influence when it comes to issues of global significance. The EU's influence over regional security politics has been historically evident in the Western Balkans where the polity has played the leading role in shaping agendas for governance and security since the early 2000s. It's primary interest in overseeing the governance of this region is directly linked with its interest in securing its periphery and its concern that political instability and conflict in countries like BiH and Kosovo may generate a 'ripple effect' with possible implications for EU member states (Buzan and Wæver 2003: 357–9).

The emphasis on securing liberal peace has thereby established a powerful impetus for the 'architects' of global liberal governance to justify their interventions in the domestic affairs of states determined to be at risk of conflict. Duffield (1999: 11) notes that during the early 1990s, this was primarily evident from 'humanitarian interventions' and by the the late 1990s, it was broadened to include the oversight of 'conflict resolution and post-war reconstruction'. Duffield describes this paradigm as 'the new humanitarianism' and suggests that it embodies the belief that international interventions have an 'ameliorative, harmonising and transformational power' that can 'reduce violent conflict and prevent its recurrence' (Duffield 1999: 11). Chandler (1999: 13) adds that the new humanitarianism reflects an emergent consensus in international policymaking circles whereby '...new democracies are seen to be so fragile that, "even without any immediate or direct threat", they may be susceptible to collapse'. In other words, this mentality demonstrates the international community's embrace of a 'regulatory' approach to promoting and supporting democratization. At the core of this approach is the belief that '[w]ithout the cultural preconditions of civil society, the institutions of liberal democracy are seen to be little more than window-dressing' (Chandler 1999: 10).

In the age of global liberal governance, the new humanitarianism assumes that the autonomy of the liberal, democratic sovereign states is problematic. This is because there is no guarantee that local democratic processes will independently and autonomously generate legislation or policies consistent with global prescriptions for liberal order. Accordingly, Chandler (2010: 3) argues that the autonomy of developing and transitional states in particular is treated as a threat to global liberal order 'rather than the unproblematic starting assumption'. It is in relation to this mentality that a paradigm of international intervention with a transformative emphasis on both liberal state-building (also referred to as 'nation-building') and democratization has emerged over the past two decades.[4]

Historically, Duffield (2007: 7) writes that there exists no 'essential relationship between liberalism and democracy'. Rather, liberalism represents a technology of government but not necessarily of democratic governance. He illustrates this claim in relation to the apparent contradiction between the emergence of liberal democratic forms of government in Western Europe during the nineteenth century and the persistence of 'non-representative and despotic forms of imperial rule overseas' (Duffield 2007: 7). This 'paradox', argues Duffield, has historically been resolved through the notion of a 'developmental trusteeship', a liberal construct which he argues 'has once again entered the political foreground following the renewed wave of Western humanitarian and peace interventionism of the post-Cold War period' (Duffield 2007: 7). The coercive and asymmetrical character of international interventions

---

[4] The terms 'nation-building' and 'state-building' will be used interchangeably in this book to refer to 'a mechanism of ongoing relationship management which is capable of ameliorating the problems of autonomy, or of government, through the extension of internationalized mechanisms of government' (Chandler 2010: 2).

designed to promote this 'new humanitarianism' is particularly evident in the case of liberal state-building projects.

In relation to liberal state-building initiatives of the past two-decades, Chandler (1999: 3) writes that the discourses associated with democratization have emphasized 'building the capacity of individuals to be able to use their already existing autonomy safely and unproblematically'. In other words, democratization as a focus of liberal state-building is not concerned with generating political freedom at the grass-roots level. Rather, it aspires to align local mentalities with global interests. This helps to ensure that political sovereignty does not conflict with global liberal order and the interests of the actors who seek to shape its contours. To promote this alignment, international actors exercise their coercive powers to shape domestic governance in weak and structurally dependent societies like BiH. Thus, while political democratization represents an important rhetorical feature of liberal state-building projects over the past two decades, the relationship between state-building and the idea of representative democratic governance is problematic. A consequence is that state-building generally operates through non-democratic practices that may also prove to be anti-democratic.[5] The international community's attempt at state-building in BiH represents a case in point.

Liberal State-building in Bosnia and Herzegovina

During the 1990s, BiH emerged as a prototypical case of international intervention and liberal state-building. Whereas the impetus to intervene in conflict-ridden states or humanitarian crises was previously evident in other countries including Somalia and Haiti, the international community's role in overseeing the peacebuilding process in BiH was unique because this intervention extended well beyond conflict management or containment and included prescriptive aspirations for reconciliation and a long-term commitment to overseeing this troubled state's 'democratic transition'.[6]

---

[5] Non-democratic governance serves as an antonym for democratically responsive governance while anti-democratic governance refers to governance that actively inhibits democratic processes (see Aitchison and Blaustein 2013: 507).

[6] Other attempts at 'third-party state-building' during the mid-1990s included UN-led international territorial administrations over East Slavonia, Kosovo, and East Timor (Caplan 2004: 10).

Since the signing of the Dayton Peace Agreement in December 1995, various representatives of the international and European communities have played a significant role in steering the country's liberal democratic transition with the ultimate goal of establishing BiH as a member of the EU. It is beyond the scope of this chapter to examine the intricate and complex history of BiH and nor is there room to provide an adequate review of pre-war BiH, the Bosnian War itself, or its immediate aftermath. Rather, I seek to provide a brief account of BiH's experience as a relatively advanced case of a transitional, post-conflict society undergoing a concerted liberal state-building process.[7]

BiH declared its independence in March 1992 following its forty-seven year history as a constituent republic of the SFRY. Even prior to this event, tensions were high between the country's three constituent nationalities. The imminent prospect of conflict and its perceived threat to regional stability compelled representatives of the international community to take an active interest in BiH's projected transition to becoming an independent, democratic state. Chandler (1999: 39) describes how, in September 1991, the European Community's Council of Ministers organized a peace conference which was specifically intended 'to keep Yugoslavia as a loose federation composing one state'. This is not to suggest that the international community initially supported BiH's bid for independence but, rather, these proposals projected a future role for the international community in 'regulating' any future developments. In December 1995, the formalization of the international community's prescribed oversight over this transitional process coincided with the signing of a brokered peace agreement that ended the four-year Bosnian War. The Dayton Peace Agreement, which served as both a peace treaty and a constitution for the newly created Bosnian state, lies at the core of the coercive and asymmetric structures of liberal state-building in BiH.

---

[7] By 'relatively advanced case of a transitional, post-conflict society' I mean that BiH began its 'transition' years before other high profile examples of transitional post-conflict societies including Afghanistan or Iraq. Unlike these recent examples, the risk of a recurrence of conflict in BiH is perceived to be relatively low and external security forces play only a limited role in providing support and training to domestic providers. 'Advanced' does not imply, however, that BiH's governing institutions are comparable in terms of their functionality or legitimacy to those of advanced liberal democracies.

By drafting the Dayton Peace Agreement, the international community established for itself a normative basis for legitimating its oversight of the long-term reconstruction of the newly created BiH state (Chandler, 1999: 33). In this respect, BiH emerged as the prototypical case of liberal state-building during the 1990s, an experimental platform upon which various strategies of intervention and regulation could be tested for future application to other post-conflict societies. The legal basis for the international community's involvement in the domestic, sovereign affairs of this newly created state was established by the eleven 'Annexes' listed in the Dayton Peace Agreement (see Office of the High Representative 1995). Given that this book is primarily concerned with police reform and the governance of security, it is worth flagging up the fact that Annex 11 of the Dayton Peace Agreement formally established the United Nations International Police Task Force (IPTF) to assist the signatories with 'meeting their obligations' in terms of providing 'a safe and secure environment for all persons in their respective jurisdictions' and with 'maintaining civilian law enforcement agencies operating in accordance with internationally recognized standards and with respect for internationally recognized human rights and fundamental freedoms'. However, the most influential source of enduring power for the international community in BiH is Annex 10 of the Dayton Agreement which established the Office of the High Representative in BiH (OHR) as the institution tasked with overseeing 'civilian aspects of the peace settlement'.

The OHR was initially established to function as the UN's formal representative in BIH. Accordingly, the OHR's mandate was officially endorsed by Resolution 1031 of the UN Security Council in December 1995 (United Nations Security Council 1995 as cited by Aitchison 2011: 51). The true extent of this institution's power can be inferred from Article V of Annex 10 of the Dayton Agreement which states that '[t]he High Representative is the final authority in theatre regarding interpretation of this Agreement on the civilian implementation of the peace settlement' (Office of the High Representative 1995).

Caplan (2004: 55) suggests that although the institutional mandate of the OHR was initially weak compared to those prescribed for other 'UN transitional administrators' in Eastern Slavonia, Kosovo, and East Timor, its powers were subsequently bolstered in December 1997 as a result of the Peace Implementation Council

(PIC) meeting in Bonn. Aitchison (2011: 50) adds that the institutional enhancement of the OHR was most evident in relation to the greater executive function which the PIC afforded it. Notably, the Council concluded that the High Representative should have the power 'to make binding decisions, as he judges necessary (Peace Implementation Council 1997)'.[8] The enhanced authority of the High Representative was specifically intended to address those cases where domestic actors were unable or unwilling to fulfil their legal obligations as defined by the Dayton Peace Agreement. Aitchison's (2011: 51) analysis suggests that these newly afforded powers had a direct and immediate impact on the ability of the High Representative to make decisions. For example, only one decision was released through the OHR in 1997 but once the OHR was afforded its 'Bonn Powers', this number increased to thirty-one decisions in 1998 and to ninety-one decisions in 1999. The nature and scope of these prescribed powers have lead Knaus and Martin (2003: 59) to characterize the OHR as a 'European Raj' with respect to its capacity to 'interpret its own mandate' and its 'essentially unlimited legal powers' meaning that '...it is not accountable to any elected institution at all'.

The international community's self-prescribed role in BiH has subsequently prompted influential academic dialogues relating to the apparent normative and ideological contradictions associated with this form of prolonged international intervention. For example, Chandler's (1999: 4) critique of the international community's approach to democratization in BiH establishes that '[t]he agency of democratisation is no longer held to be the "demos" or people, through the growth of political freedoms or liberties, self-government and sovereignty, but the international regulatory bodies which are now overseeing the political process...'. In other words, the international community's prolonged intervention in BiH created 'relations of dependency' rather than relations conducive to empowerment and the activation of newly established BiH political institutions. Chandler accounts for this trend by arguing that democracy, as a blanket prescription for governance in

---

[8] Aitchison (2011: 50) adds that these conclusions were formally endorsed by the UN Security Council via Resolution 1144 in December 1997 (United Nations Security Council 1997b) and reaffirmed by Resolution 1184 the following year (United Nations Security Council 1998).

transitional societies, describes a 'moral category' rather than one with political significance. This leads him to conclude that 'the process of democratization concerns societal values and attitudes rather than political processes' (Chandler 1999: 28). He adds that the moralization of democracy is fundamentally problematic in BiH because it undermines the ability of a society to independently govern itself in a manner responsive to public interests.

The actualization of liberal, democratic values and political processes is precluded by prevailing governing structures that advance the interests of international actors and domestic political elites while simultaneously limiting opportunities for local citizens to meaningfully shape this agenda. His analysis further suggests that there is a functionalist logic underpinning liberal state-building projects. In the aftermath of the Cold War, he writes that 'the drive behind democratisation can be located in the needs of international institutional actors for new forms of co-operation and new ways of legitimating their international regulatory role' (Chandler 1999: 93). In other words, Chandler argues that democratization served as the 'perfect form for this ongoing process of international co-operation because there is no fixed end-point' (Chandler 1999: 193). An important consequence of 'mission creep' in BiH is that the capacities of domestic political institutions remain limited as local political elites have been rendered 'superfluous to policy development and implementation' (Chandler 1999: 194–5; also Belloni 2001).

Building on his arguments in *Faking Democracy After Dayton*, Chandler (2006) has subsequently characterized the enduring presence of the international community in BiH as evidence of an 'informal trusteeship'. He concludes that after ten years of concerted state-building initiatives, 'the main transition which has taken place [in BiH] has been from the ad hoc policy-ownership of self-selected members of the Peace Implementation Council (PIC) to direct regulatory control under the aegis of the European Union (EU)' (Chandler 2006: 8). In other words, Chandler's analysis suggests that the overall effect of this transition is that BiH ownership of these newly created institutions remains 'limited' and that '[t]he Bosnian public has effectively been excluded from the transition process' (Chandler 2006: 32–3). In this respect, it is evident that the political institutions established by the Dayton Peace Agreement do not constitute a deliberative model of democratic governance.

Cooke (2000: 947) defines deliberative democracy as, 'a conception of democratic government that secures a central place for reasoned discussion in political life'. He adds that different political theorists have articulated diverse, and at times dissimilar, prescriptions for achieving deliberative democracy as well as arguments regarding the significance of deliberation (for example, Habermas 1994 and Rawls 1997). In linking this concept to Chandler's (1999) critique of the liberal state-building process in BiH, I draw from Dryzek's (2002: 17) related concept of 'discursive democracy' which itself represents a critique of mainstream 'liberal constitutionalist' approaches which assume that the procedural and distributive shortcomings of democratic systems of governance can be resolved via constitutional amendment or legislation. Instead, Dryzek's work on discursive democracy stresses that formal institutions of liberal democratic governance are themselves incapable of providing redress to those who have been structurally excluded and politically disenfranchised by the status quo. By implication, additional mechanisms must be developed to promote inclusion and participation from those who are ordinarily marginalized. To this effect, deLeon (1992: 125) argues that the existence of participatory mechanisms, be they organic or invented, is vital to the perceived legitimacy of a system of governance because participation helps to bridge the gap between the interests of policymakers and those of policy recipients. In *Deliberative Global Politics* (2006: 25), Dryzek elaborates on this idea of discursive democracy by discussing how it might be actualized at the transnational level:

Transnational discursive democracy does not have to be integrated with a particular set of formal institutions (though it can target influence over many such institutions, including states). Democracy is about communication as well as voting, about social learning as well as decision-making, and it is the communicative aspects that for the moment can most straightforwardly be pursued in the international system. This project is especially urgent in light of an international system whose dominant actors seem intent on rolling back democratic rights and freedoms in the name of global security.

The idea that participation, 'critical self-reflection' (Wendt 1999: 375: cited by Dryzek 2006: 25), and communicative action can foster empowerment represents a core theme for the remainder of this book.

The 'New Humanitarianism' as Liberal Governmentality

Chandler's (1999) discussion of liberal state-building in BiH serves as an important platform for his later work which explores the motives underpinning international interventions in other post-conflict societies during the 2000s. Focusing his analysis primarily on American and British-led interventions in Afghanistan and Iraq, Chandler (2002: 224) associates these motives with the need for liberal actors to bolster their own domestic legitimacy 'by exaggerating the legitimacy problems of peripheral or pariah states'. In other words, he suggests that powerful international actors embrace this 'new humanitarianism' narrative because it enables them to mask their own deficiencies by focusing on those of developing and transitional states like BiH. He argues that the actors who steer these interventions do so for reasons other than pragmatic security concerns associated with the idea of 'human security'. This argument also introduces an important distinction between 'liberal imperialism' of the twenty-first century and that of the eighteenth and nineteenth centuries. Whereas the historical variant was commonly associated with economic interests and empire-building, Chandler (2002) argues that interventions pursued within the discourses of the 'new humanitarianism' must outwardly respect enduring norms of non-intervention, global justice, and liberal peace.

Seeking to legitimate these interventions, the architects behind liberal state-building projects employ a 'practice of denying empire' in order to present their motives as apolitical and deontological (Chandler, 2006: 190). Denying empire relies heavily on the invocation of discourses of 'empowerment' and 'capacity building' which portray state-building processes as being primarily responsive to local development needs. Chandler (2002: 230) is of course dismissive of the possibility that externally-driven democratization processes actually contribute to the 'empowerment' of individuals in recipient societies. Instead, he argues that prolonged external oversight of internationally governed democratization or state-building processes undermine local responsiveness by ensuring the 'dismissal of the political sphere as a viable mechanism for generating this change in recipient societies' (Chandler 2002: 230). This leads Chandler (2006) to conclude that politically ambiguous prescriptions for state-building and democratization which emphasize the language of 'local capacity building', 'local ownership', and 'empowerment' are frequently compromised by the underlying structural politics of global liberal governance. The symbolic transfer of power and responsibility for liberal governance from international actors to domestic political institutions of weak and structurally dependent societies is therefore important because it outwardly constructs the international community as apolitical.

From Chandler's work, it is clear that liberal state-building is driven by the interests of powerful, supranational actors and assemblages and that 'the new humanitarianism' promotes the relative subordination of local interests to those of powerful global actors. The need to establish a moral basis for legitimacy further implies that liberal state-building constitutes an important technique of global liberal 'governmentality'. Foucault (1991: 102) defines 'governmentality' as:

The ensemble formed by the institutions, procedures, analyses and reflections, the calculations and tactics that allow the exercise of this very specific albeit complex form of power, which has at its target population, as its principle form of knowledge political economy, and as its essential technical means apparatuses of security.

The humanitarian discourses surrounding these interventions and the conflation of development and security are important in this respect because they enable powerful global actors to transpose their designs for governance upon domestic political institutions in weak and structurally dependent societies from a distance (Duffield 2007). In this respect, interventions pursued within this 'new humanitarian' framework can be said to constitute important mechanisms for reproducing and securing upwardly-responsive, glocal order in states that are either unable or unwilling to do so without prompting.

From Ignatieff's (2003) work, it is also clear that these techniques of governmentality structure the work of the international development system over the past two decades. Specifically, he describes how powerful international actors use their political influence and economic capital to steer the work of international organizations operating in transitional, post-conflict societies:

These agencies—UNICEF, UNHCR, the International Committee of the Red Cross—are dependent on Western governments for their funding, yet they struggle to keep a space free to meet humanitarian need irrespective of the political wishes of their paymasters. Yet humanitarian relief cannot be kept distinct from imperial projects, not least because humanitarian action is only possible, in many instances, if imperial armies have first cleared the ground and made it safe for humanitarians to act. (Ignatieff 2003: 20)

Ignatieff's (2003) analysis of the relationship between humanitarian aid organizations and 'imperial powers' focuses on the early stages of a post-conflict intervention but his critique is consistent with Hulme and Edwards's (1997) analysis of the structural politics of the international development system more generally. Specifically, Hulme and Edwards (1997: 12) account for a burgeoning interest amongst international donors in development work and NGO activity since the late 1990s. They argue that development aid and assistance allows these donors to influence agendas for development work without becoming directly involved in interventions or state-building processes. Conditionality is attached to development aid and this allows powerful donors like the EU and the United States to transpose their policy preferences on developing and transitional states by proxy. International development assistance programmes enable donor governments to assert their interests using various 'aid frameworks' that include provisions for non-core funding that can only be accessed by those development agencies and NGOs that align their goals with donor interests.

Linking the structural politics of the international development system with his discussion of global liberal governance, Duffield (2007: 118) writes that international development aid (and specifically non-core funding) 'offers donor governments several points of engagement with state incumbents and opportunities for selective capacity building without necessarily legitimising those incumbents'. In relation to the liberal emphasis on maintaining a balance between freedom and order, Duffield adds that this form of governmentality is particularly innovative because it maximizes the social distance between powerful donors and the recipients of their aid. Conditionality represents an important theme of my analysis of the first case study which focuses on UNDP's Safer Communities project in BiH. The remainder of this chapter introduces the literature on police development assistance to consider how its associated practices are used to foster upwardly-responsive, liberal orders in weak and structurally dependent societies like BiH.

Police Development Assistance as Glocal Policing

Police development assistance projects are designed to indirectly contribute to the reproduction of liberal order within developing and transitional states by facilitating the development of globally-responsive policing. In other words, their financiers aspire to align the mentalities and the practices of domestic policing agents with the interests of the architects of global liberal governance who view local policing as an important ordering mechanism. This process is described by Goldsmith and Sheptycki (2007) as the 'crafting of transnational policing'. From Stan Cohen's (1988*a*: 177) work it can be inferred that this type of transnational policing is crafted, at least in part, on the basis of a 'Durkheimian' assumption 'that crime is one of the many problems associated with "development", an invariable by-product of modernization and progress'. Accordingly, Cohen writes, '[t]he control implications...are seen as relatively straight-forward: we have seen it all before, and with our sophisticated knowledge we can help [developing nations] to avoid most of the mistakes that [developed nations] made' (Cohen 1988*a*: 178).

In practice, the aspirations of securitization, alignment, and accelerated modernization are infrequently realized in their entirety. This is due to the fact that the policy outputs introduced by reformers are invariably transformed during the transfer process and shaped in relation to the capabilities, interests, and values of their benefactors, their proponents, and their recipients.[9] The policy outcomes generated by these mediated policy outputs also deviate from the initial aspirations of donors as a result of cultural and contextual differences 'on the ground'. This means that 'Western' prescriptions for 'community policing' and 'community safety' which represent templates for establishing 'democratic policing' may be understood and implemented differently depending on the contexts in question. They may also be experienced differently by local citizens and produce different outcomes. For all of these reasons, it is impossible to reduce the complex mechanics of police development assistance programmes and the glocal policing outcomes they generate to their prescribed functions. Rather, the collective agency of these transnational networks is simultaneously responsive to 'global' and 'local' influences, albeit

[9] This argument is the focus of Chapter 4.

not necessarily in equal measure. The most we can say about the relationship between police development assistance programmes and local order in the context of developing and transitional states is that the former influence the latter but they are not determinative of what Hills (2009: 14) describes as 'behaviour and consequences that display predictability in the rules that govern them'.

Policing and Glocal Order

Hills (2009: 12) observes that 'order implies a degree of predictability, regularity and stability to social and political relationships, institutions and behaviours'. The concept is central to police sociology (for example, Ericson 1982) and explicit in Reiner's (2010: 5) oft quoted definition of policing as 'the set of activities aimed at preserving the security of a particular social order, or social order in general'. This important distinction between a 'particular' or 'specific' order and 'social order in general' is described in further detail by Marenin (1982: 382):

A concrete order...has two aspects: a general-order aspect reflecting the interest of all in regularity—that is what the relative autonomy of the state means—and a specific-order reflecting the use of state power to promote specific interests—that is what the concept of 'domination by the state' means.

Modern police, argues Marenin, have traditionally played an important role in reproducing both general and specific orders. He adds, 'the police make real, by what they do or fail to do, the intentions and interests of the state and of those groups that attempt to control the state' (Marenin (1982: 379)).

The distinction between general and specific-order policing is elaborated on by Walker (1994: 25–6) who suggests that the former involves '...preserving public tranquility...' while the latter is concerned with '...protecting the interests of those in a dominant political and social position...'. Referencing Engels, Marenin (1982) writes that the analytical distinction between general and specific order is universally applicable insofar as social organization and subordination are components of every society. However, the rules intrinsic to general order inevitably differ in different societies due to their distinct cultural and historical experiences. Marenin illustrates this by describing how '[t]he conception of general order during the cultural revolution in China is far different from that held in the Soviet Union under Stalin or from the liberal conception of the "rule of law" ' (Marenin 1982: 383).

The advent of global liberal governance during the 1990s gives us cause to reflect on the enduring relevance of this claim. In other words, we must consider whether processes associated with globalization have contributed to increased levels of cultural and structural convergence between different nations and how this has impacted the construction of local orders. The work of Duffield (2007) and Chandler (1999; 2002) suggests that in weak and structurally dependent states, the contours of general order are no longer primarily defined by domestic governing institutions and processes.[10] Rather, they are increasingly defined from above through the intervening mechanisms of global liberal governmentality. The implication of this analysis is that the distinction between general and specific order remains relevant to our understanding of policing in the context of police development assistance projects but the primacy once accorded to the state as an ordering mechanism appears questionable today. Rather, the state (at least in the global South) is today treated as an important building block of a global liberal order and the international legitimacy of a particular national regime is defined from above on the basis of its willingness and its capacity to comply with these processes of structural alignment.

The previous section illustrated that a perceived failure or neglect of this responsibility may establish a liberal justification for military or humanitarian interventions. It must also be considered that ongoing doubts about the willingness or the capacity of domestic policing organizations to address local sources of global insecurity have contributed to the expansion of transnational policing power over the past two decades. Accordingly, Bowling and Sheptycki (2012: 128) write, '[s]ince the power to govern means little, if anything at all, without being able to marshal coercive power, no theory of global governance can be complete without a theory of global policing'. Bowling and Sheptycki's (2012) theory of global policing is not directly concerned with police development assistance programmes but Sheptycki's earlier work with Goldsmith indicates that these 'capacity building programmes' constitute

---

[10] Although one must also question whether local order has ever been defined solely in relation to domestic political structures and institutions.

an important form of transnational policing (see Goldsmith and Sheptycki 2007). Transnational policing is identified by Bowling and Sheptycki (2012) as a sub-category of global policing and a synthesis of these two works indicates that transnational policing represents an important driver of glocal policing throughout the developing world.

As noted in the introduction to this chapter, one must avoid using the terms 'global policing' and 'glocal policing' interchangeably. To reiterate, the distinction reflects the idea that the mentalities and practices associated with the former concept are represented as being primarily responsive to the interests of the international and supranational architects of global liberal governance while those associated with the latter concept are construed as the nego- tiated outputs of interactions between the global and the local. Simply, glocal policing is a product of interactive globalization yet Bowling and Sheptycki's (2012) theory of global policing appears to construct glocal policing to an outcome of one-sided transna- tional policy exchanges that aspire to facilitate 'the re-wiring of the local structures of policing and security' with the effect that local policing '[p]riorities, politics and practices are skewed in the interests of the powerful' (Bowling and Sheptycki 2012: 76, 132). There is no denying the asymmetrical character of interactive glo- balization and even Cain (2000: 86) acknowledges this much. She writes:

The trajectory is usually from the more to less powerful, but the recipi- ent groups may, if they choose, if they are strong enough, interact with that idea, re-situate it within their own discourses and practices, modify it, make it their own, and so create an alternative model, which, ideally should then find its own place in a global pool of possibilities.

In other words, Cain (2000: 86) accepts the fact that power imbal- ances will lead to 'skewing' but recognizes that structural asym- metries alone do not dictate outcomes. Ellison (2007: 213) has similarly acknowledged the need to account for 'the complex dynamics of the donor-recipient relationship' through the lens of interactive globalization and the theme of translation features prominently in the work of Hills (2009; 2012*a*; 2012*b*).

Hills's (2009) account of the complex relationship between order and security in the context of post-conflict cities gives us further reason to question the empirical merits of hegemonic rep- resentations of this particular variant of transnational policing power. Power and order, argues Hills, are 'the result of processes of negotiation, accommodation and coercion...structured through relations of power' (Hills 2009: 201). In post-conflict cities, she argues that international donors can only play a limited role in specifying the configuration of a transitional order because 'order depends on what went before' (Hills 2009: 203). This means that top-down attempts to produce local orders must resonate with local understandings and expectations of what local order should look like. Accordingly, Hills (2012*a*: 93) denies the existence of a global security culture because 'although certain international norms appear to modify police behaviour through temporary and localised processes of socialisation, they do so for instrumental, rather than intrinsic reasons'. In other words, local police officers adopt certain elements of police reform projects because they see it as being in their best interest to do so, not because their mentalities and ways of thinking about police work have been altered significantly by the liberal discourses associated with these initiatives.

Hills's (2009) work raises important questions about the ability of international donors and development agencies to align the work of local police with liberal objectives. For example, it indicates that responsiveness is largely determined by the power relations of the setting in question with the effect that 'order' must be understood as a 'literal' concept that 'mean[s] whatever the strongest man says' (Hills 2009: 204). While the material and diplomatic capital available to international donors certainly affords them power, their ability to translate this power into policies, mentalities, and practices that will generate stability is limited. Rather, local actors who enjoy comparatively fewer material resources may nonetheless exert greater influence over these policy outputs because they possess cultural knowledge, social and political capital, and they are more proximate to important sites or nodes at which policy decisions are made. Hills (2012*b*) illustrates this point by discussing how local political elites subverted democratic policing projects in Nigeria. Hills argues therefore that 'successful transfer requires the development of a hybrid form of understanding that accommodates aspects of both donor and local understanding' (Hills 2012*b*: 742). If a legitimacy deficit is perceived to exist between the local agents tasked with implementing international prescriptions for police reform and their international benefactors, successful transfers conducive to global alignment are even less likely to result. As the following sub-section illustrates, the legitimation of these projects through the rhetoric of 'democratic policing' thus represents an important discursive mechanism for promoting alignment.

Legitimation through 'Democratic Policing'

'Democratic policing' is touted as a one-size-fits-all prescription for police reform in advanced and transitional democratic societies alike but no consensus exists regarding what it actually means or what it should look like in practice (Aitchison and Blaustein, 2013; Ellison and Pino 2012: 57; Manning 2010). An oft-cited definition for 'democratic policing' is that provided by David Bayley who links it with:

> the idea that the police are a service, not a force, with the primary focus on the security of the individual rather than the state. Its definitive characteristics are the 'responsiveness' of the police to the need of individual citizens, and its 'accountability' for its actions to the public it serves (Bayley 2001, quoted by Hills 2009: 61).

Bayley's emphasis on responsiveness and accountability is consistent with certain articulations of liberal democratic governance more generally (Kuper 2006) but the asymmetrical structures that characterize liberal interventions often negate the prospect of actually establishing democratically responsive or even locally accountable policing. For this reason, one cannot assume that international prescriptions for 'democratic policing' constitute functional models for establishing legitimate policing if legitimacy is to be measured from the perspectives of those being policed or even those doing the policing.

The audience's role in conferring legitimacy is described by political theorist David Beetham (1991: 16) who writes:

> Power can be said to be legitimate to the extent that: (i) it conforms to established rules; (ii) the rules can be justified by reference to beliefs shared by both dominant and subordinate; [and] (iii) there is evidence of consent by the subordinate to the particular power relation.

Subsequent work by Bottoms and Tankebe (2012) indicates that the audience perspective provides only a partial account of the dialogic relationships through which legitimate power is negotiated. For this reason, it is also necessary to consider the legitimacy of police development assistance programmes from the perspective of 'power holders'. Accordingly, my argument is that we must treat 'democratic policing' as a moral category that is used by reformers to legitimate both the policing models they are promoting and their ability to influence domestic policymaking through indirect coercion or conditionality rather than relationships based on organic consent. This position is consistent with Chandler's (1999: 28) argument that 'democracy' itself represents a rhetorical device used by proponents of liberal state-building in BiH to legitimate their power rather than a genuine political reality for those being subordinated. It also echoes Dryzek's (2006: 108) claim that '[t]he more important transnational or global governance becomes, the more its legitimacy will have to rest on some notion of democracy' and Ellison and Pino's (2012) argument that the rhetoric of democratic policing provides international donors with an important framework for legitimating the conditionality attached to the non-core funding they allocate to security sector reforms. In recognizing the politicized character of 'democratic policing' and the coercive and asymmetrical nature of the international development system, Ellison and Pino (2012: 1) add that 'policing and police reform cannot be divorced from other forms of [international development] assistance' because what they describe as 'neoliberal development' work has 'at its core some level of geostrategic manipulation and an emphasis on donor/national interest' (Ellison and Pino 2012: 35).

Returning to the idea that legitimation operates as a dialogue between those who hold power and those they seek to govern, the invocation of democratic policing by reformers can be understood as an attempt to establish a common moral platform or a basis of shared beliefs upon which reformers can justify their intervention to local policy actors. In relation to police capacity building programmes, this argument is supported by Goldsmith and Sheptycki (2007: 15) who write:

In an era in which the words 'imperialism' and 'colonialism' continue to carry negative economic as well as political connotations, it is widely seen in foreign policy circles as in the interests of all parties that capacity-building exercises be based upon partnerships with and the general consent of local participants ...

Establishing a common platform for moral legitimacy is particularly important in countries like BiH where the normative basis for intervention has been established by architects of global liberal governance rather than through domestic political processes.

Insofar as democratic policing is primarily a rhetorical device, Ellison and Pino (2012: 35–6) write that its prescriptions are unlikely to generate anticipated outcomes because they '[promote] a universalistic one-size fits all paradigm with similar development/reformist templates used in a variety of contexts that often differ greatly in terms of history, politics, culture and levels of social and economic equality'. Elsewhere, Manning (2010: 9) adds that the prospect of establishing democratically accountable forms of policing in transitional, post-conflict societies like BiH is particularly problematic because these contexts foster 'institutional and cultural structure[s] that [do] not possess or support democratic policing' (or indeed, deliberative forms of democracy). Accordingly, while no consensus appears to exist regarding what 'democratic policing' looks like in practice, critical scholars do agree that the concept is ambiguous, politically-loaded, and empirically vacuous. These criticisms have also been levelled at two popular templates for promoting 'democratic policing' locally in weak and structurally dependent states: community policing and community safety partnerships.

Community Policing

Brogden (1999: 168) writes that community policing emerged as a North American invention that has since spread throughout Western Europe as a result of '... the hegemony of North American scholarship in police studies'. It has since been embraced by policy entrepreneurs and reformers around the world as an important template for establishing democratic policing at the local level (Ellison 2007). A comparative typology of different international models of community policing is provided by Wisler and Onwudiwe (2008) who distinguish between 'top down' and 'bottom up' models of community policing; 'state initiated' and 'social' models of community policing; and models designed to control social behaviour and those designed to control crime. As an 'export commodity', state-initiated models of community policing are the norm as international reformers primarily focus their efforts on developing the institutional capacities of the public police rather than traditional or informal mechanisms of policing and social control that may also contribute (or have previously contributed) to communal security governance.[11] Beyond this distinction, the policies and

[11] Although some international organizations including the Saferworld have started to recognize the importance of engaging non-state security providers with community-based reforms.

practices associated with different models of community policing that have been introduced around the world are diverse. This suggests that the popularity of community policing reforms is a function of its rhetorical appeal as a 'buzzword' (Skolnick and Bayley 1988: 4) rather than the demonstrated effectiveness of a particular set of practices that serve to improve local cooperation between the public and the police. Indeed, Bayley (1992: 10) acknowledges that most community policing programmes 'work best in relatively affluent, ethnically homogenous middle-class areas' where, Ellison (2007: 209) adds, 'they are needed least'.

Given the underlying discourse which presents community policing as a strategy for improving collaboration between the public and the police and the historical appeal of this notion to domestic reformers in the global North, especially in times of institutional crisis (Alderson 1979; Bayley and Mendelsohn 1969), it is hardly surprising that this paradigm has gained credibility as a template for improving relations between the police and local populations in conflicted or underdeveloped societies. In fact, Ellison (2007: 215; also Brogden 2002) argues that community policing has become 'commodified' internationally as 'the export model of choice for many Western donors'.

Documented examples of community policing projects being introduced to transitional and developing societies can be found throughout the Caribbean (Deosaran 2002); Latin America (Frühling 2007); Northern Ireland (Topping 2008a; 2008b); South East Europe (Ryan 2007; Vejnovic and Lalic 2005); and Sub-Saharan Africa (Brogden 2002; Brogden and Shearing 1993; Ruteere and Pommerello 2003). According to Brogden (2005: 67), a combination of 'individuals, policing agencies, nongovernmental organisations (NGOs), national governments, and private corporations' are responsible for exporting community policing models to developing and transnational countries. These exchanges take place through the following transfer mechanisms which are concisely summarized by Ellison (2007: 213 paraphrasing Brogden 2005: 68–71) below:

... (1) private corporations who offer community policing for hire on the global market ...; (2) [community policing] gurus, private consultants ...; (3) transnational cooperation between state enforcement agencies ...; (4) international organisations such as UNPOL working under the aegis of the United Nations; (5) a range of NGOs and aid agencies who engage with overseas police organisations on a bilateral and multilateral *basis; and (6) the overseas development branches of Western/Northern Governments who have also been particularly active in sponsoring and funding overseas [community policing] projects.*

While international actors and organizations are clearly driving community policing reforms throughout the developing world, Hills's (2012*a*; 2012*b*) work indicates that domestic policymakers, local practitioners, and even academics can play an important role in facilitating or restricting these policy exchanges. What this means is that the community policing practices and structures that are generated by these policy transfers often deviate from their initial design. In Chapter 4, I elaborate on these transformational processes using the concepts of 'policy transfer' and 'policy translation' and in Chapter 6, I elaborate on the implementation challenges associated with community policing reforms in modern, bureaucratic police organizations. For the discussion at hand, it suffices to note that the practices and mentalities that are prescribed by reformers tend to reflect an amalgamation of various national models that have been promoted or imposed upon this context by different policy entrepreneurs and adapted selectively and strategically by international development agencies and local actors (Brogden and Nijhar 2005). This is also true of community safety partnership reforms which are often introduced to complement community policing initiatives.

Community Safety Partnerships

Proverbial depictions of the public police in the Anglo-American context describe this institution as the 'thin blue line' between order and disorder (Waddington 1998: 4).[12] Over the past three decades, the primacy of the public police in advanced, liberal democratic societies has been challenged by the realities of an increasingly pluralistic policing field. European crime control policies oriented towards prevention and partnership did not evolve uniformly but rather, Crawford (2009: xvi) argues, these 'models were heavily influenced by political ideology and

---

[12] This assertion primarily references the Anglo-American policing tradition which dominates the mainstream sociological discourse on both the observed and the theoretical relationship between this institution and modern societies.

different cultural assumptions about crime, behavioural motivations and appropriate ways of organising regulatory responses'.

Among the five common structural factors (or perhaps more accurately trends) identified by Crawford (2009),[13] there is one factor which resonates particularly well with Foucault's (1991: 102) concept of governmentality and the argument that the public police are playing an increasingly limited role in reproducing social order: a '[g]rowing acknowledgement of the limited capacity of formal institutions of criminal justice to adequately reduce crime and effect change in criminal behaviour, spurred by a recognition that the leavers of crime lie beyond the reach of formal institutions of control' (Crawford 2009: 2; see also Garland 1996). It is in relation to the proliferation of these mentalities that models for coordinating and governing the provision of plural policing have grown in popularity since the 1980s and 1990s. Notably, Rose (2000: 323) suggests that in Anglo-American contexts, this mode of thinking was symptomatic of 'advanced liberal' forms of government that involve 'a widespread recasting of the ideal role of the state, and the argument that national governments should no longer aspire to be the guarantor and ultimate provider of security...' but rather act as a 'partner, animator and facilitator for a variety of agents'.

Crawford (2009: 8–11) acknowledges significant cross-national (and even intrastate) variance in terms of how community safety and crime prevention policies have manifested themselves in Europe and he observes that many of the national 'models' with their distinctive character and origins have in fact become 'hybridized' in recent years. Drawing on the case studies included in this edited volume, Crawford suggests that hybridization is particularly evident in relation to the emergence of crime prevention policies in Southern European states including Italy (Melossi and Selmini 2009) and in former Soviet-bloc countries such as Hungary and Slovenia where 'the development of crime prevention strategies and an infrastructure to deliver them has been closely

[13] Other factors listed by Crawford (2009: 2) include: public perception of crime and fear of crime linked with rising trends in property ownership; social fragmentation and the disruption of informal social control; a growing aversion to social–welfare based policies, and; 'a political desire to explore alternative means of managing crime that avoid the economic, social and human costs associated with over-reliance on traditional punitive—"law and order"—responses'.

associated with the processes of transition' (Crawford 2009: 13). This analysis fits with the idea that the EU plays an important role in facilitating policy transfers, both within its borders and beyond (see Bulmer et al. 2007). Promoting convergence through policy transfers therefore enables the EU to manage potential sources of insecurity through its attempts to harmonize security governance at the national and sub-national level.

In acknowledging the convergent character of recent European manifestations of crime prevention policies, specifically 'community safety partnerships', Crawford (2009: 14) attributes these convergent trends[14] and the 'internationalisation of crime prevention' to 'the development of transnational and supranational networks' including the European Forum for Urban Security (EFUS), the UN-HABITAT Safer Cities programme, and the European Crime Prevention Network (ECPN) among others. These networks overlap with elements of the transnational policy communities that contribute to the dissemination of community policing to developing and transitional societies around the world. They have been particularly susceptible to the influence of British and Dutch policy entrepreneurs which Crawford argues has contributed to the popularization of situational and technological forms of crime prevention such as closed-circuit television (CCTV) (Crawford 2009: 14).

The influence of the British[15] model which aspires to '[cultivate] community involvement and the dissemination of crime

---

[14] Crawford elaborates on these convergent trends by citing the work of Jones and Newburn (2007) who suggest that the nature of this convergence has more to do with rhetoric than with actual policy content. This is an important consideration which I will return to when I examine the role that UNDP played in introducing the Safer Communities model to BiH.

[15] The British model I speak of refers to developments in England and Wales during the early 1990s. Specifically, I reference the 'Safer Cities Programme' initiated during the late 1980s (Crawford 2009) and 'Safer Communities' which began in 1991 (Edwards and Hughes 2009). Note that this does not account for developments in Scotland that emerged in response to similar contextual circumstances as those which prompted important policy developments in England and Wales during the 1990s but were ultimately oriented towards social justice outcomes rather than 'an unnecessarily narrow criminal justice agenda' (Henry 2009: 87). The Scottish experience as well as the experiences of many other European nations have undoubtedly contributed to hybrid manifestations of CSPs in these transitional and developing contexts, however, it is beyond the scope of this research to explore the composition of these projects.

prevention ideas and practices' (Garland 2001: 16) is especially evident in relation to the ongoing efforts of international organizations and development agencies to establish community safety partnerships in transitional and developing countries since the mid-1990s. Noting variation between community safety partnerships across England and Wales, Edwards and Hughes (original emphasis 2009: 67) describe community safety partnerships as a 'hybrid' policy which 'sits at the intersection of attempts by the state to deliver welfare and security, *and* policing and control in local communities'. In the context of England and Wales, this emphasis on 'community' as the territorial unit best positioned to generate improved security and to implement crime prevention strategies and technologies reflects a neo-liberal aversion to welfare-based approaches to preventing crime during this period. As Rose (1996: 331) argues, this aversion has compelled policymakers to embrace 'the community' as 'a new plane or surface upon which micro-moral relations among persons are conceptualized and administered'.

The Safer Cities Programme is one prominent example of the application of community safety partnership initiatives in transitional and developing societies. Created in 1996 'at the request of African Mayors seeking to tackle urban crime and violence in their cities', the Safer Cities Programme was developed by UN-HABITAT in cooperation with EFUS and the International Centre for the Prevention of Crime to improve urban safety in the developing world (UN-HABITAT 2007: 2). The language employed by UN-HABITAT to promote this initiative clearly echoes important discursive elements of the 'preventative turn' in Europe. The UN-HABITAT brochure for the Safer Cities Project clearly states:

Local authorities have a key role to play in addressing the rising public demand to reduce crime and violence. Success depends on partnerships between local governments and other stakeholders (UN-HABITAT 2007: 3).

Other examples of community-based crime prevention initiatives in the context of transitional and developing countries include UNDP 'Safer Communities' projects (BiH, Croatia, and Kosovo) and similar projects initiated by development agencies and NGOs including the UK Department for International Development (BiH), the Swiss Agency for Development and Cooperation (BiH and Romania) and the Saferworld Group (Kosovo, Bangladesh, Kenya, Nepal, Sudan, and Somalia). While the specific activities and structures prescribed by these projects vary, their rhetorical emphasis on improving the provision of local security and safety through partnership and prevention remains consistent. It is also apparent that the pursuit of these initiatives is often linked with attempts to implement localized forms of community policing. The following section draws from the work of Ryan (2011) and Cohen (1988*a*) in considering potential consequences of community policing and community safety partnership reforms in transnational and developing countries.

Police Capacity Building and Political Disempowerment

In *Police Reform and Statebuilding*, Ryan (2011) argues that plural forms of policing and security governance in the Western Balkans reflect a broader shift of reformative emphasis away from the language of 'police reform' and in favour of the 'holistic' language of 'security sector reform' (henceforth 'SSR'). This is problematic, writes Ryan (2011: 12), because it contributes to the erosion of political freedom in recipient societies by 'institut[ing] mechanisms that would activate liberal sources of power and marginalize alternatives'. Ryan (2011: 7) writes that police reform in the context of liberal state-building describes an important form of 'securitisation' (Buzan et al. 1998)[16] which serves to supplant the 'political freedom' of the recipient society with what he labels the 'freedom of security'. The distinction between 'political freedom' and the 'freedom of security' is central to Ryan's critique of police development assistance projects. 'Political freedom' is defined by Ryan (2011: 90) as, 'the freedom to question the validity of the status quo'. 'Freedom of security' can be understood in relation to the work of influential modern political theorists like Hobbes and Kant which accounts for the relationship between governance and security.

---

[16] Buzan et al. (1998: 25) describe 'securitisation' as the 'the intersubjective establishment of an existential threat with a saliency sufficient to have substantial political effects'. They add that '[a] discourse that takes the form of presenting something as an existential threat to a referent object does not by itself create securitization—this is a securitizing move, but the issue is securitized only if and when the audience accepts it as such'.

It is in relation to the work of Hobbes (1947) and his idea that 'security is a unifying project' that Ryan (2011: 22) locates the utilitarian emphasis of police reform as a technology of liberal governance. Ryan (2011) describes how Hobbes's (1947) *Leviathan* posits that a symbiotic relationship exists between the values of freedom and security, one which suggests that 'security is *instrumental* to the perpetuation of the common good' (quoting Ryan 2011: 22, original emphasis). Hobbes equates the common good with the values of liberty and freedom but he suggests that these values must be 'moulded to a common [sovereign] will' (Ryan 2011: 22). In this respect, Ryan notes that the Hobbesian perspective distinguishes between acceptable and unacceptable forms of freedom. Whereas acceptable forms of freedom refer to rational thoughts and actions that enable society to thrive, unacceptable forms of freedom refer to 'the chaotic plurality of wills one finds amongst the heathen' (quoting Ryan 2011: 7). Referring to the metaphor of the police as a 'thin blue line', Ryan adds that the police represent 'an elemental aspect of liberal modern governance' that provides security necessary for sustaining acceptable variants of freedom while simultaneously suppressing those manifestations that threaten to compromise this social and political order (Ryan 2011: 7).

While Hobbes's work informs Ryan's account of why policing is seen by reformers to be necessary for securing order, he argues that it was Kant's ideas that have had the greatest influence upon discourses of global liberal governance since the 1980s. Specifically, he argues that liberal internationalists of the 1980s articulated their 'philosophy of control and order' on the basis of 'selective readings' of Kant's 'perpetual peace thesis' (Ryan 2011: 24). For Kant, Ryan argues that freedom represents a moral ends in its own right. Whereas the Hobbesian perspective views freedom as a necessary component of social and political order, Ryan writes that the Kantian perspective emphasizes that '[h]ow we discipline ourselves in our minds and create our inner freedom is postulated as a framework, and a starting point, for how we secure our societies and our international system' (Ryan 2011: 23). In other words, the Kantian perspective posits that a liberal society must be comprised of liberal subjects who internalize its values and advance its cause.

Drawing on Adorno's (2007) reading of Kant, Ryan (2011: 24) notes that the Kantian prescription for freedom is in practice problematic because the actualization of perpetual peace requires 'coercive institutions capable of securing and liberating the individual'. This suggests that individuals, or in the case of global liberal governance, individual states, must be compelled to voluntarily embrace liberal values. As evident from the previous section's discussion of the 'new humanitarianism', coercion is necessary and indeed justifiable for the purpose of activating liberal values through processes of governmentality. Critiquing the paradigms of liberal peace and the global liberal governance, Ryan references Arendt's (2000) critique of Kant in arguing that 'a key feature of modernity' involves 'the colonization of freedom by security' (Ryan 2011: 25). This suggests that liberal forms of governance do not identify freedom as an ends in itself but rather they treat it as 'a marginal phenomenon' (Arendt 2000: 443, again quoted by Ryan 2011: 25). Building on this critique, Ryan (2011: 25) writes, '[f]reedom has become so instrumentalized, so existential to the status quo, that it is indistinguishable from necessity...'. This leads Ryan to conclude that liberal governance renders the pursuit of freedom and security as indistinguishable phenomena. The cumulative effect of their conflation for recipients of police reforms and SSR in weak and structurally dependent societies like BiH is that 'political freedoms' are supplanted by a 'freedom of security' that is ultimately responsive to the interests of powerful global actors like the EU. This is suggestive of Chandler's (2006: 6) critique of liberal state-building processes which describes how '[t]he functional capacity of state institutions is privileged over their representational or policy-making autonomy and increasingly understood in technical or administrative terms'.

Iatrogenesis and the 'Subculture of Transnational Policing'

Political disempowerment describes but one way in which international police development assistance projects can prove harmful for recipient societies. Bowling and Sheptycki (2012) also argue that the proponents of transnational policing contribute to the global dissemination of harmful models, mentalities, and practices because their work is primarily structured by a 'subculture of transnational policing' which is grounded in an ethnocentric assumption that 'policing agents can be solutions to problems of authority'. In other words, Bowling and Sheptycki (2012: 78) argue that participants in these transnational policy communities share a common world view or habituated understanding of the importance of their work. The archetypical personas of those identified by Bowling and Sheptycki (2012: 87–93) as responsible for the crafting of transnational policing are thus described as follows:

- The **technician** *'is broadly concerned with the efficient gathering and management of data'* and represents *'an appendage of the surveillant assemblage'*.
- The **diplomat** is *'attuned to the nuances of legal, bureaucratic and political difference found in the multi-institutional settings in which policing takes place'*. They link different policing agents and organizations by formal inter-agency cooperation and partnership.
- The **entrepreneur** is a proponent of the *'technical wizardry of scientific policing'* who is also prone to *'moral entrepreneurship'*.
- The **public relations expert** *'acts to repress and circumvent some dilemmas in policing and dramatise others'*. They play an important role in shaping *'the contours of the global policing mission'*.
- The **legal ace** is responsible for the creative application of *'civil, administrative and regulatory law as tools of disruption'*.
- The **spy** is the *'agent provocateur'* of transnational policing whose covert techniques and utilitarian mindset *'further colour[s] the legitimacy of an already tainted occupation'*.
- The **field operator** is the *'workhorse of policing'* who *'manages both immediate issues of public safety and aim[s] to avert future ills'*.
- The **enforcer** *'maximises the assertion the use of force is the core task of policing'*.

Central to this 'subculture of transnational policing' is a functionalist assumption of the need to enhance the capacities and global orientation of formal mechanisms of social control in developing and transitional countries. This, argue Bowling and Sheptycki (2012: 25), is perceived by these actors to be necessary for developing coordinated responses to local and transnational security risks that pose a potential threat to global order and stability. Accordingly, the rationale for participating in the project of global policing is linked with its theorized aspiration to expand the reach of control so that it covers every corner of the globe. Bowling and Sheptycki (2012) do not go as far as to suggest that the motives of these agents are sinister. Rather, they draw from the work of Cohen (1988a) in suggesting that even well-intentioned or 'benign' interventions may generate harmful or 'iatrogenic' policy outputs. In other words, the models, the mentalities, and the practices that are prescribed for transplant in developing and transitional countries may produce unintended consequences that are more damaging than the risks or the institutional deficiencies that they are developed to address.

Drawing on the work of Ivan Illich (1977a; 1977b), Cohen (1988a: 191) identifies three different types of harm which may be generated by Western criminal justice reforms in the 'Third World'. The most straightforward of these, 'clinical iatrogenesis', accounts for the criminogenic effects of policies, similar to what Cohen describes as 'the harmful side effects of drugs, doctor-inflicted pain, unnecessary surgery, and the like' (Cohen 1988a: 191). In the context of criminology, Cohen likens clinical iatrogenesis to 'the ironic ways in which control agencies create and stabilize deviance' through their efforts to control it (Cohen 1988a: 191). The second type of harm described by Cohen is 'cultural iatrogenesis' whereby new categories of deviance are established in recipient societies so as to replace Western interests and cultural sensibilities about crime. Cohen's concern is that the displacement of local mentalities and strategies for coping with disorder may lead to cultural homogeneity and greater intolerance of once accepted behaviours and values. The third form of iatrogenesis described by Cohen is 'social iatrogenesis'. This describes the propensity of Western models and mentalities to increase insecurity and dependency on formal institutions of social control responsible for state provision. In developing nations, this dependency is said to be especially problematic because institutions like the police lack the experience or the resources of their counterparts in the global North.

It is beyond the scope of this book to provide a comprehensive critique of the typology developed by Bowling and Sheptycki (2012) but the convergence of development and security discourses in the age of global liberal governance suggests that this list is neither comprehensive nor universally applicable. In other words, these characterizations appear to be drawn from anecdotal evidence encountered by Bowling and Sheptycki (2012) who conducted empirical research on transnational policing in the Caribbean and Western Europe, respectively. Thus, if we look to Ellison and Pino's (2012) comparative research on police capacity development projects (which account for a type of transnational policing), Hills's (2012*a*; 2012*b*) research on police reform in Nigeria, or consider the growing popularity of partnership-based approaches to community policing and human security management in developing and transitional countries, it is clear that the range of actors and organizations responsible for crafting transnational policing is more expansive than argued by Bowling and Sheptycki (2012). In other words, transnational policing is crafted by a combination of global and local actors who need not represent the interests of institutions with a formal policing mandate or security remit. It is therefore necessary to question the degree to which the work of agents such as international development workers or members of international organizations like the OSCE is structured in accordance with the posited subculture of transnational policing. Furthermore, if indeed the 'crafters' of transnational policing do subscribe to a common worldview,[17] its values and discursive origins are inevitably more diverse, complex, and nuanced than has been suggested by Bowling and Sheptycki (2012). Accordingly, the reasons why different actors engage with transnational policing as a field of policy and practice are varied as are their means of interpreting their work.

Towards a 'Transnational Criminology of Harm Production'

My final task for this chapter is to introduce a reflexive discussion about the purpose of criminological engagement in transnational fields. Referencing Cohen (1988*a*: 172), Bowling (2011: 366) writes that 'criminologists, crime control officials, international agencies, and various other "experts"' are also complicit in what are, in practice, not-so-benign transfers.[18] Because of this, he adds that ethnocentric functionalist assumptions about the nature of crime and its control have also impeded upon the development of what he describes as a 'transnational criminology' that 'requires detailed knowledge of various geographical locations and transnational

---

[17]   Like Hills (2009; 2012*a*), I am sceptical of this argument.

[18]   Further to this point, Bowling sings candidly in his 2012 single, '...I'm a criminologist/What am I supposed to do?/It's crime that pays my wages/I'm telling you it's true'. Bowling, B. 'Criminal Injustice' by Doc Bowling and the Blues Professors. Pink Usagi Studies, 2012.

processes as well as theoretical and methodological flexibility' (Bowling 2011: 364).[19] Citing a second essay written by Cohen (1988*b*), Bowling (2011: 374) writes that '[i]n order to live with the awful products of the system that we observe, write about, advise on, and sometimes contribute to, criminologists use "techniques of neutralization" to deny the victim and deny the harm...'. To minimize the risk that criminologists will contribute to iatrogenic outcomes through their engagement with transnational fields, Bowling concludes:

Perhaps we need a criminology of harm production emphasizing the role of the discipline in documenting the harms produced by global crime control practices and the role of criminologists of speaking truth to power... (Bowling 2011: 374).

In the field of criminology, the phrase 'speaking truth to power' is attributed to Phil Scraton (2011: 35) who writes:

Critical research, publication and teaching within criminology has a significant role in resisting the political and ideological imperatives of official discourse, state-sponsored evaluations of official policy initiatives and the correspondence of vocational training to the requirements of the crime control industry.

Scraton adds:

Those who endure institutionalised harm at the hands of advanced democratic states more readily now raise their voices to demand thorough investigations, effective inquiries, disclosure of information and the fair administration of justice. They are voices that will not be hushed (Scraton 2011: 37).

In summary, 'speaking truth to power' means using one's expertise and intellectual capital to draw attention to gross injustices and inequalities in order to give a voice to those who are otherwise disempowered and potentially vulnerable. In the context of a 'transnational criminology of harm production', Bowling's (2010; 2011) work highlights the idea that critical criminologists must continuously challenge the assumption that the growth of

---

[19] Bowling (2011: 365) characterizes the distinction between a 'transnational criminology' and 'global criminology' as 'one of scope'. He adds, '...the latter [speaks] to the idea of process that involve, or at least aspire to involve, the whole world *considered in a planetary context*' (*ibid*, original emphasis).

transnational policing and the global dissemination of Western policing and crime control models and mentalities are of benefit to weak and structurally dependent nations of the global South. To this effect, he poses two important questions that should guide future research in this area: '…how far can theories of crime, criminal justice and punishment actually travel?; [and] To what extent, if at all, is western criminology applicable to Latin America, Africa, or Asia?' (Bowling 2011: 375). To answer these questions and, thus, 'speak truth to power', Bowling (2011: 375) concludes that '[c]riminologists should be working to understand the application of their theories and methods to other places'.

In *Policing the Caribbean*, Bowling (2010) 'speaks truth to power' by critically examining how the international 'war on drugs' has impacted law enforcement practices and culture throughout the region. Reflecting on his extensive qualitative fieldwork, Bowling concludes:

…with only a few exceptions, life in the countries of the regions has become far more dangerous than ever before. Moreover, public debate about security has been diverted from some of the most pressing economic, political, and environmental dangers that face the region and threaten to do great harm to its people. The clandestine trade in narcotic and psychotropic drugs and the armed violence that springs from it are, of course, major security threats. But these are not problems of the region's own making; they are the collateral damage of a failing war on drugs (Bowling 2010: 311).

Bowling's analysis echoes Cohen's (1988a) warnings about the potentially iatrogenic effects of Western-initiated reforms. It also illuminates the asymmetric power relations that shape the flow of crime control policies and practices from the United States and Britain to Caribbean nations and the fact that these transnational policing activities have emerged in response to the geo-strategic significance of the Caribbean as a transit region for narcotics. His concern is therefore with the lack of 'openness, transparency and accountability' associated with these transnational policing networks (Bowling 2010: 314). He goes on to argue (sic), '[i]n future, such activities should be accountable to local communities *and* subject to a robust and transparent system of supranational oversight'. This prompts him to identify the need for policymakers to address underlying structural and economic sources of global inequality in order to combat the 'global drug trade' and the harms it generates (Bowling 2010: 314).

'Resisting political and ideological imperatives' (paraphrasing Scraton 2011: 35) represents a worthy goal for transnational criminology but one must also consider that researcher reflexivity is central to any research that aspires to interpret and reconstruct global, comparative, and transnational dimensions of crime and its control (Blaustein 2014a). Reflexivity in the context of a transnational criminology of harm production can be understood as the idea that '[t]here is no one-way street between the researcher and the object of study; rather, the two affect each other mutually and continually in the course of the research process' (Alvesson and Sköldberg 2009: 79). Similarly, Dryzek (2006: 111) writes '[r]eflexive actors are aware of their status "inside" the world, and of the fact that their actions and messages help constitute or reconstitute the world in which they are operating'. The reflexive praxis described by Alvesson and Sköldberg and Dryzek holds important methodological implications for criminologists who are interested in studying globalization 'as an interactive rather than a hegemonic process' (Cain 2000: 252); in other words, a process that is continuously shaped by local and global forces and susceptible to transformation. 'Policy translation' and 'policy ethnography' which I discuss in Chapter 4 represent important conceptual and methodological tools for actualizing a critical-yet-reflective research agenda for transnational criminology. These tools are useful for illuminating the subjective perspectives of different stakeholders who may or may not share the researcher's initial assessment of a glocal situation or the discourses and structures underpinning it.

Discussion

Critics of international policing reform projects in the context of weak and structurally dependent societies generally suggest that prescriptions for 'democratic policing' overwhelmingly reflect the interests of powerful international actors who use their power to generate policy alignment and structural convergence from a distance. What this implies is that the policing practices and structures generated by foreign assistance programmes lack clear channels of local accountability and responsiveness. For this reason, the concept of democratically responsive policing which I introduced in Chapter 1 establishes a better framework for supporting local policing practices that are primarily responsive to the interests and needs of local citizens as opposed to international elites. Community policing and community safety partnerships are templates for supporting locally responsive policing but their commodification through transnational policy networks combined with the structural challenges facing recipient societies imply that they may not achieve their envisioned functions of controlling or empowering local citizens.

A dilemma confronting the Northern transnational criminologist with critical inclinations is as follows: should I seek to 'educate' my research participants about the potential dangers of transnational policing and the global structures and networks that generate convergent and potentially iatrogenic ways of thinking about crime and security, or should I adopt a more cautious and relativistic approach whereby I aspire to learn from my research participants in order to identify and understand the nuances and the diversity of their viewpoints? Bowling (2010) has done well to balance these objectives through his research on transnational policing in the Caribbean so perhaps we need not treat them as incompatible. For this reason, my stance is that transnational criminologists, in particular those of Northern origin, have an obligation to speak *truths* to power rather than a singular truth. In other words, Northern criminologists as cultural and contextual outsiders often lack local knowledge and, in many cases, a moral basis to directly and intentionally influence decision-making processes that shape local manifestations of transnational policing. Epistemologically, this argument is consistent with Raewyn Connell's (2007: 207) advocacy of what she identifies as 'dirty theory' whereby 'the goal . . . is not to subsume, but to clarify; not to classify from the outside, but to illuminate a situation in its concreteness'.

This is not to suggest that Northern criminologists must distance themselves from the key deliberative processes or policy nodes through which transnational and glocal policing are crafted. Nor do I believe that objective detachment is truly possible given the 'expert' status that is commonly ascribed to the Northern criminologist in these fields. Rather, it is because the Northern criminologist is frequently ascribed 'expert' status that they should exercise modesty by limiting their aspiration for generating 'impact' to co-producing knowledge that assists reformers, policymakers, and practitioners in formulating and implementing policies that empower local citizens. In some instances, there may also be further scope to use their intellectual, social, and political capital to improve the accessibility of key governing processes and nodes to local stakeholders who otherwise lack a voice. Returning to Connell's (2007: 213–14, paraphrased) work, speaking truths to power can be seen as part of an agenda for 'undoing the erasure of experience from the periphery for the purpose of re-working the relations between the periphery and the metropole to make a shared learning process possible'.

To perform this role, Loader and Sparks (2010: 122) have elsewhere articulated a form of criminological engagement labelled 'democratic under-labouring' in which the criminologist 'explicitly seek[s] to understand and improve politics rather than replace it with expert-led calculation (Latour 2007: 5)'. The warning against 'expert-led calculation' applies not just to criminological research that seeks to promote evidence-based solutions to the criminal question or experimental methods in the developing world (see, for example, Neyroud and Wain 2013; Sherman 2012) but also to that which prioritizes critical theorization with the effect of obscuring the complexities of the field and, thus, marginalizing the viewpoints and preferences of those for whom critical criminologists claim to speak. Accordingly, 'speaking truths to power' is about accessing and activating a diversity of viewpoints so they factor into the deliberative processes that govern crime and its control.

3

Reforming the Police in Bosnia and Herzegovina

When I commenced my fieldwork in early 2011, the existing body of literature on police reform in BiH consisted of post hoc assessments of macro-level police reform initiatives (Hansen 2008; ICG 2002, 2005; Muehlmann 2008; Wisler 2005); critiques of the goals and objectives that had been pursued by international actors such as the United Nations Mission in Bosnia and Herzegovina (UNMBiH) (Vejnovic and Lalic 2005) and the EUPM (Collantes-Celador 2007, 2009; Maras 2009; Merlingen and Ostrauskaite 2005); analyses of the circumstances that drive policing reform initiatives in this context (Collantes-Celador 2005; Venneri 2010); and localized empirical evaluations of specific policing reform initiatives (Deljkić and Lučić-Ćatić 2011). This body of work afforded me valuable background information that was essential for undertaking detailed ethnographic studies of police capacity building projects in this context. It drew my attention to the role that international reformers had played in shaping the rhetoric and content of policing and security governance in BiH and it fostered my awareness of the presence of hierarchical and non-democratic power structures. I recognized that many of the reforms being introduced to BiH were modelled on 'Western' policing mentalities and practices and so my initial inclination was to interpret my cases through the lens of policy transfer. By nature of my access agreement with UNDP I quickly realized, however, that the data I was generating captured more than a linear and one-directional exchange of ideas. Rather, the ideas themselves were being altered and modified during their transmission. I also recognized that along with my temporary colleagues at UNDP, I was an active participant in this transformational process.

Building on the previous chapter's discussion of police capacity building, this chapter situates my ethnographic research by providing a focused review of the police reform process in BiH that highlights the asymmetrical character of the governance of security in this transitional society. The chapter begins by reviewing the police reform process in BiH chronologically, initially accounting for macro-level initiatives that were designed to 'democratize' the police throughout the country. It then proceeds to discuss the implementation of local community policing projects throughout the country and discusses the early contributions of UNDP's predecessors including DFID and the SDC in the lead-up to the Safer Communities project which was launched in 2009. The review draws primarily from a substantial body of secondary literature on police reform in BiH and this is supplemented by primary analysis of project documents that I gained access to through my fieldwork as well as data generated through interviews and personal observation.

Policing Before 'Dayton'

Policing in the SFRY remains poorly documented in the English language policing literature[1] but it is clear that institution exhibited elements of what Brodeur (1983) describes as 'high' and 'low policing'. High policing was evident from the centralized, state policing body known as the 'Resor Državne Bezbednosti' (RDB). The RDB was responsible for intelligence and counter-intelligence activities and was comprised of a paramilitary force of approximately fifteen thousand officers who '… could be deployed in times of political unrest or disorder when the local police were expected to side with the populace against federal authorities' (Soper 2007). This suggests that the RDB primarily performed a specific order maintenance function within the SFRY by working to insulate the Yugoslav Government and its political ideology from political dissidence. By contrast, low policing responsible for maintaining general order within the SFRY was decentralized and administered by

---

[1] I searched English-language scholarly databases and asked fellow researchers from BiH to search local academic libraries for any Serbo-Croat resources on policing in the former Yugoslavia. The only Serbo-Croat reference that I have located on policing in the former Yugoslavia (pre-1991) was a National Criminal Justice Reference Service (NCJRS) Abstract for Anzic (1992). The abstract indicates that the article focuses on the repressive function of high policing in Yugoslavia but I have been unable to access the full text.

each of Yugoslavia's six individual republics following liberalization initiatives of the 1960s and 1970s (Stojanovic and Downes
2009: 75–6).[2]

The fact that each individual republic had a certain degree
of control over local 'milicija' (public police) suggests that local
policing varied throughout the SFRY. While descriptive accounts
of low policing in each of the constituent republics are scarce,
anecdotal evidence does suggest that its provision was generally
viewed more favourably by the Yugoslav public than its state-level
counterpart. This was at least the case in the Republic of Bosnia
and Herzegovina where Bringa (1995: 74) suggests that the local
milicija derived a certain degree of legitimacy from its capacity to
act as a *de facto* arbitrator of inter-ethnic disputes. The milicija
may have therefore performed an important order maintenance
function in the Republic of Bosnia and Herzegovina but this is not
to suggest that the institution was highly regarded by the public
it served. Nor does it appear to be the case that members of the
public were overly keen to engage with their local police officers. I
personally encountered anecdotal evidence of the public's aversion
to police contact during one of my interviews with a senior police
officer in Sarajevo. The officer suggested that, even today, older
generations in BiH continue to mistrust the police because they
associate the current sector-based policing model with neighbourhood policing styles of the Yugoslav era.[3] A 2003 project proposal
for DFID's community-oriented policing project (discussed later in
this chapter) also supports this analysis by suggesting that neighbourhood policing in the SFRY was characterized by 'a lack of
trust between police and communities' (Atos KPMG 2003: 2).

State policing in the SFRY does not appear to have been considered 'democratic'[4] but its legacy during the Bosnian War was

---

[2] Prior to liberalization, public policing was overseen by the Federal Secretariat
of the Interior. The six constituent republics of the SFRY included the Socialist
Republics of Bosnia and Herzegovina, Croatia, Macedonia, Montenegro, Serbia,
and Slovenia.

[3] Interview with RPZ1's Station Supervisor on 4 April 2011.

[4] This is not to suggest that an objective benchmark or threshold exists for
measuring the 'democratic' character of this institution but rather that it was not
intended to be 'democratic' and nor does the limited anecdotal evidence suggest
that it was viewed as democratic by citizens of the SFRY or prominent Western
political scientists of the era like Rummel (1997) who associated the RBD with
'democide'.

clearly 'anti-democratic' (Aitchison and Blaustein 2013: 502–3). Bieber (2010) describes how the collapse of SFRY during the early 1990s prompted the local police to redefine their function for the duration of the conflict while Aitchison (2007: 327–8) observes that, between 1992 and 1995, local police officers actively participated in various human rights violations including acts associated with ethnic cleansing, forced population transfers, mass detention, and mass murder. The role of the public police during the war and its complicity with these human rights abuses inevitably tarnished the reputation of this institution as a legitimate provider of public security and this further diminished the institution's operational capacities for maintaining general order. It was in relation to the perceived non-democratic character of policing in the SFRY and its anti-democratic character during the Bosnian War that international reformers identified police reform as an important state-building priority in BiH beginning in the late 1990s.

Towards 'Policing for Democracy' in Bosnia and Herzegovina

As noted in Chapter 2, the international community's mandate for supporting police reforms in BiH was established by Annex 11 of the Dayton Peace Agreement which established the IPTF to assist the 'Parties' with overseeing the implementation of police reforms that would establish a 'a safe and secure environment for all persons in their respective jurisdictions, by maintaining civilian law enforcement agencies operating in accordance with internationally recognized standards and with respect for internationally recognized human rights and fundamental freedoms' (OHR 1995). Underpinning the international community's interest in reforming the police was an assumption that a 'democratic' model of policing was necessary for re-establishing general order throughout BiH and for ultimately establishing and sustaining liberal democratic governing institutions prescribed by the Dayton Peace Agreement. Elsewhere, I have argued with Aitchison that, between 1996 and 2003, the IPTF's primary contribution to the police reform process in BiH involved fostering a model of public policing that was necessary for establishing democratic governance: 'policing for democracy'. Reflecting on the international community's role in supporting police reform in BiH, we define 'policing for democracy' as '…policing which does not damage, but rather actively supports, the development of the core elements of a democracy and of democratic consolidation' (Aitchison and Blaustein 2013: 499). This definition emphasizes the need for the institution of policing to demonstrate restraint with respect to their use of coercive force as well as their positive obligation to use their coercive powers to protect key democratic processes and institutions including fair and free elections.

During the IPTF's first year (January–December 1996), the most immediate priority was to address the public order security gap that existed in the aftermath of the war. Aitchison (2011: 82) elsewhere has written that the IPTF's prescribed role emphasized 'monitoring and facilitating law enforcement activities, offering advice and training to police forces, advising government bodies, assessing threats and evaluating capabilities, accompanying and assisting police, and reporting human rights violations to the authorities…'. In other words, the IPTF lacked a formal policing mandate[5] and was instead tasked with overseeing various police reform initiatives that were designed by the UNMBiH to improve the institutional capacities of BiH's 'decentralised and dysfunctional' police forces (ICG 2002: 1; also Wisler 2005: 140).[6]

In December 1996, Aitchison (2011: 82) notes that the IPTF's mandate was formally extended by UN Resolution 1088 (also Wisler 2005: 147). As stated in a 2002 report produced by the International Conflict Group titled *Policing the Police in Bosnia*, the renewal of the IPTF's mandate included a call for a greater focus on 'the protection of citizens' rights [through] the articulation of specific, observable standards' (ICG 2002: 7; quoting Dziedzic and Bair 1998: 20, 28). Aitchison (2011) argues that, around this time, the IPTF also became involved with a 'lustration' process designed to transform the police into a trusted institution via the implementation of a three-tiered

---

[5] As Wisler (2005: 145) notes, the United Nations International Civilian Police (UN CIVPOL) mission (which included the IPTF) 'was unarmed and not entrusted with law enforcement capacities'.

[6] A 2002 report from the ICG suggests that the state and governmental structures that were prescribed for BiH by the Dayton Agreement would actually create major challenges for the IPTF and subsequent agencies involved with police reform initiatives because it effectively established fourteen different police forces which lacked a mechanism of central coordination or an inclination towards cooperation (ICG 2002).

accreditation process.[7] The first stage of this process required individual police officers to register with a national database. The second stage involved screening every officer 'by means of a self-completed questionnaire' (Aitchison 2011: 83). During the third stage, police officers were required to pass individual background checks to ensure that they had not been involved with human rights abuses or war crimes (Wisler 2005: 148). Finally, before these officers could be certified and issued a UNMBiH identification card, they were required to complete mandatory training courses that covered human rights issues and training on more programmatic aspects of 'democratic policing'.

In terms of its overall impact and legacy, the IPTF mission played an important role in re-establishing the general order maintenance capacity of the public police in BiH (ICG 2002: 1). This suggests that the IPTF contributed to the establishment of 'policing for a democracy' in BiH but was less influential in terms of developing the police into a democratically responsive institution.[8] Specifically, the IPTF struggled to address the issue of police interference from nationalist politicians in the RS while the fragmented political structures in FBiH limited its capacity to implement reforms uniformly throughout its ten cantons. The IPTF's attempts to 'socially engineer' the police in BiH (Collantes-Celador 2005: 373) further highlights the non-democratic character of the transnational governance of security in BiH. The powers afforded to the IPTF via Annex 11 of the Dayton Peace Agreement and UN Resolution 1088 effectively rendered it an important architect of structural alignment in BiH, its work primarily accountable and responsive to international interests like the UNMBiH and the Office of the High Representative (OHR) which viewed the police as an important 'transmission mechanism'[9] that served to impart liberal democratic values throughout the wider social and political architecture of the newly established BiH state (Collantes-Celador

---

[7] This accreditation process was initially introduced to FBiH in 1998 and only subsequently implemented in RS in 1999 due to ongoing resistance from nationalist political elites.

[8] The IPTF was not the only organization/agency involved with police reform during this period, however, it was the most influential. Other contributors ranging from the U.S. Department of Justice's International Criminal Investigative Training Assistance Program (ICITAP) to the OSCE are listed in ICG (2002: 7).

[9] Collantes-Celador (2005: 373) borrows this term from Paris (2002).

2005: 373). The rhetoric of 'democratic policing' was attached to this transformative agenda (see, for example, UNSC 1997*a*) yet the governance of the police reform process remained inaccessible to democratically-elected BiH politicians who lacked the authority or the influence to positively shape these prescriptions. Instead, their designated role involved acting as intermediaries and, in theory, legitimating the international community's prescriptions for state-building through domestic governing institutions.

Europeanization and Policing Reforms

On 1 January 2003, the EUPM replaced the IPTF as the primary agency tasked with overseeing the police reform process in BiH. The convergence between international and EU interests in BiH was effectively cemented in 2003 when the OHR took on the role of the European Union Special Representative in BiH thus entangling the agendas for democratization and Europeanization in this context. As the coordinating agency tasked with overseeing BiH's democratic transition as well as the fulfilment of various prescribed EU pre-accession criteria, the OHR played a significant role in subsequently shaping the agenda of the EUPM.[10]

Wisler (2005: 153, original emphasis) argues that this transition 'opened the door to a new era of *realpolitik* in Bosnia by the EU...', one that would signify a reformative shift from peacebuilding towards a specific, European brand of liberal state-building that called for BiH's gradual integration into the structures and institutions of the EU (see also Centre for European Perspective 2008: 7). The EU's interest in overseeing the police reform process in BiH was linked with its Common Security and Defence Policy. Notably, Osland (2004: 544–5) argues that police reform was viewed as a means of combatting the risks associated with state failure on the EU's periphery, specifically organized crime, terrorism, and narcotics trafficking. Juncos (2007: 46) adds that BiH would come to serve as an important 'security laboratory' for the EU which, according to Buzan and Wæver 2003: 343) had emerged as one of two powerful 'regional security actors' in this region.[11]

---

[10] The European Commission also served as an important source of influence over the EUPM's agenda as it was responsible for overseeing BiH's pre-accession negotiations.

[11] The other regional hegemon being the Russian Federation.

Through its prospective role in overseeing the state-building process in BiH and, more specifically, its oversight of the police reform process, Osland (2004: 545) argues that the EU sought to generate important credibility for its *European Security Strategy* (see Solana 2003) that was adopted in December 2003 and which subsequently served as an important test of the EU's capabilities as a legitimate, regional security actor.

Drawing from the experience of its predecessor, the IPTF, the initial aims of the EUPM were to 'improve [police] governance on the middle and higher levels' and to 'de-politicise the police' (Osland 2004: 553). During its initial three-year mandate,[12] the EUPM worked closely with the OHR to address the issue of political interference through a plan which called for extensive restructuring of the police throughout BiH. In response to conclusions published in a 2003 *European Commission Feasibility Study* that stipulated the need for European reformers to restructure the police in BiH (see Muehlmann 2008: 4–5), High Representative Paddy Ashdown and the OHR established the Police Restructuring Commission (PRC) in 2004 as a vehicle 'for proposing a single structure of policing for Bosnia and Herzegovina under the overall political oversight of a ministry or ministries in the state-level Council of Ministers' (PRC 2004). The impetus behind this proposal also stemmed from the realization that the established policing structures that the EUPM had 'inherited' from the IPTF were highly fragmented, dysfunctional, and susceptible to corruption. In other words, they were thought to represent a significant vulnerability to the prospect of establishing 'rule of law' in BiH. Accordingly, existing policing structures in BiH were identified as a major impediment to BiH's progress in its pre-accession negotiations with the European Commission and the prospect of it signing a *Stabilization and Association Agreement* (Muehlmann 2008: 3).

---

[12] The EUPM's mandate was initially prescribed to last for only three years (January 2003–December 2005). Osland (2004: 552-3) suggests the EUPM's initial plan was to carry out its work over three stages. The planning stage was expected to overlap with the work of the IPTF and was intended to ensure a smooth transition between the two agencies. The second stage involved implementing various projects in order to 'transform the BiH police into a professional, political and ethnically neutral institution for judicial enforcement'. Finally, the third stage emphasized handing over power to domestic actors and ensuring that the outputs generated were in fact sustainable.

The EUPM's main contribution with respect to the PRC's proposal for a single policing structure in BiH involved designing the 'second level of policing' structures in BiH. This new design called for establishing new police regions that transcended the inter-entity boundary line between FBiH and RS. This proposal was viewed as a 'contentious' issue by Bosnian Serb members of the PRC who considered it a threat to RS's autonomous oversight of the police. Their concern was that creating these new inter-entity regions could ultimately lead to the discontinuation of the RS Ministry of the Interior which had previously been responsible for coordinating all policing activities within RS (Muehlmann 2008: 7). Ultimately, resistance on behalf of RS politicians undermined the OHR's attempt to restructure the police in BiH.

While the EUPM's involvement with the PRC was an important aspect of its first mandate, Collantes-Celador (2009: 240) notes that another issue which confronted the EUPM stemmed from plans to introduce 'European standards practices' for policing to BiH. In fact, Collantes-Celador suggests that the EUPM's preoccupation with restructuring 'led to the interruption or slowing down of programmes/projects under EUPM's first mandate' with the effect that its mission would subsequently be extended for another two years (January 2006–December 2007).[13] The EUPM's difficulties in supporting programmatic reforms during its first mandate can be partially attributed to ongoing resistance and political interference from domestic politicians. However, Collantes-Celador adds that the OHR's focus on restructuring also contributed to a reduction in 'political energy and resources available for crime-fighting' and other programmatic and technical initiatives like community policing (Collantes-Celador 2009: 240). These obstacles, combined with what Juncos (2007: 46) describes as the EU's relative inexperience 'in the field of civilian crisis management' and operational issues including the EUPM's scattered presence throughout BiH prompted important questions about the purpose and capabilities of the Mission. These concerns compelled the EUPM to redefine its mandate to focus exclusively on high profile issues like building the capacity of the BiH police to combat organized crime and political corruption as these issues

---

[13] Note that the EUPM's mandate would be formally extended on two more occasions from January 2008–December 2009 and from January 2010 until 30 June 2012.

were determined to represent significant impediments to the country's prospective accession to the European Union (EUPM 2011). Subsequent reforms which dealt with local policing structures and practices were left to international development agencies, specifically DFID and the SDC, which took the lead in drafting a national *Strategy for Community-based Policing* in 2007 (henceforth '*Strategy*', referenced as 'BiH Ministry of Security 2007').

Towards Community Policing and Community Safety Partnerships

In the previous chapter, I discussed how community policing has been embraced by policy entrepreneurs and reformers as an important prescription for democratic policing in the context of transitional post-conflict societies. As an export commodity (Brogden and Nijhar 2005: 4), community policing provides reformers with an important 'buzzword' (Skolnick and Bayley 1988: 4) and a 'plastic concept' (Eck and Rosenbaum 1994: 3) used to describe an array of activities relating to low policing. While various models of community policing exist, the Peelite narrative that underpins community policing presents it as the antithesis of 'military-style policing with a central bureaucracy obedient to directive legislation which minimizes discretion' (Brogden and Nijhar 2005: 2). In the context of weak and structurally dependent societies like BiH, community policing usually exists as an amalgamation of different national models that have been promoted or imposed upon this context by different policy entrepreneurs, international development agencies, and domestic reformers who collectively constitute an important transnational policy community. This section presents a detailed account of the various initiatives and models that contributed to this amalgamation process in BiH.

Macro-level Initiatives

The rhetoric of community policing was first introduced to BiH in the late 1990s by the IPTF and has since served as a recurring focus of international reformers. The IPTF's role in initially introducing the rhetoric of community policing to BiH is documented in a 2003 report by DFID which also describes the involvement of the United States Department of Justice International

Criminal Investigative Training Assistance Program (ICITAP) (Atos KPMG 2003: 2). This report also accounts for an early discursive link between community policing and democratic policing by suggesting that ICITAP's aim in the late 1990s was 'to create a community-oriented police force that abided by democratic standards and observed and protected human rights' (Atos KPMG 2003: 2). A subsequent report published by the US Institute of Peace also accounts for the collaborative relationship between ICITAP and the IPTF by describing how '... [ICITAP] trained and equipped local police directly or provided curriculum and equipment to the IPTF, which trained the Bosnians' (Perito 2007: 8).While these documents demonstrate that the rhetoric of community policing has been present in BiH since the early phases of the police reform process, the lack of documentation relating to these early initiatives indicates that their programmatic influence over subsequent community policing projects has been rather limited.

Between 2000 and 2002, more concrete attempts by the IPTF to promote community policing in BiH become evident. In 2000, the IPTF implemented a mandatory training course for all police officers that provided them with a basic understanding of the community policing philosophy (UNSG 2000: 3). This initiative complemented the three-stage lustration process described by Aitchison (2011). It is difficult to assess the impact that this educational initiative had on subsequent community policing practices in BiH or the extent to which officers at the time actually understood or embraced these lessons, but one indicator of the IPTF's success, at least in terms of disseminating the rhetoric of community policing, is that, by July 2001, '[t]he community policing programme [had] been completed in 60% of the Federation and 88% of Republika Sprska' (UNSG 2001: 2). The novelty of this concept from the perspective of local police officers in BiH is questionable however. For example, the 2003 Atos KPMG report commissioned by DFID notes that many of the rhetorical elements of the IPTF's training programme including its emphasis on the need for police to maintain a presence within the communities they served and the importance of information sharing were already recognized by BiH police officers as important components of the Yugoslav model of 'sector policing' (Atos KPMG 2003: 2). This indicates that the IPTF's training may not have actually introduced ideas like problem-solving and information sharing to BiH but rather provided the officers with a fresh, democratically-compliant vocabulary for describing familiar practices.

International support for macro-level community policing reforms began to dwindle under the direction of the EUPM between 2003 and 2005 and a 2010 evaluation report commissioned by the SDC notes that, by 2008, the EUPM had 'retreated from local policing issues' altogether (Wisler and Traljic 2010: 23). A project associate working for the SDC's community policing project accounts for the EUPM's decision to withdraw its direct support for community policing reforms by suggesting that the EUPM viewed them as time consuming, resource intensive and difficult to implement uniformly given the absence of a universal legal framework to compel interior ministries throughout BiH to adopt the reforms.[14] This analysis is supported by Collantes-Celador's (2007: 6) description of the EUPM as lacking '...adequate resources and personnel...' to simultaneously focus on macro-level restructuring and local improvements in the delivery of policing.

Community Policing as International Development Assistance

By late 2003, police officers throughout BiH had been introduced to the rhetoric of community policing but the training that they had received from the IPTF and through the police academies in Banja Luka and Sarajevo included limited emphasis on the actual skills or practices required for doing community police work. Nor did this curriculum encourage police managers to incorporate this 'policing style' into their 'every-day operations' (Atos KPMG 2003: 2). Seeking to advance the programmatic development of community policing and community safety partnership schemes across BiH, DFID and the SDC initiated parallel projects in 2003 which introduced two different community policing and community safety partnership models to select municipalities throughout the country. The 'lessons learned' from these projects served as a platform for the agencies' future contributions to the development of the national *Strategy*.

DFID oversaw the larger of the two initiatives in terms of both scale and budget and established community policing and

---

[14] Interview with 'SDC Project Associate' on 22 June 2011.

community safety partnership pilot projects in Žepče and Prijedor. This initiative formed part of the agency's Safety, Security and Access to Justice Programme (SSAJP) which was financed by the UK Government's Conflict Prevention Pool (Atos KPMG 2003: 3). The logic of pursuing community-oriented policing reforms as part of DFID's broader interest in conflict prevention and stability in the Western Balkans demonstrates that the agency subscribed to the 'human security' narrative discussed in Chapter 2. The holistic emphasis on conflict transformation through development is evident from DFID's 2003 technical proposal for the project which stated, '...the goal of the project is that public bodies implement justice strategies that reduce local tension, conflict and prevent crime and disorder' (Atos KPMG 2003: 3). According to the cluster manager for the SSAJP project, Prijedor and Žepče were specifically selected as the pilot sites for local community policing projects because they were identified as likely hotspots for future ethnic conflict.[15] This indicates that DFID embraced community policing as a potential mechanism for managing local conflict through the police as local security institution. By translating the community policing 'philosophy' into strategic programmes that could be implemented within these two municipalities, DFID also sought to contribute to increased levels of trust and cooperation between uniformed police officers and members of the public because it was thought that this would improve the police's ability to address any tensions and to manage the risk of escalation (Atos KPMG 2003: 4). The emphasis on community policing reform was further complemented by a second component of the project that involved establishing community safety partnership schemes at both sites to improve cooperation between the police and public agencies which had previously struggled with communication and had failed to address public security and safety issues in a collaborative manner (Atos KPMG 2003: 4).[16]

The pilot project was designed and implemented by a team of UK-based consultants employed by Atos KPMG which had been contracted by DFID. The team was led by a 'Project Manager' who had previously worked as an Assistant Chief Constable in Scotland and had subsequently served as an advisor for police

---

[15] Interview with a former DFID Cluster Coordinator on 26 July 2011.
[16] Also, interview with a former DFID Cluster Coordinator on 26 July 2011.

reform projects in Namibia and Jamaica. It also featured four project associates who had previously advised or consulted on policing matters in Albania, India, Kosovo, and Serbia and Montenegro. All of these individuals possessed previous experience working with community policing and community safety partnership schemes in the UK. At each pilot site, one associate was responsible for community policing while their counterpart was responsible for the community safety initiative. In addition to the project's international consultants, the team also employed local consultants 'on a needs basis' because it was recognized that the 'core team' lacked 'local expertise' (Atos KPMG 2003: 15). This suggests that during its pilot phase, DFID's community policing project was primarily developed and implemented by members of a transnational policy community who Ellison (2007) and others have associated with the global export and commodification of community policing.

The specific model for community policing that DFID introduced to these pilot sites reflected an amalgamation of the best community-oriented policing practices from the UK and the developing and transitional countries where its project members had previously worked. According to the former Cluster Coordinator, the Atos KPMG team advocated a two-component model for establishing community-oriented policing which could be readily adapted to local circumstances and structures.[17] The first component focused on 'institutionalizing' the idea that every police officer should perform their duties in a manner that reflected the philosophy of community policing. It also involved establishing 'strategic boards', comprised of local officials and senior police officers, to: 'review progress as community-based policing is introduced'; 'advise on the strategic direction and endorse key decisions'; and 'establish mechanisms to monitor and evaluate the introduction of community-based policing' within these municipalities (DFID 2005: 8). The second component focused on developing and managing 'strategic partnerships' at these sites to: 'strengthen the capacity of the police to solve community problems'; 'secure joint commitment across government to the new model...'; and 'assist the police in developing and implementing local policing plans...' (DFID 2005: 10).

In 2004, the SDC initiated its own pilot project for community policing, initially in Zenica (FBiH) and subsequently throughout

---

[17] Interview with the former DFID Cluster Coordinator on 26 July 2011.

the entire Zenica-Doboj Canton (DeBlieck 2007: 23). Smaller than its UK-funded counterpart, the SDC project team consisted of two full-time project associates from BiH and a Project Manager who was based primarily in Switzerland. The SDC worked to implement its own brand of community policing locally throughout BiH but it did not reject or oppose DFID's aim of institutionalizing the community policing philosophy. Rather, the SDC project associate who I interviewed stated that the SDC recognized the importance of ensuring that every police officer conducted their work in a manner consistent with the philosophy of community policing while questioning whether meaningful outputs could be generated and sustained through institutionalization alone.[18] These concerns prompted the SDC to advocate 'strategic' prescriptions for developing teams of local community policing specialists who would take a proactive role in implementing a problem-oriented approach to policing that was grounded in the 'Scanning, Analysis, Response, Assessment' (SARA) methodology.

Between 2004 and 2006, the SDC provided training for community policing specialists in Zenica-Doboj Canton and it also trained police managers 'in areas such as field work, management, communication and public relations' (BiH Ministry of Security 2007: 17). It further established a citizen security forum in Zenica and provided financial assistance for crime prevention campaigns, police station refurbishments, and the implementation of a public perception survey designed to identify local community safety issues. My interview with an SDC project associate revealed that the agency may have had multiple motives for supporting community policing reform in BiH. On an idealistic level, the project worker believed that the Swiss Government wanted to make a meaningful contribution to the post-war reconstruction and state-building process in BiH. On a pragmatic level, they added that the project and the SDC's work with community policing reforms in Romania reflected the Swiss Government's belief that investing in SSR in proximate countries undergoing transition would support a long-term reduction in Switzerland's immigrant population and indirectly contribute to a reduction in levels of petty crime. While this analysis must be treated as highly speculative, the suggestion that the SDC's motives were more instrumental than idealistic is

---

[18] Interview with an SDC Project Associate on 22 June 2011.

credible given the documented convergence of development and security discourses in the aftermath of the Cold War and the fact that an estimated 74.3% of prisoners in Switzerland are foreign nationals.[19] Instrumental motives are also described by Hvidemose and Mellon (2009: 3) who suggest that the primary objective of the SDC's regional programme for police reform known as 'Phase 10' was to '...help law enforcement improve its ability to fight transnational crime, and [to] promote community policing as a means of conflict prevention' (see also Uster 2007: 4).[20]

A National 'Strategy for Community-based Policing in Bosnia and Herzegovina'

In attempting to pilot their respective community policing projects, DFID and the SDC encountered significant institutional resistance from senior police officers who proved hostile to change or failed to follow through on their assurances of support. One reason for this institutional resistance was the lack of a formal framework (either legal or policy-based) that necessitated managerial cooperation and compliance. Another obstacle described by the former DFID Cluster Coordinator was that police managers failed to recognize the strategic utility of the reforms and did not appreciate the instrumental value of community policing. Rather, he described how they referred to it as 'child policing' or associated it with 'helping old ladies'.[21]

Despite the indeterminate success of their pilot projects, DFID and the SDC drew upon the lessons learnt from their pilot projects and supported the federal Ministry of Security in developing the national *Strategy for Community-based Policing* which was

[19] See 'Switzerland'. *World Prison Brief.* International Centre for Prison Studies, n.d. Web. 23 Apr 2014. <http://www.prisonstudies.org/country/switzerland>.

[20] The third rationale which was presented by the project associate from the SDC was that Switzerland 'is only a small country with an interest in showing the world that they know something' (paraphrasing a personal communication with an SDC project associate on 22 June 2011). This rationale perhaps explains why the SDC continued to promote its particular brand of community policing in BiH despite the fact that the 2007 national *Strategy* formally adopted DFID's approach but as an explanation for why the SDC initially decided to invest in this project, it appears to be less convincing than the instrumental account.

[21] Interview with a former DFID Cluster Coordinator on 26 July 2011.

approved by the BiH Council of Ministers in 2008 (BiH Ministry of Security 2007). The 'Foreword' to the *Strategy* states that it was developed by a working group that included representatives from key state, entity, and cantonal ministries as well as representatives of different policing agencies and the EUPM but my interviews with the SDC Project Associate and the former DFID Cluster Coordinator revealed that the majority of its content was influenced by DFID. DFID played the greatest role in steering the implementation of the national *Strategy* between 2008 and 2010 because its budgetary resources enabled it to fund a Secretariat position for the National Implementation Team which was responsible for disseminating the *Strategy*'s prescriptions throughout BiH, facilitating implementation, and monitoring progress. By funding this post, DFID was able to subsequently reduce its direct oversight of localized community policing projects and instead focus its resources on specific activities linked with the third Strategic Objective of the *Strategy* which emphasized establishing 'Community Safety Boards and prevention campaigns' to support the implementation of this *Strategy* in new locales (Wisler and Traljic 2010: 21). This Secretariat position provided DFID with a means of shaping the implementation of the *Strategy* from a distance in a manner consistent with the techniques of global liberal governmentality described by Duffield (2007) and Ryan (2011).

In authoring the template for the *Strategy*, DFID also intentionally left certain areas of the framework 'broad' in order to accommodate the Swiss model where it was believed to be contextually relevant. It was anticipated that this would encourage the SDC to continue to support the implementation process despite the SDC's doubts about the philosophy-based approach. Accordingly, the SDC subsequently focused its attention on supporting police-oriented activities rather than those which focused on mobilizing community resources or generating support from local public officials.[22]

Between 2007 and 2011, the SDC continued to support the implementation of the national *Strategy* through the following activities: implementing opinion polls designed to identify local priorities for community police work; coordinating prevention campaigns that would assist RPZ officers in addressing these issues; providing RPZ officers with training that reflected the 'best

[22] Interview with a CSS Project Associate on 28 April 2010.

practices' of community policing in Switzerland; providing managers with training on community policing; contributing to the National Implementation Team's development of an *Operational Handbook on Police-Community Co-Operation* (BiH Council of Ministers 2010);[23] and lobbying for adjustments in performance management systems in order to account for the flexible nature of community policing. Seeking to facilitate greater trust between the police and the public, the SDC also provided officers with training in concepts like 'transactional analysis' and 'security marketing' aimed at generating greater public awareness of community policing (Schorer 2007; Wisler and Traljic 2010).[24] Finally, the SDC subsidized the refurbishment of public reception areas at police stations throughout the country including Banja Luka and Novi Grad in Sarajevo in order to improve the institution's public image.[25]

By supporting the objectives identified by the national *Strategy*, the SDC continued to promote its specialist model of community policing and, in 2007, the SDC introduced it to two municipalities in Sarajevo Canton and throughout RS (Petrovic 2007). In July 2010, the SDC commissioned an external review of its community policing project in BiH that was conducted by Dominique Wisler, a Swiss community policing expert with significant previous consulting experience, along with a former member of DFID's SSAJP project. The findings of this unpublished report indicate that the SDC was relatively successful in generating outputs that were consistent with the objectives that it set back in 2007. However, the report also recognized that the SDC's working methodology was output-oriented meaning that the SDC struggled to define or measure its 'successes' in relation to the actual impact of these reforms.[26] In the following chapter, I note that focusing on outputs rather than outcomes is common practice for international development agencies that embrace the idea of 'results-based management' (henceforth 'RBM'). It is also symptomatic of the fact that international development workers struggle to measure and

---

[23] The Saferworld Group and the Sarajevo-based Centre for Security Studies (CSS) were the main supporters of this 'Handbook'.

[24] These are reviewed in greater detail in Chapter 6.

[25] Personal communication with an officer from RPZ1 on 7 March 2011.

[26] Wisler and Traljic's (2010) evaluation of the second stage of the SDC's community policing project provides valuable insights into the working methodology of this organization's approach to implementing police-oriented activities in BiH. The analysis presented in this 2010 review is also noticeably more detailed than in

anticipate the long-term outcomes of their work due to the limited time frames for implementation and assessment.

The report went on to conclude that the SDC made significant progress in developing self-sufficient training regimes for RPZ specialists at the police academies in Sarajevo and Banja Luka. The evaluators stated that this progress was promising in terms of promoting sustainability for the project's outputs and that 'neighborhood policing is capable of reproducing itself as far as training is concerned without further technical assistance' (Wisler and Traljic 2010: 13). They then describe numerous successful applications of the specialist model in order to provide an indication of its potential to generate favorable outcomes at other sites. Many of these examples are drawn from the work of an RPZ team operating in Sarajevo Canton since 2007 which the evaluators suggest, has 'clearly invested a great deal of intellectual effort into understanding the concepts involved and translating this into practice' (Wisler and Traljic 2010: 5). Perhaps the most important conclusion of the evaluation report was that the SDC project required a one-year extension (through 2011) so that the SDC could use its political influence to promote the legal institutionalization of community policing and the RPZ role within entity and cantonal ministries throughout the country. They write, 'considering the nature of the administration in BiH, the adoption of the aforementioned bylaw is a requirement for ensuring that CP stabilizes completely: currently, its implementation depends heavily on the police management good will' (Wisler and Traljic 2010: 7). Ultimately, the evaluators concluded that the lack of a legal framework to support community policing served as a major impediment to the successful implementation of the *Strategy*.[27] Recognizing the challenge of

Uster's (2007) evaluation as it includes critical reflections on the value and impact of specific aspects of the SDC's work in the country.

[27] This sentiment that the National Implementation Team had been unsuccessful in implementing the *Strategy*'s recommendations was shared by representatives of UNDP's Safer Communities project during our initial meeting in April 2010. These individuals suggested that the difficulties generated by this lack of a legal framework were further compounded by the National Implementation Team's lack of budgetary and human resources which served to restrict its presence on the ground (personal communication with an undisclosed colleague from the Safer Communities Team' on 26 April 2010). Further information regarding the Baseline Assessment exercise which generated these conclusions is provided in Chapter 5.

achieving legislative support at the state or entity-level in FBiH, they specifically advocated that the SDC pursue an 'early-riser' approach to promoting legal institutionalization that would focus on compelling 'cantons/entities that present the best conditions for an early adoption' to make necessary changes to their book of rules as a model for others to subsequently follow (Wisler and Traljic 2010: 7). On the basis of these recommendations, the SDC was granted a one-year extension by the Swiss Government and its community policing project concluded in January 2012.

Discussion

There is no denying that the so-called 'architects' of global liberal governance provide financial support to promote templates for 'democratic policing' through police capacity building projects in countries like BiH because it is in their interests to do so. It is also difficult to refute the argument that these financiers aspire to promote specific variants of liberal order which, if successfully reproduced in weak and structurally dependent societies, may undermine political freedoms by disempowering local stakeholders. Nor is the intent of this book to deny the risk that attempts by these 'architects' to 'rewire' the 'local structures of policing and security' (Bowling and Sheptycki 2012: 76) may facilitate the dissemination of liberal or 'neo-liberal' policies and values (Ellison and Pino 2012) and potentially introduce harmful outputs (Cohen 1988a). Rather, it is important to consider that selfish and short-sighted intentions are not deterministic of the actual policing mentalities and practices generated from these projects. In other words, police development assistance programmes may generate harms but, in certain contexts, they may also assume the role of the 'local repair workshops' described by Bauman (2013: 2) at the start of the previous chapter. Along these lines, Hills (2012b: 740) recognizes that 'concentrating on recipient response...rather than the content of the message or the bureaucratic logic and organisational culture of the police institution, runs the risk of producing a descriptive account that leaves transmission, transmitters and knowledge under-theorized, and the operationalization of terms such as transmission ambiguous'. This theme of translation is the focus of the following chapter.

4
Policy Translation

The concept of 'policy transfer' has been embraced by criminologists as an important framework for analysing convergent and divergent trends in criminal justice policymaking around the globe. Jones and Newburn (2007) employ this concept to analyse convergence between the United States and England and Wales over the past two decades while contributors to an edited collection by Newburn and Sparks (2004) explore this concept in relation to the role that domestic political cultures play in shaping divergent criminal justice policymaking outcomes in different nations.[1] Growing literatures on comparative, international, supranational, and transnational aspects of criminology and criminal justice policymaking also highlight the need to acknowledge the significance of policy convergence more generally (for example, Aas 2013; Melossi, Sozzo, and Sparks 2011; Nelken 2010; Sheptycki and Wardak 2005). Aitchison's (2011) work further suggests that these concepts are helpful for understanding the drivers of criminal justice transformation in the context of transitional societies.

Within the sub-discipline of police sociology, this concept is implicit in a burgeoning literature that explores the prospect of democratizing the police in developing, transitional, and failed states. Examples can be found throughout Goldsmith and Sheptycki's (2007) collection, *Crafting Transnational Policing*, as well as in Bayley's (2006) analysis of American foreign assistance to police reform projects in post-conflict societies. Policy transfer is also central to Brogden's (2005; with Nijhar 2005) critique of the global export of community-based policing as a 'one-size-fits-all' template for democratizing the police and implicit in Marenin's (2007) idea of a policing transnational policy community which

---

[1] This latter assertion is consistent with the claim of Dolowitz and Marsh (2000) that with the advent of globalization, governments are increasingly likely to look abroad for policy 'solutions'.

suggests that human agency has played an important role in facilitating the growth and spread of transnational policing power since the Cold War.

Despite the discipline's embrace of these concepts, it has yet to fully incorporate the alternative concept of 'policy translation' into its analytical toolkit.[2] This is hardly surprising given that the concept has only recently started to gain purchase in the field of comparative social policy where it originated less than a decade ago (see Lendvai and Stubbs 2006, 2007, 2009). Ignoring its relative obscurity, this introductory chapter reviews the conceptual lineage of the term and its methodological implications. It begins by rooting the term in the literature on 'policy convergence' and 'policy transfer' and proceeds to differentiate between the two concepts by drawing on the work of Lendvai and Stubbs. My argument is that 'translation' lends itself to an interpretivist, ethnographic approach while the concepts of 'convergence' and 'transfer' are better suited to reductionist, post hoc analysis. Both of these approaches have their place in criminological research but the case studies presented in this book seek to illustrate the benefits of the former. The chapter concludes by elaborating on the methodology used for each of these case studies and the advantages and limitations of employing participatory and non-participatory methods to interpret active policy translation processes.

Policy Convergence and Policy Transfer

Convergence, according to Evans (2004: 2), describes:

'a process of external "hollowing-out" [of the state] . . . as a consequence of the differential impact of processes of globalization on domestic policy formation' and '[a] process of internal "hollowing-out" . . . in different countries as a consequence of the differential impact of processes of privatization, the marketization of public services, and decentralization on both the institutional architecture of the state and domestic policy formation'.

Evans's linkage of globalization with 'internal' processes of 'privatization', 'marketization', and 'decentralization' highlights the neo-liberal character of policy convergence. One must also

---

[2] But it is worth noting that the concept of 'translation' has appeared in work by Ellison (2007) and Melossi, Sozzo, and Sparks (2011).

consider the ideology's role as a driver of policy convergence in an age of economic globalization. This is the argument of Wacquant (2009) who attributes global convergence in the sphere of criminal justice policy to the influence of 'hegemonic neo-liberalism' and the appeal of certain models, generally grounded in discourses of what criminologists might associate with 'right realism', to address the angsts and insecurities of a post-Keynesian world (see also Melossi, Sozzo, and Sparks 2011: 7).

The concept of agency is central to understanding how policy convergence actually operates. Attempts to reduce this phenomenon to the presence of hegemonic global structures or discourse will obscure the complexity of the actual processes and networks that in practice generate ideologically similar but culturally and contextually mediated policy outputs and outcomes. Narrowing in on this issue of agency, Bennett (1991) identifies four processes that may generate seemingly convergent policy outcomes: 'emulation', 'elite-networking and policy communities', 'harmonization', and 'penetration'. Emulation, argues Bennett, cannot be reduced to a simple process of policy diffusion, or the idea that comparable policy outcomes can be attributed to mere imitation. Rather, Bennett writes that emulation involves 'the utilization of evidence about a programme or programmes from overseas and a drawing of lessons from that experience' with the effect that 'the policy of another country is employed as an exemplar or model which is then adapted and, one would hope, improved upon' (Bennett 1991: 221). This description acknowledges that the outcomes of policy emulation and by extension policy transfers cannot merely be inferred from the inputs of the exchange. Rather, the process and its outputs are actively shaped by policymakers who acknowledge that imported policies must be adapted to local contextual circumstances before they can be implemented.

Recognizing the centrality of agency to policy convergence processes does not mean ignoring the important role that macro-structural factors play in shaping these adaptive processes. Rather, policy convergence is best studied in relation to a continuous interplay between structure and agency and can therefore be interpreted through the lens of structuration theory (Giddens 1984). To this effect, Bennett (1991: 2, original emphasis) writes that in the case of 'harmonization', 'convergence is driven by a recognition of *interdependence*' that 'facilitates the shaping of a common response to common problems, to mitigate the unintended external consequences of domestic policy'. With respect to police development assistance work, the paradigm of global liberal governance and the politics of the international development system account for important structural factors that shape policy convergence by producing powerful pressures for reformers to utilize policy transfers and lesson learning to facilitate policy synchronization. Policy transfers thus describe mechanisms that may facilitate different processes of policy convergence in which 'knowledge about policies, administrative arrangements, institutions etc. in one time and/or place is used in the development of policies, administrative arrangements and institutions in another time and/or place' (Dolowitz and Marsh 1996: 344).

A key point about policy transfers is that they describe 'an intentional activity involving the movement of ideas between systems of governance in the aspiration of forging policy change' (Evans and Davies 1999: 251). Evans and Davies add that '...intent may be ascribed both to those who seek to borrow and to those who seek to impose' (Evans and Davies 1999: 366). The transfer agents best positioned to initiate voluntary policy transfers in the context of mature liberal democracies are domestic participants in policymaking processes. Nutley and Webb (2000, 15) associate this category of actors with 'government ministers, senior civil servants and co-opted policy advisors' as well as '[p]oliticans and elected officials at local government level and other activists' including 'professional associations', 'pressure groups', and 'journalists'. Conversely, an episode of policy transfer might be characterized as coercive if the transfer agents that facilitate this exchange are compelled to do so by external pressures. According to Dolowitz and Marsh (1996: 347–8), these pressures may be either 'direct' or 'indirect'. Direct coercion occurs 'when one government forces another to adopt a policy' while indirect pressures that generate coercive policy transfers are said to result from 'the role of externalities, or functional interdependence' which 'push government[s] to work together to solve common problems' (Dolowitz and Marsh 1996: 348–9).

Reflecting on Duffield's (1999; 2007) analysis of the development-security nexus which was discussed in the previous chapter, one can safely assume that policy transfers initiated by actors external to the state in the context of an overarching process of liberal state-building will invariably entail some degree of coercion. This argument is consistent with Ellison's (2007) critique of the 'commodification' of community policing. To this effect, Ivanova and Evans (2004: 96) write that policy transfers which occur between developed and developing societies contribute to, and are therefore constitutive of, a process of overarching structural transformation. Accordingly, they refer to these developing societies as 'transitional societies' because the latter term emphasizes the presence of a programme for prescriptive transformation which assumes that the existing structures and institutions are inadequate for synchronization with the emergent global prescriptions for liberal order and neo-liberal globalization. While Ivanova and Evans acknowledge that voluntary forms of policy transfer do occur in transitional societies, they conclude that ultimately 'this transformation must arise, at least initially, from policy transfer from exogenous sources' (Ivanova and Evans 2004: 96–7). Once again, this fits with the review of community policing as a focus of police capacity building presented in Chapter 2, specifically Brogden's (2005) description of the different transfer mechanisms and agents. The implication here is that a certain degree of coercion inevitably characterizes these exchanges and 'governments in developing countries are often compelled... to introduce policy change in order to secure grants, loans or forms of inward investment' (Evans 2004: 3).

Adding to this point, one might also consider that not every policy transfer that occurs between structurally empowered liberal democracies can be reduced to voluntary episodes of 'lesson drawing'. This concept assumes that policymakers facing similar policy dilemmas seek to 'learn from how their counterparts elsewhere respond' (Rose 1991: 4). To this effect, Wacquant (2009: 172) writes that 'neo-liberal hegemony' does prompt voluntary policy exchanges between 'collaborating countries' in the sphere of criminal justice but it also supports more coercive methods of policy diffusion consistent with what Bennett (1991: 227–8) elsewhere identifies as 'penetration'. Written nearly two decades prior to Wacquant's (2009) *Punishing the Poor*, Bennett's (1991: 228) description of convergence as a 'penetrative process' implicitly touches upon its neo-liberal character at the time:

Most evidence of convergence through penetration lies in the role of multi-national business in successfully securing, for example, a common regulatory framework for its products.

My specific concern is not with the penetration of government policymaking processes by the private sector but, rather, with the penetration of the policymaking processes in weak and structurally dependent states by actors and institutions which represent the interests of foreign governments and international organizations. These interests may still be regarded as 'private' in the sense that they are not synonymous with the 'public' interest if the public interest is to be articulated on the basis of the needs and policy preferences of local citizens. While it is beyond the scope of this discussion to provide a detailed exploration of neo-liberalism or the extent to which its theorized 'hegemony' has evolved since the early 1990s, it is worth briefly elaborating on the relationship between neo-liberalism and globalization because this theme is central to Ellison and Pino's (2012) critique of the international development system and its support for police reform throughout the global South.

At the core of Ellison and Pino's (2012: 16) argument is the idea that proponents of globalization, including major global financial institutions, have deliberately contributed to the international diffusion of neo-liberal policies. They add that this project (or collection of projects) aspires to 'promote dependency and exploitation' and thus, amounts to a new form of 'imperialism' (Ellison and Pino 2012: 13). The impact of these policies in the global South is described by Ellison and Pino (2012: 62) as reinforcing 'conditions of inequality' that are recognized by the international community as a potential proxy for conflict. Police development assistance and SSR are therefore treated as logical strategies for managing the destabilizing structural consequences of neo-liberal policy diffusion through securitization. Essentially, Ellison and Pino (2012) are arguing that economic, political, and ideological convergence in the global South has indirectly prompted the use of further policy transfers as a means of dealing with their consequences.

Analysing Policy Transfers

The conceptual foundations of policy convergence and policy transfer have further implications for our ability to research these phenomena. For example, Dolowitz and Marsh (1996: 349–50) suggest that policy transfers might refer to 'policy goals, structure and content; policy instruments or administrative techniques; institutions; ideology; ideas, attitudes and concepts;

and/[or] negative lessons'. Along these lines, Evans and Davies (1999: 382) distinguish between 'soft' and 'hard' forms of policy transfer[3] but recognize that one could potentially define the 'object' of a specific episode of policy transfer in terms of the ideas that prompted the exchange or the specific policies or practices that the idea spawned. Accordingly, they suggest that most policy transfer processes exhibit a combination of 'soft' and 'hard' policy content. This complexity can be illustrated in the sphere of criminal justice policy through a brief review of Jones and Newburn's (2007) analysis of 'zero tolerance' policing in England and Wales. Jones and Newburn suggest that, initially, the mantra of 'zero tolerance' was articulated to '[convey] a determination to use the criminal law to "crack down on" something that has previously flourished' (Jones and Newburn 2007: 224–5) While this concept was perhaps most visibly associated with a policing strategy made famous by former New York Mayor Rudolph Giuliani and former Chief of the NYPD Bill Bratton in 1994, its discursive origins can actually be traced back to Ronald Reagan's 'war on drugs' in the mid-to-late 1980s (Jones and Newburn 2007: 106). Interestingly enough, the first reference to 'zero tolerance' in UK police circles also predates its association with policing as evident from a 1992 campaign against domestic violence in Edinburgh (see Jones and Newburn 2007: 108). Despite its multi-faceted lineage, Jones and Newburn (2007) note that the term 'zero tolerance' was only applied to policing in England and Wales following widespread media coverage that touted the model's contribution to the 'New York Miracle'. Small-scale, zero tolerance policing 'experiments' were subsequently initiated throughout the UK, most notably by the Metropolitan Police in London and the Strathclyde Police in Glasgow.

Jones and Newburn (2007) go on to argue that 'zero tolerance' policing had a limited impact on the provision of policing throughout the UK. Specifically, they describe how the 'zero tolerance policing' model was widely opposed both in principle and practice by most police chiefs in the UK who acted as an important source of institutional resistance to the policy. On an ideological level, however, they recognize that the mentalities

---

[3] 'Soft' policy transfers refer to 'ideas, concepts, attitudes' while 'hard' policy transfers are said to involve 'programmes and implementation' (Evans and Davies 1999: 382).

underpinning the 'zero tolerance' philosophy may have actually had a greater discernible impact on UK policy. This is particularly evident with respect to New Labour's embrace of right realist discourse (see Murray 1996) and 'broken windows' theory (Wilson and Kelling 1982) during the late 1990s and their decision to incorporate these ideas into the 1998 Crime and Disorder Act and the 2003 Anti-Social Behaviour Act (Jones and Newburn 2007: 110–11).

Whether one decides to prioritize soft content or hard content in their analysis is largely a matter of preference and there are advantages and limitations to each approach. Focusing on policy outputs and thereby treating the policy transfer as the independent variable may cause the analyst to neglect important contextual factors which are necessary for developing detailed case studies. Conversely, treating the policy transfer as a dependent variable by focusing solely on the diffusion of ideological content or discourses may obfuscate the elements of agency and intentionality (Evans and Davies 1999: 370). One solution for potentially reconciling these competing approaches is offered by Evans and Davies who draw upon Wendt's (1987) articulation of structuration theory to propose a 'multi-level' framework for interpreting policy transfers as the 'dialectical synthesis' of macro-level structures and micro-level agency (Evans and Davies 1999: 370). They go on to argue that the benefit of this meso-level approach is that it allows the research to 'overcome the subordination of one to another'. Methodologically, this meso-level approach involves identifying and mapping the networks of and nodes of power that facilitate the transfer of policy meaning and content between contexts. Because policy meaning 'may be *discovered*, as well as "lost" ' (see Melossi, Sozzo, and Sparks 2011: 2) through these networks, it is questionable whether 'transfer' is in fact the most appropriate verb for analysing how policies travel.

'Translation'

According to Lendvai and Stubbs (2009: 677), the conceptual distinction between 'policy transfer' and 'policy translation' is grounded in Latour's (2005) differentiation between the roles of 'mediator' and 'intermediary'. Whereas an intermediary 'transports meaning or force without transformation', '[m]ediators transform, translate, distort and modify the meaning or the elements that they are supposed to carry' with the effect that '[t]heir input is never a good predictor of their output' (Latour 2005: 39). Mediators represent active participants in a process of transformation while intermediaries merely serve to transmit policies between contexts. Lendvai and Stubbs (2009: 677) proceed to criticize the mainstream policy transfer literature for what they identify as its tendency to represent these exchanges and their outputs as 'binary oppositions'. They characterize these 'oppositions' in the following way:

> ...either policy is institutionalised in another place or resisted; it either 'fits' or it does not fit; it is picked up by institutions and actors or it is blocked by veto players and/or at institutional veto points (Lendvai and Stubbs 2009: 677).

This criticism, along with Melossi, Sozzo, and Sparks's (2011) critique of the methods used by criminologists to research and reconstruct the complexities of 'the international and intercontinental mobility' of policies, calls for further consideration of the conceptual and methodological advantages of 'translation' as opposed to 'transfer'. Put simply, the argument of Lendvai and Stubbs (2009) is that the study of how policy meaning and content travel between contexts cannot be reduced to narratives of resistance or compromise. Rather, policy meaning is negotiated through sites or nodes of power. Borrowing from Mary Louise Pratt (1991), Lendvai and Stubbs (2007: 6) describe these spaces as 'contact zones'.

According to Pratt (1991: 6, quoted by Lendvai and Stubbs 2007: 15), 'contact zones' describe '...the spatial and temporal co-presence of subjects previously separated by geographic and historic disjunctures, and whose trajectories now intersect'. Contact zones are important social fields in which different actors interact and compete to shape policy meaning and content in relation to their individual and institutional preferences (Lendvai and Stubbs 2007: 16). Contact zones are actively constructed 'through actor networks' and therefore they do not represent 'pre-existing categories' (Lendvai and Stubbs 2006: 6). In other words, a contact zone represents a shared site at which various stakeholders seek to translate their institutional preferences into policy prescriptions and, ultimately, policy outputs.

Actors in the politicized space constituted by a contact zone as well as the security nodes that they bridge utilize available resources to advance individual or collective preferences within a shared system.[4] Accordingly, Lendvai and Stubbs (2007: 16, original emphasis) write, '[i]n the "contact zone" encounters are rarely, or rarely *only*, about words and their meaning but are almost always, more or less explicitly, about claims-making, opportunities, strategic choices and goals, interests and resource maximization ...'. Drawing on institutional resources, these translators compete to shape the language and prescriptions for policies in ways that reflect their own habitus. The process of channelling one's habitus through a universally appealing framework affords a translator a symbolic mark of legitimacy that serves to authenticate their subjective world view and objectify it through the doxa of the contact zone. A similar argument is also put forth by Freeman (2009: 435) who writes that within these spaces '...some kinds of association or translation are legitimated and authorised just as others are excluded or denied'. Actors who possess capital possess the means to shape policy and align it with their chosen discourse. Those who lack this capital may struggle to do so. This process of contestation occurs at multiple stages of the translation process and the actions and decisions that collectively shape a policy in one contact zone will have implications for subsequent stages of what one might crudely describe as a transfer cycle. Methodologically, the implication is that the power relations that occur within contact zones must be actively interpreted and reconstructed.

Before I elaborate on the participatory and non-participatory methods that I used to study policy translation in BiH, it is worth briefly clarifying the conceptual relationship between 'contact zones' and what Johnson and Shearing (2003) describe as 'security nodes'. Johnston and Shearing's (2003) work on nodal security governance illuminates a similar relationship between the different actors, institutions, and assemblages within these polycentric fields. Emphasizing the mediated character of nodal security governance, they write:

...[this] *model refuses to posit any correspondence between mentalities, the objectives, institutions and technologies associated with them, and governmental 'outcomes'. For that reason we have been able to ask...whether the same mentality might, under different conditions,*

---

[4] Here Lendvai and Stubbs (2007: 5) draw explicitly on the work of Bourdieu and Wacquant (1992).

*support normative programmes and substantive outcomes different
from those with which it is normally associated* (Johnston and Shearing
2003: 160).

Whereas security nodes describe concrete and relatively stable
sites through which security is governed, contact zones may also
refer to impermanent spaces between security nodes that may or
may not be located in a concrete institutional setting. This idea
is consistent with Lendvai and Stubbs's (2006: 6) argument that
contact zones are actively constructed 'through actor networks'
and thus do not represent 'pre-existing categories'. By contrast,
security nodes can and often do refer to pre-existing categories.
Concrete or institutionally-based contact zones can be studied
in relation to newly established nodes developed to improve or
facilitate policy coordination or coherence within a pre-existing
network of governance. With reference to police capacity building projects, concrete contact zones may be identifiable in relation to internationally-funded development projects that seek to
implement community safety partnership schemes at the local
level. These projects simultaneously function as contact zones
and security nodes in the sense they constitute important links
between local and global actors and because they ultimately
shape the 'governance of governance' (Wood and Shearing
2006: 113) within their respective local contexts. Analysing the
dispositions that emerge from translational policy processes
affords researchers valuable insights into the politicized character of these nodal settings.

In recognizing the analytical potential of 'policy translation', it is
necessary to briefly acknowledge the fact that Lendvai and Stubbs's
work does appear to understate the sensitivity of other policy (and
legal) theorists to the transformational nature of policymaking
processes. For example, Susanne Karstedt's (2004: 23–4) work
on 'path dependency' recognizes that '[t]he concept...implies the
use of loosely coupled concepts instead of "strong", unilateral and
deterministic ones' and she adds that '[i]n socioeconomic theories
of modernisation the unilateral model and the idea of convergence
have been substituted by the concept of "path dependent" modernisation'. A similar rejection of determinism is evident from debates
arising from Alan Watson's (1974: 21) work on 'legal transplant'
which he describes as 'the moving of a rule or a system of law from
one country to another, or from one people to another'. Watson

acknowledges that 'a successful legal transplant...will grow in its new body, and become part of that body just as the rule or institution would have continued to develop in its parent system' (Watson 1974: 27). He adds, '[s]ubsequent development in the host system should not be confused with rejection'. Watson's concept emphasizes adaptation as an important aspect of this transplant process. While Watson's concept can certainly accommodate the possibility of transformation, it is Pierre Legrand's (2001) critique of 'legal transplant' that truly draws attention to 'disturbances' akin to those described by Lendvai and Stubbs (2009). Legrand's (2001: 57) argument is that the concept of 'legal transplant' embodies a flawed assumption that 'law is a somewhat autonomous entity unencumbered by historical, epistemological, or cultural baggage'. Thus, he writes:

There is more to ruleness than a series of inscribed words . . . A rule is necessarily an incorporative cultural form. As an accretion of cultural elements, it is buttressed by important historical and ideological formations. A rule does not have any empirical existence that can be significantly detached from the world of meanings that defines legal culture; the part is an expression and a synthesis of the whole: it resonates (Legrand 2001: 58).

The same critique can be applied to policymaking processes. In other words, policy outputs or outcomes cannot exist in rhetoric only; they must take on form and meaning, both of which will be shaped by the specific cultural and contextual experiences of agents at the recipient loci. This argument is consistent with Jean-Yves Tizot's (2001: 305) prior assertion that '..."exact" translations are impossible because of the irreducible differences between ideological contexts and historical evolution from one country to another, and...transfers are always imperfect and impure'.

Policy Ethnography

The challenge of attempting to construct a multi-level analysis of a specific episode of policy transfer as a policy 'outsider' is evident from the work Ivanova and Evans (2004) who provide a case study of local government reforms in the Ukraine. Ivanova and Evans (2004) provide a compelling description of the structural circumstances that prompted local governments in the Ukraine to band together and form a policy transfer network but their analysis treats the outcomes of these policy transfer processes as the focal point thereby obscuring the deliberations and interactions that produced them. Aitchison (2011) describes similar methodological difficulties that he experienced while researching criminal justice transformation in BiH:

While international aid and assistance may have brought numerous potential agents for transfer into the country, the multitude of nations represented within the international community suggests that the process of policy learning is complicated in these circumstances...Moreover, a simple line cannot be drawn between the country of origin of a particular expert and the model they advocate, even though respondents in the field sought to suggest that this was so...Thus while a large international presence may facilitate the exchange of policy ideas and models, it may in turn create a dynamic and multi-dimensional version of lesson drawing where policy and laws are not transferred or transplanted from one particular source country, but in which the local is merged with various different models available according to perceived needs and available resources (Aitchison 2011: 207).

This excerpt reinforces the idea that the dynamics of the policy translation process are inherently difficult to interpret and reconstruct post hoc from the perspective of an outsider. Accordingly, my argument is that proximity, and wherever possible, participation in an active policy process enhances one's ability to generate a detailed, interpretive account. As stated in my introductory chapter, it is impossible for a researcher to embed themselves throughout the entire policy translation process so an aspiring policy ethnographer must work to generate detailed 'snapshots' of what are (hopefully) active and relevant contact zones.

Each of my case studies involved the use of different methods consistent with the policy ethnography approach. My first case study with UNDP is based on a participatory policy ethnography whereas my second case study which focuses on a Swiss-initiated community policing reform project in Sarajevo involved the use of non-participatory methods. Insofar as proximity to an active contact zone constitutes an important determinant of one's ability to study policy translation, participatory methods are preferable to non-participatory methods when feasible. Unfortunately, opportunities to conduct participatory policy ethnographies are limited. The remainder of this section draws from my experiences to sketch out the main methodological advantages and limitations of each approach.

Case Study 1: Participatory Policy Ethnography of UNDP's Safer Communities Project

My first case study focuses on how UNDP in BiH's Safer Communities project shaped the contours of an 'off-the-shelf model' for governing local security. As one of four individuals who collectively comprised the Safer Communities team,[5] I was directly involved with important decision-making processes involving the project's design and conceptualization. Participating in these tasks afforded me insights relating to how the interplay between individual, institutional, and structural factors shaped key decisions and deliberation processes. I never achieved full membership in this setting but my status as an active participant did allow me to document the team's activities on a continuous basis. The ethnographic methods that I used to generate this data were largely determined by my access and the participatory nature of my fieldwork. As Neyland (2008: 10) observes, the need for researchers to 'develop their method in association with the field being studied' is important for all forms of ethnography. My primary method consisted of openly documenting my participant observation in this active policy node in my field diary. My 'jottings' established a record of the project's activities between January and April 2011, including those with which I was directly involved. They also account for my conversations and interactions with colleagues at UNDP in BiH as well as meetings I attended with representatives from 'partner' institutions including international organizations, non-governmental organizations, local government, and the police. My field diary provided me with a means of continuously recording my personal reflections as a temporary participant in the field. These reflections proved valuable when it came time to analyse my data because they allowed me to reflexively reconstruct these experiences and recognize how my immersion would subsequently shape my interpretations of the field.[6] Additional data sources included

[5] I introduce these individuals in Chapter 5.

[6] The team's Project Manager was briefed about my aims and intentions prior to the research, and a 'Terms of Reference' document was developed and agreed upon prior to the commencement of my fieldwork. The 'Terms of Reference' document established my right to use the internship as a platform for conducting my research, my ownership of the data, and my right to reference my field notes in scholarly publications. It further informed my colleagues of my preliminary research questions, my proposed methods, and my ethical protocols. Key to this collaboration was a mutual commitment to transparency and a shared

various project documents and working drafts of a policy brief that I authored during my time with UNDP.

There are numerous factors that restrict researchers from directly immersing themselves in an active and relevant contact zone. First, there are informal restrictions on access. Specifically, security nodes can only be studied as contact zones if they are actively contributing to a policy translation process. Insofar as access to contact zones is temporally sensitive, the researcher must be in the right place at the right time in order to generate a first-hand account of their trans-lational activities. From the researcher's perspective, this can be quite problematic as the contact zones which present themselves as accessible may not actually fit with their initial research plan. For example, the initial focus of my research in BiH was on community policing reforms. It was only after my initial meeting with represent-atives from UNDP in April 2010 that I decided to expand my focus to include community safety partnerships. The Safer Communities Project Manager's subsequent invitation to join the project in order to conduct my research allowed me to immerse myself in this contact zone and carry out the fieldwork for this case study.

My experience further suggests that contact zones may come to exist as a result of changes to policy discourse. In this case, the international community's advocacy of 'community policing' reforms in BiH had been gradually supplanted by a consensus that previous initiatives had yet to achieve their anticipated 'results' due to poor cooperation between the police and other local agen-cies. Accordingly, the rhetoric of 'partnership' gained purchase throughout this network and came to define a future trajectory for SSR projects in BiH. As described in the following chapter, UNDP

expectation that the research would be mutually beneficial. I received no financial compensation for my participation in this internship and I was only reimbursed for research or travel expenses which related directly to my work with the Safer Communities project. I continued to maintain regular contact with members of the Safer Communities team until the project started winding down in March 2012. This afforded me regular updates about the project's future plans and access to project documents which allowed me to consider how the discourses surrounding the project had evolved since I exited the field. In exchange for these updates, I provided my former colleagues with feedback on various project doc-uments including a final project report (unpublished). I also provided my col-leagues with the opportunity to review and feedback on a draft of the case study presented in Chapter 5 prior to its publication as Blaustein (2014*b*) in *Policing & Society*. One member of the Safer Communities team read the article prior to its publication and provided a positive assessment of my analysis.

in BiH piloted the Safer Communities project on the basis of an expectation that it would resonate with donors and attract funding. This is not to suggest that UNDP in BiH initiated the project for purely selfish reasons but, rather, that the translational work which takes place within active contact zones is inevitably structured by a broader policy context.

A second issue of access relates to the formal restrictions put in place by the institutions that populate or participate in activated policy nodes. The issue is that many of these concrete contact zones lack transparency and access is permitted or restricted by institutional gatekeepers. Formal access to these sites may be restricted as these gatekeepers and the institutions they protect 'have a practical interest in seeing themselves and their colleagues portrayed in a favourable light' (Atkinson and Hammersley 2007: 50–2). Allowing an outsider to access these spaces for the purpose of interpreting the activities and discourses that influence policy meaning and content is potentially risky because this level of transparency has the potential to undermine the ability of the host institution to legitimate their participation in the policy translation process.

Considering these potential barriers to access, there have only been a few prior examples of scholars using participatory ethnographic methods to develop meso-level accounts of active international development projects. Perhaps the most notable example is Mosse's (2005) *Cultivating Development: An Ethnography of Aid Policy and Practice* which provides a detailed, reflexive account of his direct participation as an 'anthropologist-consultant' with an aid project in India which was funded by DFID during the 1990s. As with my own fieldwork, the interpretive approach which Mosse (2005) employs is based on the policy anthropology tradition, specifically the work of Shore and Wright (1997). Mosse's (2005) experiences lead him to conclude that a significant gap exists between development policy and practice, a theme which also emerged from my own fieldwork in BiH. They further attune him to the fact that different policy stakeholders derive and exercise power through translational processes inherent to international development work. He writes,

Donor advisers, consultants and project managers are able to exert influence only because the ideas or instructions they purvey can be translated into other people's own intentions, goals and ambitions (Mosse 2005: 8).

A second example is Harper's (1998) *Inside the IMF*. Harper's (1998) research employed ethnographic methods to understand organizational processes for the purpose of supporting managerial and technological improvements within the organization rather than as tools of critical interpretation. The distinction between the aims of Mosse's (2005) and Harper's (1998) research illustrates Hammersley's (1992) argument that an 'ethnography of an organisation' and an 'ethnography for an organisation' constitute different types of research. My research with the Safer Communities project was intended to function as an ethnography of an organization (i.e. critical interpretation) but the data I generated through my participant-observation proved valuable to my colleagues at UNDP who embraced (or perhaps more accurately, tolerated) me as a critical friend. For example, my insights supported the Project Manager and Community Policing Advisor in their ongoing efforts to ensure that the project simultaneously resonated with local and international discourses relating to crime and security. At times it also prevented them from contributing to potentially harmful outcomes. For example, there was one instance when I was able to convince a colleague to abandon the idea of organizing a women's self-defence seminar as part of a domestic violence awareness campaign that the Safer Communities team was organizing in partnership with one of the citizen security forums. My concern was that this approach might lead to either the women or their partners being harmed. Accordingly, while I believe that there is merit in maintaining the distinction between ethnography *of* and ethnography *for* an organization, we must also consider that these two approaches might be reconciled if a solid foundation of trust exists between the researcher and the institutional host.

Another important method that I used to complement my use of participant-observation was informal, ethnographic interviewing. Ethnographic interviewing was employed as part of my ongoing, daily interactions with my colleagues and I also used this technique during my fieldwork with community police officers in Sarajevo Canton. Ethnographic interviews are distinct from formal interviews in that they represent a distinct kind of 'speech act', one which Spradley (1979: 331) loosely equates with 'a friendly conversation'. In other words, the informant is aware of the fact the conversation is 'supposed to go somewhere' but 'only has a hazy idea about this purpose' (Spradley 1979: 331). Over the course of these conversations, Spradley adds that 'the ethnographer gradually takes more control of the talking, directing it in those channels that lead to discovering the cultural knowledge of the informant' (Spradley 1979: 335). A successful ethnographic interview requires the researcher to subtly educate or prompt the informant with regards to the type of cultural data which is being sought. This is achieved through the use of subtle cues and mutual feedback which, over time, enables the researcher to manage this series of interactions in a manner that reinforces trust and generates honest and insightful data.

The data that I generated from these conversations was valuable because it afforded me candid insights as to my colleagues' perceptions of the structural context and institutional culture surrounding the contact zone. As Serber (2001: 71) suggests, accessing this type of data can be particularly difficult in institutional settings 'because a structural requirement of such institutions is to conceal the actual organisational processes that generate industry orientation'. Once again it is worth emphasizing that it was my prolonged immersion in the setting that allowed me to establish a necessary foundation of trust with my colleagues who acted as my interviewees. However, my immersion and the relationships that I formed did lead to the issue of 'over-rapport' (Miller 2001: 170). On more than one occasion, I found myself presented with sensitive or potentially disruptive information relating to the project or UNDP that I could not explicitly reference in my field notes. One such incident took place during a meeting with a senior manager at UNDP in BiH. This individual presented me with two options at the start of the interview: they would speak to me candidly about their role with the organization and the challenges of development work in BiH if I agreed not to take notes or make reference to their comments in publications. The alternative option was that they would provide me with the 'official' institutional response which they acknowledged would be of limited value to my research. I decided to go with the former option because I assumed that the authentic perspective would at least be useful for refining my developing analysis of the contact zone.

Case Study 2: Non-Participatory Policy Ethnography of the SDC's Community Policing Project

My second case study draws from qualitative data generated during a five-week study of the implementation of a Swiss community policing project in Sarajevo Canton. This multi-site case study was initiated with the support of UNDP in BiH in order to explore how local community police officers (henceforth 'RPZ officers') in Sarajevo were working to implement, or impede the implementation of, a Swiss community policing project. Access to conduct this fieldwork was negotiated by UNDP and approved by the Ministry of the Interior for Sarajevo Canton (MUP KS) in February 2011. My permission to reference this data for scholarly publication was established in my 'Terms of Reference' with UNDP and in the research protocol approved by the MUP KS.

The ethnographic data was based on over seventy hours of observation[7] completed with two units operating out of different urban sectors in the city. These units were purposively selected for the study following consultations with colleagues at UNDP and the RPZ Coordinator for the Sarajevo Canton Police which revealed them to be the most experienced policing units in Sarajevo Canton. This was important because it ensured that the officers were already well-versed in the SDC's model and, thus, any shortcomings could not be attributed to inexperience. The ethnographic data is further complemented by my notes from ethnographic interviews conducted with members of the units, their colleagues, and various 'partners' from the community. During the final week of fieldwork, I also conducted semi-structured follow-up interviews with station supervisors, colleagues from other RPZ units, the RPZ Coordinator, a project worker from the SDC, and the external evaluator for the SDC's project. None of the interviews were tape-recorded in order to facilitate candid and honest discussions. Adnan Fazlić, a graduate student at the University of Sarajevo, acted as a translator and interpreter for my observation with RPZ2. He was also present at the semi-structured interviews and his personal reflections provided an important source of inter-coder reliability that enhance my interpretation of key events and interactions.[8]

---

[7] This included observation of the officers during their shifts and at meetings that I attended at which the officers were present.

[8] The identity of the officers, their units, and the specific location of their sectors has been obscured. All quotations are paraphrased unless explicitly stated. The author did not have a formal working relationship with the SDC or any personal interest in the evaluated 'success' or 'failure' of their community policing project.

As an evaluative piece of research, the limitations of the methods and the methodology were numerous. Perhaps this was excusable given the context within which I was operating and the limited time frame for carrying out the fieldwork but this is beside the point. As an exploratory piece of research that provided me with unique insights into how an externally defined community policing model was being received and resisted by local police officers, the fieldwork naturally lent itself to an interpretivist approach. My analysis presented in Chapter 7 details how police officers from one unit (RPZ1) used their agency to support the initiative by facilitating cultural validation of community policing in their sector. The success of RPZ1 is contrasted with the experience of the officers from a second unit (RPZ2) who struggled to demonstrate progress towards implementing the reform in their sector due to a combination of contextual obstacles and limited managerial support. In their case, these 'Western' discourses proved to be less influential than localized, sub-cultural understandings of crime and police work.

The possibility of using participatory policy ethnography to conduct this fieldwork was negated by my status as both a cultural and a contextual outsider. In other words, there was no prospect of me taking on the role of either one of the officers tasked with implementing the policy or a 'partner' in the community. As an outsider, I approached this study with two separate, albeit complementary, research agendas. My 'official' agenda was linked with UNDP's desire to develop a better understanding of the SDC's progress towards implementing its community policing model. This interest stemmed from UNDP's recognition of the fact that the SDC's budget for community policing related activities in BiH was scheduled to expire at the end of 2011. This promised to create a future policy vacuum as to which agency would continue to provide ongoing support for micro-level community policing reforms in BiH. My 'official' or primary objective as a representative of UNDP undertaking this research was therefore to determine if the Swiss model of community policing had been successfully implemented, if it was having its intended effect, and if not, why not? My 'scholarly' agenda stemmed from my broader interest in examining the transformation of micro-level community-oriented policing reforms in BiH and I approached this fieldwork with a tentative hypothesis that community-oriented policing reforms are not only susceptible to transformation at their design stage, but that the meaning and content ascribed to them are also trans-formed through the practice of the policy recipients tasked with implementation.

Accordingly, the methods available to me were for the most part non-participatory because my access never allowed for me to achieve membership status in the setting. This in turn restricted my proximity to decision-making processes but the methods were nonetheless useful for developing a deeper understanding of the extent to which this model resonated with the officers and the context. Comparing my observations and my interview data with the policy prescriptions developed by the SDC also afforded me insights into the translational process that occurred through the interactions between local police officers, the SDC, and different 'partners' in the community.

An interpreter was not used for my fieldwork with the offic-ers from RPZ1 because three of the four community policing spe-cialists spoke English and actively assisted me with interpreting different events and conversations. The fact that I depended on these officers for interpretation amounted to a significant limita-tion of the fieldwork because it restricted my ability to indepen-dently access and reproduce certain interactions. This issue was most problematic when it came to comprehending the content and nuances of dialogue and interactions that took place in Bosnian. In this respect, the language barrier provided my research subjects with a powerful means of controlling my access to the field. In order to study these interactions, I was forced to rely on mediated accounts of various events or meetings that were provided by my hosts. This limited my capacity to objectively evaluate their work but it was useful for developing a limited basis of trust with the officers and for accessing their subjective understandings of what community meant and how it should operate in practice.

As my observation of RPZ1 progressed, it was also clear that the language barrier and the privacy that it afforded these officers actually helped me to establish positive rapport. For one thing, it made my physical presence amongst the officers less threatening because I struggled to grasp all but the most basic conversations in Bosnian. This allowed the officers to ignore me while carrying out their work and they knew they could conduct private and sensitive conversations in my presence. It also meant that my unannounced and unanticipated presence at meetings between the police and their 'partners' in the community was less problematic from an ethical standpoint and the officers acted as a filter for any personal or sensitive information. In this respect, I argue that this relationship of dependency actually empowered my research subjects while simultaneously sensitizing them to my personal limitations as a 'foreign' researcher keen to access this field. By providing me with their interpretations, these officers functioned not only as research participants, but as key informants who facilitated my comprehension and reproduction of the field within my notes.

My observation with the officers from RPZ2 proved less fruitful because none of the team's three officers spoke English so I was accompanied in the field by my interpreter Adnan Fazlić. As a native Bosnian speaker with an academic background and local knowledge of the police, Adnan's presence improved my comprehension of the various events and interactions which occurred in our presence. This proved valuable because it helped us determine that many of the various meetings, activities, and interactions we observed had been staged for our benefit. For example, during our first day of observation with RPZ2, we went on 'patrol' with one of the officers who took us around their assigned neighbourhood. The officer proceeded to introduce us to various 'partners' in the community but none of these encounters seemed to generate information that was relevant to the work of the officers. Rather, the interactions focused on our presence as researchers and the 'partners' were told to answer my questions. It must be considered then that Adnan's ability to understand private conversations and to make sense of different interactions and events on the basis of the local knowledge he possessed may have actually acted as a limitation. Regardless, my experiences with each of these units highlight the fact that reflexivity constitutes a fundamental component of policy ethnography, regardless of the methods utilized. In other words, self-awareness represents an important determinant of a researcher's ability to faithfully interpret and reconstruct 'glocal' interactions including those which occur as policy translations.

Discussion

With this chapter I have sketched out my argument for why the concept of policy translation provides a unique framework for studying how and why policy inputs are mediated and transformed into outputs through international criminal justice policy transfer processes. I have also argued that proximity and participation are helpful to accessing the contact zones at which key transformations take place but that participatory methods are not always feasible. Linking this methodological point to Chapter 2's review of the relationship between the transnational and glocal policing further illuminates the prospect of using policy ethnography to develop 'the types of rich ethnographic details that have become a mainstay of the literature on national policing' (Haggerty 2013: 366) through future empirical research on glocal policing. It was previously noted that police capacity building represents a specific form of transnational policing, itself a sub-category of global policing, and a contributor to glocal policing in developing and transitional countries around the world. Whereas glocal policing describes the idea that local policing activities are increasingly structured and influenced by policing mentalities and practices from other countries, police capacity building as a form of transnational policing is concerned with the role of policy networks in disseminating and exporting models for glocal policing. For this reason, police capacity building does not directly involve the use of coercive power to promote upwardly-responsive policing activities. Rather, it aspires to use indirect coercion to structure the ordering activities of local police officers from a distance. For researchers, this implies that policy nodes within the transnational policing networks are more readily accessible as contact zones than the actual processes through which they are implemented. The reason for this is simple: it is possible for an academic researcher to temporarily assume the role of an active policy translator (assuming they are invited to do so) but they cannot assume the role of the local police officer based in another country who has been tasked with implementing the reform and translating it into contextually viable practices.

5

Interpreting Safer Communities

Policies associated with the community safety partnership model including 'Safer Communities' and 'Safer Cities' initiatives have proliferated globally over the past two decades. An increasingly prominent feature of plural policing and crime control strategies in 'advanced' Western societies, the touted success of this model has rendered it an attractive template for reformers involved with security sector reform in developing, transitional, and post-conflict societies (Crawford 2009). Its global dissemination through transnational policy communities populated by policy entrepreneurs, international development agencies, and NGOs since the mid-1990s has contributed to significant cross-national (and even internal) variation with regards to the conceptual and programmatic features of these 'partnerships'.

In Chapter 3, it was noted that community safety partnerships were introduced to BiH between 2003 and 2006 by DFID and the SDC. Both of these agencies initially established Citizen Security Forums (CSFs) to complement their community policing projects. The logic underpinning these decisions reflected an assumption that community policing would improve the public's willingness to engage with the police while local security forums would generate greater cooperation between the police and their counterparts from other local public service providers thereby improving the capacity of these officers to address community problems through partnership. Drawing from this narrative and the work of its predecessors, UNDP in BiH launched its own community safety partnership project in 2009.

In this chapter, I introduce my ethnographic case study of the Safer Communities project in BiH by profiling the project's institutional sponsor UNDP, and by reviewing its origins as an offshoot of UNDP's Small Arms Control and Reduction Project (henceforth 'SACBiH'). The discussion constructs the habitus of the international development worker at UNDP as a product of the conflicted role of this organization and its increased dependency on non-core funding for pursuing its capacity development mandate. The chapter then proceeds to detail the institutional origins of the Safer Communities project leading up to the start of my placement in January 2011. This includes a discussion of the project's implementation which began in 2010 and an analysis of the working methodology used to pilot the project. The project's status as a contact zone which linked local community safety forums to the United Nations development system and international donors is discussed and I argue that the project's nodal positioning and limited seed funding initially enabled the Safer Communities team to design project activities that addressed local needs. These factors also afforded local partners opportunities to participate in important decision-making processes that shaped the local governance of security within their respective municipalities.

Building on this account of the habitus of the international development worker at UNDP and the origins of the Safer Communities project, the remainder of the chapter presents my policy ethnography of the Safer Communities project to examine the negotiated character of this contact zone and the policy translation process. It begins by examining the project's unique positioning as a concrete contact zone that linked local CSFs to international donors. It then proceeds to analyse how nodal positioning and structural factors influenced the work of the Safer Communities team and momentarily compelled *us* to align the project with what we perceived to be the interests of the European Commission. On one level, this process of alignment was indicative of the global liberal governmentality argument put forth by Duffield (1999; 2007) and Ryan (2011). My active participation in the project also highlighted a redemption narrative whereby we, as seemingly disempowered members of the Safer Communities team, actively worked to mitigate the potential consequences of these pressures by balancing the aim of securing funding with UNDP's commitment to capacity development.

Whereas the first part of this chapter concludes with a cautiously optimistic assessment of the prospect of maintaining a habitual emphasis on capacity development despite the limited availability of funding and structural pressures for policy alignment, the section which follows presents a somewhat bleaker analysis with respect to the issue of sustainability. An account of the difficulties faced by members of the Safer Communities team in their efforts to develop a sustainability report for the project indicates that the official aim of generating self-sustainable CSFs had, on occasion, proven difficult to separate from the team's concerns about the need to sustain the project itself and from UNDP's interest in sustaining its own oversight and proximity to this contact zone. This raises further questions about the responsiveness of this node to the needs and interests of policy recipients.

The chapter concludes by analysing the broader implications of this case study as they relate to the transnational policing literature reviewed in Chapter 2. The discussion recognizes that the habitus of the international development worker is susceptible to structural interference which, in this case, risked aligning the work of the Safer Communities team with the interests of powerful supranational actors. More promisingly, the case study also highlights our awareness of this possibility at the time and our concerted efforts to mitigate the influence of European donors over the outputs generated by the project. In this respect, the case study provides some evidence that deliberation, reflexive analysis, and creative problem-solving can allow proximate actors to facilitate a healthier balance between the global and the local in the context of police development assistance projects despite the existence of the coercive structures identified by critical theorists of transnational policing and global liberal governance.

An Institutional Profile of UNDP

Profiling an institution draws attention to the historical, cultural, and structural factors that shape the habitus of its members. This section describes the ideational and operational contours of UNDP, an international multi-lateral development agency encompassing a global network of regional and country offices by focusing on an important institutional conflict that exists between UNDP's capacity development mandate and the organization's financial dependency on external, non-core funding. The discussion draws primarily from two key secondary sources. The first source is an institutional analysis of UNDP written by Stephen Browne (2011) who spent more than thirty years working in the UN development system. The second source is Craig Murphy's (2006) history of UNDP which was officially commissioned by former Secretary of the United Nations Kofi Annan. Both sources emphasize the organization's struggle to define its purpose within the wider UN development system, an analysis which resonates with my personal observations as an intern with the organization.

UNDP was created in 1966 by a merger of two major international development funds: the 'Expanded Programme of Technical Assistance' and the 'Special Fund'. It was initially established to function as a central coordinating network that would oversee the allocation of a unified technical assistance fund and 'pre-investment' services for all development-related work being carried out within the UN development system (Murphy 2006: 5). Over the next five decades, UNDP's role as a technical assistance fund was greatly diminished as other UN agencies that depended on it sought to re-assert their organizational autonomy in this complex and competitive institutional environment. They did this by actively seeking out sources of non-core funding that would bolster their institutional resources and enable them to expand their global operations. With UNDP's levels of core funding inherently volatile and the availability of non-core donor funding increasing, UNDP began its transformation into a fully-fledged development agency during the 1990s (Browne 2011). By securing this additional non-core funding, UNDP was able to run its own projects and programmes through a network of regional and country offices that employ roughly 7,000 staff. The significance of UNDP's institutional transformation since the publication of the first *Human Development Report* (ul Haq 1990) is evident from Browne's (2011: 5) observation that, as of 2011, non-core funding accounts for 'no less than 80 percent' of the organization's annual budget. This suggests that UNDP today simultaneously functions as both a central hub for core fund disbursement within the UN development system and a fully functional multi-lateral development agency that competes with other UN agencies (as well as non-UN agencies) for non-core funding.

In its capacity as a development agency, UNDP's formal mandate emphasizes the objective of 'capacity development', a concept that can be traced back to the first *Human Development Report* (ul Haq 1990). This innovative and 'subversive' report was authored by Pakistani economist Mahbub ul Haq and introduced under the leadership of William Draper who Murphy (2006: 242) credits with embracing a greater advocacy role for UNDP, particularly in relation to issues involving gender equality and poverty reduction. Following the collapse of the Soviet Union and the outbreak of a number of localized conflicts during the 1990s, UNDP also embraced 'governance' and 'crisis prevention and recovery' as additional operational priorities (Browne 2011: 96). This ideational and operational flexibility has helped UNDP to retain its role as a pre-eminent international development organization (Murphy 2006) but its propensity to adopt vague and ill-defined mandates like 'capacity development' has also served as an important source of ontological insecurity for this institution and its staff. Browne (2011: 90) argues that UNDP's insecurity reflects the organization's concerns about its relevance and managerial efficiency as well as its awareness of the fact that it was not originally designed to function as an autonomous international development agency. He writes:

All of the entities of the UN development system were established to answer specific development needs... UNDP, on the other hand, was not so much an organization as an amalgam of two funding facilities, the 'need' for which was based on the concern at the time to facilitate the transfer of technical skills from North to South (Browne 2011: 90).

Since the 1990s, Browne (2011: 91) argues that UNDP has struggled to reconcile its prescribed role as the central coordinator and disburser for the UN development network with its invented function as an autonomous development agency:

UNDP's search for a role has not been without ambiguity, the signs of which were visible in the early days. The real strength of the field network is to keep the organization's ear to the ground, identifying the specific development priorities of each country. But while these highly differentiated needs are fed upwards, the organization has developed a set of centrally determined development priorities which it attempts to propagate downwards. One recent observer has characterized this tension as UNDP's 'riding two horses simultaneously' (Browne 2011: 91).

These conflicting roles call into question what it is that UNDP actually does. Does it serve a necessary function within the UN development system? What makes the agency unique amongst an increasingly populous field of bilateral and multilateral competitors with similar capacities and donor appeal? How can the organization actually translate abstract objectives like 'capacity development' into tangible outcomes? All of these questions contribute to the ontological and professional insecurity of the organization and its staff. Confronted by this insecurity, UNDP employees actively seek to align their work with the Programme's capacity development mandate but their ability to do so is frequently restricted by the limited availability of core funding to pursue capacity development projects initiated by staff based in UNDP country offices. Limitations on UNDP core funding thus generate strong institutional pressures for UNDP staff to pro-actively seek out non-core investment from international donors and this has the potential to conflict with their capacity development mandate (Browne 2011).

UNDP's strategy for addressing the final question which relates to the issue of measuring performance is evident from its enthusiasm for 'results-based management' (henceforth 'RBM') in its regional and country offices. A 2006 report by the Organisation for Economic Co-operation and Development (OECD) and World Bank states that '[r]esults-based management asks managers to regularly think through the extent to which their implementation activities and outputs have a reasonable probability of attaining the outcomes desired, and to make continuous adjustments as needed to ensure that outcomes are achieved' (OECD and World Bank 2006: 9).[1]

A 2007 publicly available internal document titled *Evaluation of Results-Based Management at UNDP* observes that UNDP was 'among the earliest UN organizations to introduce results-based management' back in 1999 as a strategy for 'learning from empirical evidence based on past experience and using that information to manage' (UNDP 2007: i, 5). However, the *Evaluation* concludes that by 2007 UNDP had made limited progress towards successfully implementing RBM because UNDP embodies an institutional culture that is characterized by 'a lack of clear lines of accountability' (UNDP 2007: x). The effect is that staff at country offices face competing pressures to simultaneously manage capacity development projects for outputs and outcomes. This means that the need to demonstrate effective project management to donors may consume time and resources that could otherwise be devoted to implementing the project and reflecting on whether outputs are actually developing the capacities of local partners. It also raises an important question about how the organization defines a 'successful'

---

[1] A 2007 UNDP *Evaluation of Results-based Management at UNDP* indicates that organizations employ the notion of results-based management differently. UNDP's *Evaluation* references this quote as a relevant description for how RBM is pursued at UNDP (UNDP 2007: 9).

project: is a successful project one that is implemented on schedule, produces its prescribed outputs, and keeps to its budget, or is a successful project one which generates sustainable outputs that have a measurable, positive impact from the perspectives of local partners?

Increasingly, it appears to be the case that pressures for performance management have encroached upon the idealistic aims of the organization. To this effect, Browne (2011) argues that the re-orientation of UNDP from a network coordinator into a multi-faceted international development agency has fostered an opportunistic managerial culture at its regional and country offices. He explains, '[w]herever it has become clear that donors are willing to fund a particular incentive or program, a suitable proposal is sure to follow' (Browne 2011: 119). While limited core funding continues to be disbursed to these offices to cover administrative costs, fund certain core programmes designed to address centrally defined priorities, and provide seed funding to encourage local staff to initiate projects that may potentially attract future non-core donor investment, UNDP's core budget is insufficient. This means that the majority of development projects that are implemented by UNDP staff around the world are funded by external, non-core investment provided by national and international donors including the United States and the EU member states.

Faced with the need to finance their operations via external channels, Browne (2011: 119) writes that projects implemented through UNDP's regional and country offices are increasingly being defined in relation to what are perceived to be the interests of donors rather than the needs of recipients. Browne (2011: 119) adds that '[t]here is little doubt that all these donor-driven initiatives have provided benefits to developing countries' but acknowledges that the influx of non-core investment has created significant 'operational distortions' that affect the way in which UNDP actually operates. This means that project managers based at UNDP's regional and country offices must frequently demonstrate the prospective benefits of any project they propose to donors in order to attract non-core funding. When and if this funding is secured, they must then continuously work to assure these donors that their investment is being put to good use and allocated in a manner consistent with the guidelines agreed upon in what is known as a 'project document' which effectively acts as a contract. Monitoring and evaluation activities therefore serve as important elements of RBM at UNDP.

Given that outcomes can only be measured via post hoc evaluation, continuous monitoring and evaluation procedures require project managers to invent predictive 'indicators' in order to demonstrate that the project is on-schedule, on-budget, and hitting pre-defined targets. The demands of continuous monitoring and evaluation combined with the threat that donors may potentially withdraw funding if certain benchmarks or targets are not met has rendered UNDP's managerial culture highly opportunistic. The parallel accountability structures which exist as a result of UNDP's dependency on non-core funding are also argued by Browne (2011) to compel UNDP's staff to align their projects and activities with what they identify as the interests of donors. Doing so is important for not only sustaining individual projects but also for asserting UNDP's relevance within the international development system. These pressures illustrate that the habituses of international development agencies have become increasingly structured by the interests of the architects of global liberal governance discussed in Chapter 2. The ontological and professional insecurities that these pressures generate for local staff based in UNDP country offices and the ways in which these individuals respond to them represent recurring themes of my analysis of the Safer Communities project.

Origins of 'Safer Communities'

The goal of improving cooperation between the police and other municipal service providers with a role to play in community safety and local security governance served as the working narrative for the Safer Communities project during its pilot phase which officially commenced in early 2009. The project's initial aims included supporting five previously established CSFs in Bratunac, Prijedor, Sanski Most, Višegrad, and Zenica (see *Frontispiece*) and drawing from these experiences to develop a strategic framework that would subsequently allow the Safer Communities team to support the project's expansion throughout BiH with financial support (i.e. non-core funding) from European donors.[2] With reference to

---

[2] Interview with the Safer Communities team's Project Manager on 26 April 2010. See also UNDP (2010).

Johnston and Shearing's (2003) work on nodal security governance, it is evident that UNDP aspired to develop a parallel architecture for governing security in BiH, one that it was thought
would enhance the policing capacities of state institutions through
improved links between various stakeholders including the police,
municipal officials, and other municipal-level public service providers (UNDP 2009*a*). During the pilot phase, each CSF constituted an important security node within this emergent security
assemblage. UNDP in BiH also served as an important security
node and contact zone in its capacity as an international organization and the institutional sponsor for the Safer Communities
project. Specifically, it provided the project with access to seed
funding that allowed the Safer Communities team to offer financial and technical support to these forums. To contextualize the
work of the Safer Communities team, this section examines the
origins of the project and its working methodology during its pilot
phase prior to the start of my internship in January 2011.

The Safer Communities project was established as a component
of the SACBiH. Section 1.4 of the SACBiH *Project Document*
states:

*The safer community project will demonstrate how community members
with commitment and ideas can work together to develop innovative
approaches to crime prevention and reduction of supply and demand for
SALW . . . The Small Arms Control Programme will support the implementation of the principles and characteristics of community-based
policing to allow the police and the community to work tighter in new
ways to solve problems of crime, disorder and safety issues to improve
the quality of life . . . for everyone in that community* (UNDP 2009*a*: 15).

The link between Safer Communities and SACBiH was based on a
belief that community policing and community safety partnerships
could be used to support small arms and light weapons reduction
activities (henceforth 'SALW')[3] and contribute to an overall reduction in the levels of illegal SALW ownership in BiH by improving
the overall level of security for citizens within their communities.
Essentially, the *Project Document* forecasts that the SACBiH
team's support for community policing and the partnership model
would encourage greater cooperation between the police and
other municipal officials and contribute to improvements in the

---

[3] For example, weapons amnesty programmes.

governance and provision of local security that would ultimately reduce the incentives for private citizens to own illegal weapons. The *Project Document* also states that Safer Communities would 'help communities develop and implement community-based solutions to problems that contribute to crime and SALW widespread presence' by '[b]uilding partnerships with women's organizations to encourage them to engage in the 'armed violence against women' issue and implement activities to try to understand and decrease men's motivation for gun ownership and use' (UNDP 2009a: 15).

During the pilot phase of the Safer Communities project (2009–2012), both the SACBiH project's focus on SALW control and the posited link between community policing and SALW reduction played a negligible role in terms of actually defining the range of project activities that were supported by the Safer Communities team. I never observed my colleagues from the Safer Communities team approach representatives of the five pilot CSFs about mobilizing its members or local community police officers for activities designed to contribute to a reduction in SALW ownership.[4] Nor did the Safer Communities team seemingly designate SALW collection as a strategic priority for these CSFs when helping them to develop operational plans. Rather, the majority of the project activities[5] that the Safer Communities team developed reflected a broader objective which was set out in Section 1.4 of the *Project Document*:

...to reduce crime, increase public safety and enhance public education and awareness about the causes of crime through community tailored sets of activities that entail direct support to the municipalities (UNDP 2009a: 15).

It was also evident that the Safer Communities team's Project Manager only referred to the link between SALW and Safer Communities when discussing the project with specific audiences. Not once did the issue of SALW arise at any of the four meetings that I attended between representatives from Safer Communities and local CSF representatives. Nor was it discussed at meetings between UNDP and other international agencies involved with police reform in BiH. It was, however, referenced on one occasion during a SACBiH project board meeting that was attended

---

[4] Although it is possible that such discussions took place without my knowledge.
[5] These are described later on in this chapter.

by key project stakeholders and donors including representatives from the European Commission and BiH's Ministry of Security. At the meeting, the Project Manager devoted the majority of the presentation to reviewing the SACBiH team's progress towards munitions destruction and made only a passing reference to the Safer Communities component by suggesting that it was 'linked with weapons collection activities'.[6] This example illustrates how the Safer Communities team consciously adapted the way it presented the project to different audiences. It is therefore reasonable to assume that the motives for doing so were linked to the funding pressures discussed in the previous section.

The SACBiH project's initial budgetary resources included US$7.8 million including: US$4.2 million in non-core funding from the EC; US$2.8 million in non-core funding from bilateral donors mainly from Europe; and US$695,000 in core funding from the UN Bureau for Crisis Prevention and Recovery budget (UNDP 2009a: 1). None of the non-core funding was initially allocated to the Safer Communities project. Rather, the SACBiH team was forced to delay the launch of the Safer Communities component until December 2009 while it waited to receive core funds from the UN Bureau for Crisis Prevention and Recovery.[7] The benefit of initially financing the Safer Communities component with UNDP seed funding instead of non-core funding which had been allocated for SALW-related activities was that there was no need for the Project Manager to justify this financial expenditure or utilize an RBM approach to demonstrate the value of community safety project activities to the European Commission. Rather, the Project Manager's description of the Safer Communities project at the presentation reflected the need for the SACBiH team to justify its decision to allow its members to spend time on activities that, from a donor perspective, might appear to be unrelated to munitions reduction and destruction targets established in the *Project Document*. Facing increased pressure from European

---

[6] Field notes, 4 February 2011.

[7] The Safer Communities project also attracted non-core investment from the Danish Government during its pilot phase (undisclosed amount). A member of the Safer Communities team suggested that this was a relatively small grant with limited strings attached that was intended to supplement the component's seed funding (conversation with undisclosed member of the Safer Communities team on 16 February 2012).

donors to hit these implementation targets following a series of logistical delays, the risk was that UNDP in BiH would end up alienating its donors and be forced to repay the remainder of this non-core funding if donors believed that the SACBiH team lacked focus or was misallocating its resources. Thus, the official aim of the Safer Communities component was to support the development of community-based partnerships which could help support the implementation of SALW-related activities but this appeared to have limited bearing on the type of project activities that the Safer Communities team worked to implement in partnership with CSFs.

The 'Safer Communities' Team

Biography is essential for understanding how and why individuals respond to structural and institutional pressures. Accordingly, this section provides a brief account of the agency of the Safer Communities project. Due to the need to protect the individual identities of my former colleagues, specific biographical details have been obscured and their gender is not revealed. Naturally, the need to obscure these details accounts for an important methodological limitation of participatory policy ethnographies, one which restricts the scope of my analysis.[8]

Having secured its seed funding by the end of 2009, the SACBiH team recruited a 'Community-based Policing Officer' (henceforth 'Community Policing Advisor') in February 2010. The Community Policing Advisor acted as the team's resident expert and coordinator for all operational aspects of the Safer Communities project. This individual reported directly to the SACBiH Project Manager who continued to oversee the work of the Safer Communities team until late 2011. The Community Policing Advisor had previously worked as a police officer in BiH for nearly ten years and retired in the mid-2000s to serve on a UN police mission in a developing country which had recently experienced conflict. As the newest permanent member of the SACBiH team, the Community Policing Advisor had limited previous experience of working

---

[8] Specifically, the need to obscure the identity of my colleagues limits my ability to discuss in great detail how their backgrounds and experiences shaped their individual interpretations of their institutional habitus. It further limits the possibility of reflecting on the gendered nature of their work.

for international organizations involved with policymaking and development work but had previously dealt with major multilateral organizations including the IPTF and the EUPM while serving as a senior police officer. These formative experiences helped to shape the Community Policing Advisor's negative view of the international community's 'top-down' approach to introducing their reforms to BiH. They also instilled in this individual an awareness of the risk that a 'top-down' approach may generate significant resistance from local policymakers and practitioners. Accordingly, the Community Policing Advisor readily identified with UNDP's capacity development ethos and employed it as the guiding principle for building relationships and supporting improvements in the local governance of security from the 'bottom-up'.[9]

Naturally the SACBiH Project Manager also played an important role in shaping the Safer Communities project during its pilot phase. Born in BiH and having completed a portion of their higher education studies in an EU country, the Project Manager joined UNDP in BiH in 2009 having previously worked as legal counsel for another major multilateral organization involved with security sector reforms in BiH. The individual's managerial style reflected the importance of setting tangible targets and delivering measurable results. This highlighted their susceptibility to the pressures of UNDP's RBM culture. Because of the demanding nature of the Project Manager's role in supervising the SACBiH project, their involvement with the day-to-day operations of the Safer Communities component was limited. The final member of the Safer Communities team was a Project Associate who was primarily responsible for overseeing administrative tasks for both SACBiH and Safer Communities. This individual began their career at UNDP after completing a series of unpaid or low-paying internships at other international organizations and NGOs in BiH and was simultaneously studying part-time for a postgraduate qualification in international security. They contributed to discussions and brainstorming sessions relating to the design of the Safer Communities project but played only a limited role in terms of contributing to the project's operations.

---

[9] Multiple conversations with the Safer Communities team's Community Policing Advisor which took place between January and April 2011.

As BiH citizens and residents, the Project Manager, the Community Policing Advisor, and the Project Associate were all classified as 'local staff'. This meant that, at the time of my fieldwork, they were employed on temporary contracts that were tied to the continuation of the SACBiH project. Accordingly, they enjoyed limited horizontal and vertical career mobility within the UN development system and they were paid significantly less than the 'international staff' that populated the upper echelons of management at the UNDP BiH office. Compared to the international staff, members of the Safer Communities project also lacked significant social and political capital within the UN development system and their knowledge of UNDP's funding structures and budgetary resources was somewhat limited. The Project Manager represented a partial exception because of their charisma, their previous experience of working for another major international organization in BiH, and their personal contacts amongst influential domestic political elites.

Planning 'Safer Communities'

Between April and June 2010, the Community Policing Advisor, the Project Manager, and the head of UNDP in BiH's Safety and Justice Sector conducted a series of meetings and interviews with local and international stakeholders involved with different aspects of community policing reforms in BiH. This included over fifty meetings with representatives from all levels of government; international organizations and local NGOs; the National Implementation Team for Community-Based Policing (NIT); local police officers; and representatives of other municipal-level public service providers. Following these meetings, the Community Policing Advisor and the Project Manager created a *Baseline Assessment* report (UNDP 2010; see Appendix 2) that was subsequently published by UNDP in June 2010. This report concluded that the implementation of the national *Strategy* (2007: 6) had been hindered by numerous obstacles and that cooperation between the police and municipal officials remained problematic in many urban communities that were working to implement its recommendations.

The *Baseline Assessment* report also summarized the working 'methodology' that the Safer Communities team used to select its five pilot sites. It describes how a number of possible candidates were initially eliminated due to their inadequate size. This was due to the team's belief that those municipalities which were too small were not suited to community-based policing. This elimination process was followed by a process of positive selection whereby municipalities with desirable characteristics were effectively short-listed for consideration. During my initial meeting with the Project Manager and the Community Policing Advisor in April 2010, they confirmed that the most significant factor for determining whether or not a municipality was suitable for pilot status was if key local stakeholders, including current and prospective CSF members, were motivated to implement the proposed changes. Essentially, the Safer Communities team was only keen to invest its limited time and resources into supporting CSFs in receptive communities that were unlikely to generate resistance. For this reason, the municipality of Stolać, which was initially identified by the Project Manager as one of seven possible sites for piloting Safer Communities, was eliminated from consideration after numerous unsuccessful attempts by the Safer Communities team to schedule a meeting with municipal officials to discuss the proposition.[10]

From the selection process described in the *Baseline Assessment* report it is apparent that the Safer Communities team was keen to emphasize the values of partnership and cooperation as core symbolic elements of its working methodology. These narrative elements were perhaps unsurprising given that they were consistent with what the Project Manager and a Project Associate identified as the institutional mandate of UNDP: local capacity building.[11] For the Safer Communities team, this ethos motivated them to distinguish the project's reformative approach from what colleagues identified as the top-down and coercive approach utilized by other agencies involved with policing reform initiatives in the country. For example, the Project Manager stated that the Safer Communities project was not about forcing a specific model

---

[10] Stolać was considered to be particularly attractive as a pilot site for Safer Communities because of its troubled history of policing following the Bosnian War and the fact that the town's Bosnian Croat majority continued to exercise totalizing influence over local government and the police (conversation with the Safer Communities team's Project Manager and Community Policing Advisor on 26 April 2010). Aitchison (2007: 332) has elsewhere described how majoritarian politics in Stolać created significant obstacles for the IPTF during the late 1990s.

[11] The terms 'capacity building' and 'capacity development' were used interchangeably by staff at UNDP in BiH.

or structure upon these local actors but, rather, the project's core budget would allow it to provide technical and financial assistance to pilot CSFs and to subsidize project activities designed to address the local security needs of these communities.[12] It was anticipated that this investment and the project's formal ties with UNDP would support increased collaboration between the police, local government officials, and other key public service providers who would be compelled to participate in these CSFs as a means of accessing the project's discretionary budget. Essentially, the unofficial goal of the Safer Communities team during the pilot phase was to demonstrate the value of the model by using an 'early riser' approach which it hoped would generate future interest in other municipalities.

Having selected its five pilot sites in mid-2010, the Safer Communities team hired a consultant to conduct an independent assessment of the National Implementation Team's progress towards implementing community policing reforms throughout BiH and to develop a strategic framework for operationalizing the Safer Communities model. The successful bid was tendered by a small UK-based consultancy firm (henceforth referenced as 'UK Policing Services') which at the time consisted of a retired senior police officer from England and a local research assistant from BiH. The chief consultant possessed extensive experience of overseeing operational and training aspects of community-oriented policing projects in England and had previously served as an international police adviser and consultant for two other community-based policing projects in developing countries.[13] Like the Atos KPMG consultants hired by DFID to design and implement its community policing project in BiH between 2003 and 2005, the individual represented a member of the transnational policy community responsible for the global dissemination of community policing which was described in Chapter 2.

Between 28 September 2010 and 14 November 2010, the research assistant conducted a series of seventy-eight interviews with different community policing stakeholders throughout BiH. This included police officers, local partners, and community

---

[12] Conversation with the Safer Communities team's Project Manager on 26 April 2010.

[13] Conversation with the Safer Communities team's Community Policing Advisor in February 2012.

representatives. The purpose of these interviews was to assess the NIT's progress against the fourteen key performance indicators published in the national *Strategy* and to identify important 'issues that have affected the implementation of the strategy and the delivery of the strategic objectives' in BiH (UK Policing Services 2010*a*: 2).[14] The findings of this research were submitted to UNDP as a *Community Policing Strategy Bosnia Herzegovina (BiH) Evaluation Report* (henceforth '*Evaluation*') which concluded that 'the CBP concept is embedded in police divisions throughout BiH' but police officers, including the SDC trained RPZ specialists, working to implement these reforms regularly encountered problems due to a lack of support from 'service delivery partners at the municipal and cantonal level' (UK Policing Services 2010*a*: 21–2). The *Evaluation* concluded that this lack of cooperation indicated that 'there is a **need** to migrate the CBP strategy into a CSP strategy with CBP forming a single workstream of this strategy' (UK Policing Services 2010*a*: 21–2).

UK Policing Services referenced this apparent 'need' in its *Community Safety Partnership Development Strategic Framework Document* (henceforth '*Strategic Framework*', referenced as UK Policing Services 2010*b*)[15] which translated these 'obstacles' into strategic prescriptions for operationalizing the Safer Communities model in BiH. The *Strategic Framework* recommended that the Safer Communities team should proceed by developing a functional, multi-level system for governing community safety partnerships in BiH. It also reaffirmed the team's decision to establish CSFs at the municipal level and it called for the creation of a 'Steering Group' at the national level that could oversee the expansion of this project throughout the country and serve as a hub of coordination linking these CSFs once the Safer Communities project expired (UK Policing Services 2010*b*: 11–12). During the pilot phase of the Safer Communities project, the programmatic recommendations provided by UK Policing Services played only a limited role in influencing the design of the Safer Communities project but the reports did provide the Safer Communities team with an important source of external validation which, from their perspective as both power holders and power brokers, helped them

[14] Listed in Appendix 2.
[15] Listed in Appendix 2.

to legitimate the claim that community safety partnerships represented the only logical strategy for improving the local governance of security across BiH.

Piloting 'Safer Communities'

During its pilot phase, the flexible and indeterminate character of the Safer Communities project represented an important asset to the Safer Communities team, one that allowed its members to invest the project's limited resources in project activities that it was hoped would improve the governing capacities of local political elites and practitioners throughout BiH. To this effect, the Project Manager suggested that the Safer Communities project represented a 'perfect metaphor for the work of UNDP' because 'it can be used to do anything but it is difficult to define'.[16] As noted earlier in this chapter, UNDP in BiH aspired to use the Safer Communities project to develop a parallel architecture for nodal security governance in BiH, one that could enhance existing state structures and institutions by improving the links between different agencies and security actors and rendering their governance more accessible and responsive to the needs and interests of local security consumers (UNDP 2009*a*). The remainder of this section examines the micro-politics of the Safer Communities project as an emergent contact zone by examining the team's methodology for selecting and identifying relevant project activities which were implemented through the local CSFs.

Before the Safer Communities team could develop project activities that would address local needs, the needs themselves had to be identified. To do this, the team hired a local, BiH-based 'marketing media and social research agency' in November 2010 to conduct a countrywide telephone survey that was used to measure public perceptions of community safety and security (henceforth '*Public Opinion Poll* 2010').[17] The survey's limited sample size and sampling methods raised concerns amongst members of the Safer Communities team regarding the reliability of this data. For example, the final report states that only fifty households were

---

[16] Personal communication with the Safer Communities team's Project Manager on 17 February 2011. This description is consistent with Browne's (2011) analysis of the weak and ill-defined mandate of UNDP.

[17] Listed in Appendix 2.

surveyed at each of the five pilot sites and asked about their views 'regarding the security situation in their areas of residence, their attitudes regarding the issues of safety and the level of concern shown for public safety by the authorities as well as their experiences, aspirations and trends with regard to security' (*Public Opinion Poll* 2010: 3). It was therefore clear that the sampling and data collection methods employed for this survey failed to capture the perceptions of certain groups in BiH which one might expect to be at greater risk of victimization or economic hardship (for example, Roma or 'returnee' populations). The findings published in the *Public Opinion Poll* were also determined to be problematic because they did not definitively support the team's assumption that there was local demand for improving the local governance of security. For example, the survey found that 'the highest percentage of citizens felt *mostly* safe in their municipality of residence' while 'the highest percentage of respondents (12.7%) who opted...[to identify a security issue as being most significant in their community]...considered stray dogs as the biggest problem' (original emphasis *Public Opinion Poll* 2010: 6; see Figure 5.1). These findings can perhaps be explained by the fact that 89.7% of the sample 'stated that they had not been the victim of criminal activity or any other form of socially unacceptable behaviour during the past two years'. In other words, the survey indicated that the BiH public did not feel particularly insecure when it came to the issue of criminal behaviour within their communities because the frequency of reported incidents appeared to be relatively low. Another finding that was potentially problematic for the Safer Communities team was that 'amongst the general population [only] 45.5% would like to introduce certain changes into the security management of their municipalities' (*Public Opinion Poll* 2010: 6). These findings call into question UNDP's local mandate to implement the reform in accordance with its capacity development ethos, especially because 91% of the residents sampled at four of the five sites[18] expressed that they felt 'very safe' or 'mostly safe' within their municipality of residence.

Any doubts about the necessity of the project or the legitimacy of UNDP's capacity development mandate were effectively

[18] Bratunac, Prijedor, Sanski Most, and Zenica. Višegrad was not included in the survey.

Figure 5.1 Stray Dogs in Stari Grad, Sarajevo (2011)

addressed by members of the Safer Communities team who constructed an alternative interpretation of these findings. Specifically,
it was suggested that the BiH public had limited expectations of
formal security provision in BiH, particularly in comparison to
their counterparts from Western European nations. Although
this 'theory' was never subjected to rigorous empirical testing, it
does resonate with Hills's (2009) argument that formal security
providers including the public police often play a limited role in
reproducing general order in the aftermath of conflict. In other
words, the disintegration of state control in times of conflict does
not imply a breakdown of local order altogether. Rather, informal
sources of social control including a longstanding, close-knit ethnic or religious community such as those which developed or were
strengthened throughout much of BiH during the war may step in
to fill any perceived void. In fact, it should also be considered that
the capacity of such communities to regulate the behaviour of their
members, at least in terms of their interactions with one another, may

actually be enhanced by the absence or the discrediting of formal institutions of social control given that people become less dependent on formal security providers under these circumstances.

Whereas Cohen (1988*a*) warned against the dangers of rendering citizens overly dependent on formal apparatuses of social control in weak states, the Safer Communities team's Community Policing Advisor felt that the public's low expectations and lack of dependency on formal security providers, including the police, was problematic. According to my colleague, the public's disengagement meant that the police in BiH along with their prospective partner institutions lacked an impetus to develop collaborative approaches to addressing local security problems that fell beyond their traditional, law enforcement role. The Community Policing Advisor also believed that widespread apathy would continue to contribute to a vicious cycle whereby the public would become increasingly disinvested from the governance of security within their local communities with the effect that providers and institutions responsible for governing security would become even more lethargic and less responsive.[19] Thus, rather than deterring the team from pursuing the project, these findings were interpreted in a manner which established a justification for the team's decision to proceed with the project as planned.

All of this occurred during my first few days as an intern. The discussions that took place as to whether or not there was actually a need for the project forced me to grapple with the ethical implications of my continued involvement with the project as both a researcher and an intern. My primary aim as a researcher was to avoid contributing to any activities that were likely to harm or disempower local stakeholders. This was of course challenging because I recognized that I lacked local knowledge meaning I could not predict the long-term implications of my contributions to the project. What I found perhaps most disconcerting at this early stage of my fieldwork was that my colleagues had already started to treat me like an expert on community policing due to my educational background and long-term residence in the UK.[20] According a

---

[19] Conversation with the Safer Communities team's Community Policing Advisor on 31 January 2011.

[20] The UK was viewed by my colleagues as world leader when it came to advancements in community policing. This perception was undoubtedly shaped by my colleagues' previous contact with the consultant from UK Policing Services as well as their familiarity with the DFID project which had concluded by this time.

person expert status means empowering that individual within a contact zone but I did not wish to be empowered given that my knowledge of operational aspects of community safety partnerships was almost entirely academic. Acting ethically in this situation meant intentionally distancing myself from this particular decision-making process. Rather than voicing an opinion or providing my colleagues with recommendations, I made a concerted effort to raise questions that I hoped might prompt critical reflection and stimulate dialogue about the future of the project. This process is illustrated by an excerpt from my field notes documenting a meeting with the Project Manager during the first day of my internship:

The [Project Manager] suggests that 2011 is going to be about implementation for the Safer Communities project as well as justifying the future of this project to prospective donors. The [Project Manager] suggests that donors in Brussels will not be impressed by 'stray dogs' so the challenge over the next year will be to figure out how to map the Safer Communities project onto desirable language that will appeal to these donors. [They] note that the [Safer Communities project] is more difficult than the SALW project because of its lack of tangibles.

I ask the question about relative expectations of public safety in Bosnia and Herzegovina compared to Western European countries where these donors are based. To this question, the [Project Manager] responds that communities in Bosnia are actually safer than communities in France, or at least this is what the surveys [statistics] suggest. I question whether this has to do with relative perceptions and expectations of citizen security in Bosnia given the country's recent history of conflict. The [Project Manager] concedes that this is an interesting point but that it is very difficult to measure so s/he is not entirely sure (field notes, 17 January 2011).

My ability to stimulate open, critical dialogue in this environment is documented by a second excerpt that describes a conversation with an undisclosed colleague later that month:

The discussion then shifts to the work of the UNDP in BiH thus far. I decide to be rather open with [my colleague] and share my observations thus far in order to get a sense of this individual's reaction. I suggest that I am impressed with the work that is being done through Safer Communities over the past year to which [they are] a little bit more reserved in their response. By confronting [my colleague] with a positive assessment I manage to prompt this individual to open up about [their] personal views on the project. [My colleague] feels that the whole project is understaffed and that this has prevented the team from really

*making as great an impact as this individual believes that they should
have. I sense frustration in this individual's response, particularly in
relation to the restrictions placed upon the project team by bureaucratic
issues and procedures at the UNDP. In terms of this individual's status
as a Bosnian citizen, I also got the sense that there is a deeper frustration in terms of the international community's involvement in BiH since
1996. Mainly, [their] response appears to emphasize [awareness of] the
top-down approach to state-building that these organisations are commonly said to pursue. I wonder how much this critique has been influenced by this individual's [biography].*

*As the discussion shifts back to my project brief, I am impressed by
how knowledgeable [they are] about issues of policy transfer. Notably,
about the fact that you cannot merely implant a foreign model or
policy like community policing in Bosnia without regard for local circumstances. Based on this discussion, I have a very high opinion of the
UNDP SACBiH team's approach to implementing Safer Communities.
I feel that these are local stakeholders negotiating a bureaucracy to make
things better in their country. I also question their ability to do what they
aim to because I feel like as a team, they are [spread too thin] and lack
the theoretical [knowledge] of CSPs to [design] and effectively monitor
its implementation.*[21]

I believe that my contribution to this decision-making process
was consistent with the idea of speaking truths to power. Rather
than drawing from my undeserved expert status in order to challenge my colleagues' assumptions about the need for the reform,
I used my participation to prompt them to question it themselves.
Their responses highlight their ability to recognize the limits and
potential consequences of their actions. Of course, the discourses
that shape and are shaped within any contact zone are inevitably
bounded to some extent by institutional and structural factors but,
if nothing else, deliberation improves the reflexive credentials of
the decision-making process.

The public's limited expectations of formal security provision was also viewed by my colleagues as a significant managerial obstacle because it meant that it would be inherently difficult
to demonstrate the value of the project's outputs using an RBM
framework. This was due to the fact that many of the local public safety issues that were identified by the *Public Opinion Poll*
did not relate to crime so progress could not be measured using

---

[21] Field notes, 25 January 2011.

available indicators such as police statistics. Investing in project activities designed to address the country's stray dog population might improve the public's sense of security in many communities but the problem confronting the Safer Communities team was that it was difficult to convey the value of such activities to potential donors . This touches upon an important difference between how local citizens and international donors understood the concept of security. For local citizens, the *Public Opinion Poll* indicated that security was associated with a feeling of safety within your neighbourhood. International donors on the other hand associated security with regional stability.

Despite uncertainty about how the team might implement and manage this project for 'results', the Community Policing Advisor presented the findings of the *Public Opinion Survey* (2010) to representatives from each the five CSFs. Following a series of consultations, the Safer Communities team identified a range of tailored project activities that addressed local security issues defined by each of the municipalities. During its pilot phase, the Safer Communities team used its seed funding to support the construction of stray dog shelters in Sanski Most, Višegrad and Zenica. In Bratunac and Prijedor, it also invested in projects designed to improve road safety and CCTV technology was introduced to all of the municipalities. My concerns about the potential ethical and social problems of introducing CCTV through the forums were to some extent allayed by the Community Policing Advisor who also recognized the risk that there could be problems. My field notes describe a meeting with CSF representatives in Bratunac at which my colleague spoke openly about their concerns:

[The Community Policing Advisor's] main concern is that people will disapprove of this technology on the grounds that it represents a form of 'big brother'. [They] also however recognize that there are arguments in favour of prevention. All of this [they] present openly to the CSF members in order to gauge their stance on the matter and to prompt them to devise a plan for selling the technology to the public as a 'good thing'.

The Police Chief provides the police point of view on the matter. He openly acknowledges that citizens will have concerns about privacy and that this is a potential concern but he does assert that the surveillance has shown improved results when used effectively. In particular he seems keen to deploy CCTV to monitor major roads in and out of Bratunac as he feels quite confident that this will help with the apprehension of criminals. He notes that they have previously seen this success through use of

CCTV cameras at gas stations outside of the city. He concludes by again asserting that these cameras should not intrude on people's private life.

[The Community Policing Advisor] describes the privacy concerns and a recent consultation with a CCTV designer regarding possibilities for masking non-essential visuals on the cameras and ensuring that the technology is not abused.

The Police Chief steps in and asserts that the only reason they want CCTV is for road coverage anyway, not buildings and that this is to see who comes and goes. He notes that buildings are not interesting to them. My guess is they will not have these cameras actively monitored anyway due to lack of human resources and budget.

[The Community Policing Advisor] concludes this matter by reiterating that either way citizens must be better informed of this impending technology.

The Mayor then provides further reassurance that the problems associated with CCTV in 'developed countries' won't be relevant here anyhow because there are no resources to have staff constantly monitoring the cameras anyway. Instead they are used to provide evidence and provide information for incidents.

[The Community Policing Advisor] then notes that CCTV represents a dangerous area in terms of politicization and asks what the CSF's plan is for dealing with this. [They] proceed to ask about whether they have come up with their strategic plan yet and states that while they have no doubt about [the forum's] ability to implement improvements, they are interested in seeing their procedure.[22]

Following the meeting, the Safer Communities team reflected on these issues and took the decision to require the CSFs to sign up to the 'Charter for a Democratic Use of Video-Surveillance' published by the European Forum for Urban Security in order to receive money for CCTV (see European Forum for Urban Security 2010). The Safer Communities team also subsidized the construction of a designated youth centre in the municipality of Bratunac after members of its CSF suggested that it might help to prevent antisocial behaviour. In Višegrad, the Safer Communities team purchased a lifeboat following a number of accidental drownings

---

[22] Field notes, 8 February 2011. The conversation was translated by the Community Policing Advisor. Also in attendance was a representative from another international organization involved with community safety reforms at the time. I am fairly confident that the translation provided by my colleague was faithful to what was actually being said because the English-speaking representative from the other organization was able to actively participate in the meeting.

in the Drina River and in Zenica, it worked with the local CSF to develop a curriculum for addressing gender-based violence through a training seminar.

The Safer Communities team's decision to support these low profile project activities illustrates UNDP's influence within this contact zone. This investment afforded to the Safer Communities team the chance to exercise a significant degree of autonomy in terms of how it chose to conceptualize the project and define its projected outputs so that they could address local issues without fear of under-delivering. In this respect, the designated 'results' for the pilot phase of Safer Communities remained largely intangible. UNDP's economic resources in the form of seed funding also ensured that Safer Communities would be designed, managed, and implemented by UNDP employees. While the Safer Communities team's role in governing the governance of security is suggestive of what deLeon (1992: 125) labels the 'elite characterization' of policy actors, their 'elite' positioning did not appear to create a cultural or discursive 'disconnect between policy actors and local users' because the Safer Communities team continued to implement these project activities in a manner reflective of UNDP's capacity development ethos which advocated 'policy sharing' as a means of identifying local needs. This involved maintaining regular channels of communication with local political elites involved with the forums and employing local BiH citizens to manage and implement the project as members of the Safer Communities team. Local staff at UNDP represented a particularly important mechanism for exercising operational reflexivity and their presence in this contact zone fostered policy sharing by ensuring that their collective habitus was at least to some degree shaped by their personal interest as citizens in achieving meaningful and sustainable improvements in the local governance of security in BiH.

The Safer Communities project also functioned as an important link between local CSFs and other security nodes operating in this network. For example, representatives from the Sarajevo-based Centre for Security Studies (CSS), the OSCE, and the London-based Saferworld group were invited to attend a series of meetings between the Safer Communities team and local CSFs in February 2011. During these meetings, these different organizations presented CSF members with educational resources covering issues like community engagement and responding to hate crimes.[23] The majority of the interactions[24] that took place during these meetings were consistent with UNDP's capacity development ethos in that there was no expectation from these different organizations that CSF members would utilize their resources or enter into collaboration unless it was in the interest of their local communities to do so. In this respect, the Safer Communities project and its individual members played a role in empowering local CSFs by allowing them to govern security within their communities in relation to local preferences. Of course, there was no way for UNDP to be certain that local politicians or bureaucrats would implement the project activities faithfully and as my second case study which focuses on the implementation of the SDC's community policing reform project in Sarajevo Canton demonstrates, the impact of these activities is at least partially determined by the willingness and the ability of designated end users to see them through.

Habitus is Mutable

The capacity of the international development worker at UNDP to act as a policy mediator in the sphere of transnational policing is linked with the fact that their habitus is simultaneously responsive to global and local factors. On one level, the international development worker might be described as an ancillary of global liberal governance and global policing who works to reproduce upwardly-responsive policing models, mentalities, and practices in the context of developing societies. On another level, the international development worker recognizes that they have an ethical obligation to promote initiatives that develop the capacities of local partners. Insofar as the habitus of the international development

---

[23] Field notes, 8–10 February 2011.

[24] One example of an interaction that I observed which does not fit this analysis was between a representative from another international organization involved with SSR in BiH and members of the CSF in Prijedor. The representative attended the meeting to inform the police officers in attendance about new procedures that were being introduced throughout the RS for reporting hate crimes. The representative stated that these officers would need to familiarize themselves with these new procedures and that the police in RS would need to take responsibility for maintaining a database of all hate crime incidents as this was a condition of their organization providing assistance. This is indicative of the susceptibility of this nodal assemblage to externally-responsive forms of governance (field notes, 10 February 2011).

worker at UNDP reflects the ontological insecurities of the organization and the pressures that these insecurities generate, it can be described as conflicted and malleable. It is at once idealistic and opportunistic and this renders the international development worker both principled and savvy. It is an actor whose transient interest in policing and police reform projects is predicated on the circumstantial demand for such projects and the availability of funding to support such activities. For this reason, it is impossible to reduce the international development worker's contribution to the sphere of transnational policing and the project of global policing to either control or empowerment. It is also difficult to distinguish between their idealistic and opportunistic motives in the context of key decision-making processes such as those documented in this chapter unless one possesses an intimate understanding of the actors, their backgrounds, and the institutional and structural pressures they face.

Duffield's (1999; 2007) work calls into question the possibility of distinguishing between development and security agendas in the age of global liberal governance but the international development worker's ephemeral interest in police and security sector reform projects indicates that development and capacity building may still be perceived as ends in their own right. In other words, the conflicted capacity development ethos may compel development workers to engage with the governance of security in order to achieve broader outcomes linked with development, local ownership, democratization, and liberalization. Their institutionalization ensures that they define their role through discourses of capacity development rather than securitization. Accordingly, the Manichean world view that Bowling and Sheptycki (2012) associate with their posited 'subculture of transnational policing' does not appear to be characteristic of the habitus of the international development worker who nonetheless represents a transnational policing actor. In other words, development workers do not uncritically assume that more policing or better forms of policing represent the ideal solution to problems of order and instability. The discussion of the ethical and social implications of CCTV is particularly telling in this respect given that the Community Policing Advisor's concerns were a product of their awareness of the public's aversion to state surveillance during the Yugoslav era. It must be considered then that the habitus of the international development worker is mutable (Wacquant 2011; also Bourdieu 1977: 73–5) and susceptible to modification as a result of historical experiences and contemporary circumstances as well as the cultural, social, and political processes that contribute to the objectification of subjective dispositions, norms, and values within a contact zone.

Translating 'Safer Communities'

The lack of clarity surrounding the conceptual and programmatic contours of the Safer Communities model was advantageous because it allowed the project team to focus on capacity development. It was also problematic from a performance management perspective because it led the project team to assume that capacity development outcomes would not in themselves appeal to prospective donors who were interested in tangible outputs.[25] As a project dealing with security sector reform in the Western Balkans, it was also believed that the European Commission represented the only remaining source of potential investment as most alternative sources of bilateral assistance to BiH had dried up by this point. Confronted with a need to attract a new source of revenue to sustain the Safer Communities project beyond 2011, I spent a significant portion of my time working with colleagues to negotiate and translate the conceptual and programmatic contours of the Safer Communities model into language that we hoped would appeal to the European Commission.

Articulating a new identity for the project proved challenging because neither my colleagues nor I understood how to go about attracting non-core investment from donors. There was also confusion about the types of policing reform projects, if any, that the European Commission might be keen to invest in given the extensive history of police reform in the country. As noted earlier in this chapter, my colleagues from the Safer Communities team were BiH citizens who lacked first-hand experience and knowledge of the higher echelons of both the UN development system and the international community's network of governance in BiH.[26] As junior staff in the UNDP BiH country office, the team's

---

[25] Conversation with the Safer Communities team's Project Manager on 17 January 2011.

[26] As a non-BiH citizen, I would have been considered 'international staff' had I been salaried during this internship. I initially lacked intimate knowledge of the key structures and processes involved with governance in BiH and, more importantly, I lacked the social capital necessary for acquiring this knowledge without introductions provided by the Project Manager.

Community Policing Advisor and Project Associate lacked the social capital necessary for directly acquiring this information from senior UNDP managers with a better understanding of the UN development system. While the Project Manager could periodically access these individuals, this individual was frequently preoccupied with addressing various obstacles that had arisen with the SACBiH project meaning that the Community Policing Advisor, the Project Associate, and I were left to explore these questions through regular brainstorming sessions that generated different concept notes. These concept notes were used by the Safer Communities team as a way of articulating a vision for the project and for clarifying its aims and objectives for external audiences including prospective donors. Reflecting on the development of these documents provides insight into how the team's habituated view of the project changed during this period. My participation calls for an auto-ethnographic account of this translational process in order to present the data reflexively.

Renegotiating 'Safer Communities'

Admittedly, the process of translating the Safer Communities model into something that might resonate with donor preferences proceeded on the basis of imperfect information about what the European Commission was actually willing to finance. The limited information that was available to us was supplied by the Project Manager who suggested that we would need to identify a 'selling point' for Safer Communities that would readily answer the question, 'what is it that these forums actually do?'.[27] The Project Manager added that Safer Communities projects in other transitional countries were linked with specific, topical issues designed to attract investment. In Kenya, for example, they noted that a 'Safer Cities' project had been implemented by UN-HABITAT which focused on the issue of developing safer housing. In Croatia, UNDP's Safer Communities project stipulated that 20% of the project's budget must be spent on gender-related activities. By citing these previous examples, the Project Manager was implying that the Safer Communities project in BiH would only appeal to donors if it was marketed as a strategy for achieving a clearly defined goal

---

[27] Paraphrasing a conversation with the Safer Communities team's Project Manager on 17 January 2011.

as opposed to marketing it as a template for improving the local governance of security. From our perspective, empowerment was not recognized by donors as an attractive development goal in its own right.

Similar ideas were expressed by a colleague at UNDP who suggested that 'the European Commission and other donors are only interested in seeing progress in the short term, demonstrated through tangible outputs'. They recognized, however, that this would be problematic for the Safer Communities project because 'CSFs are ultimately successful when they are operating and being utilised to deal with local issues without an overreliance on external support and resources'.[28] In other words, they believed that aligning the project with donor interests risked compromising the model's value as a mechanism of local capacity development. Despite these concerns, the team's Project Manager remained adamant that the European Commission would only invest in projects that could be measured and evaluated.[29] These assumptions informed our search for a 'greater selling point' and they prompted us to conceive of ways of demonstrating that the Safer Communities model could be aligned with the European Commission's efforts to facilitate BiH's accession to the European Union.

One of the first concept notes that we developed proposed that CSFs might serve as useful platforms for combatting rising levels of social exclusion in BiH. Social exclusion was an issue which was previously identified as important by a 2009 UNDP Human Development Report for BiH titled *The Ties That Bind* (UNDP 2009b).[30] This report states, 'the use of *štela*—personal and family connections—is widespread' in BiH with the effect that different populations enjoy differential access to important networks of governance. The report adds that those populations[31] which lack these connections are 'network poor' meaning they 'have lower

---

[28] Paraphrasing a conversation with an undisclosed colleague at UNDP which took place in January 2011.

[29] Conversation with the Safer Communities team's Project Manager on 17 January 2011.

[30] I took the lead in developing this report and feedback was later provided by the Project Manager and Community Policing Advisor.

[31] The report suggests that '[g]roups most likely to suffer from social isolation include [internally displaced persons], minority returnees, the elderly, women in rural areas and people with lower education' (UNDP 2009b: 22).

levels of social capital and higher levels of material deprivation'. This implies that they are ultimately disempowered within and beyond their respective communities and prone to social exclusion (UNDP 2009b: 22).

Building on the theorized relationship between differential access to networks and social exclusion, I composed the following introduction to a draft of a concept note titled 'Safer Communities Project 2012–2015: Security Governance as Social Capital'[32] in February 2011:

> *The Safer Communities Project aims to reinvigorate meso-level social bonds in Bosnia and Herzegovina through the establishment of Citizen Security Forums (CSF) that serve to enhance the accountability and transparency of the process by which local security governance is provided. As it currently stands, the key structures and institutions that are tasked with governing security in Bosnia and Herzegovina are largely exclusive in that opportunities for citizen participation are limited and the availability and functionality of formal communicational channels designed to encourage information sharing remain underutilized and ultimately inadequate.*

Later in the concept note, I also drew attention to the 'tangible' security risks associated with social exclusion in order to amplify the significance of this project for prospective donors.

In an admittedly desperate attempt to bolster the empirical credibility of the proposal, I drew upon the *Public Opinion Poll* (2010) and summary data from the two consultancy reports produced by UK Policing Services (2010a; 2010b) which provided some empirical support for the posited link between social exclusion and insecurity. I also invoked the 'common-sense' wisdom of the Broken Windows Theory (see Wilson and Kelling 1982) to provide theoretical support for the proposal because I thought it would be accessible to non-specialist reviewers in Brussels. The draft of this concept note which I submitted to the Project Manager in February 2011 stated:

> *This notable gap between security 'providers' and citizens is inherently problematic in that it serves to continuously erode the latter's trust and confidence in the former. Furthermore, this lack of information sharing serves to negate the capacity of 'providers' at all levels of government*

---

[32] Listed in Appendix 2.

*in Bosnia and Herzegovina from effectively addressing key safety and
security issues of relevance to citizens. This contributes to a vicious cycle
resulting in two significant outcomes that represent fundamental threats
to the long term sustainability of Bosnia and Herzegovina as an independently governed state. The first 'outcome' is that citizen expectations
decrease, particularly in relation to the provision of public safety and
security. Related is the second 'outcome' whereby the impetus for 'providers' to provide such services is thus reduced accordingly...*

*...Not only does this cycle serve to deprive these citizens and com-
munities of these socio-economic benefits but perhaps most problematic
of all it contributes to the normalization of this social deprivation in the
eyes of these 'consumers'...*

*...In linking this dynamic to the 'broken windows' theory, the mutu-
ally-dependent relationship between democratically responsive structures for local security governance and social capital is clear. Broken
windows theory suggests that ineffective security governance within a
community is likely to prove conducive to petty crime and anti-social
behaviour. Over time the overt occurrence of this behaviour combined
with its social and physical effects will ultimately be normalized in the
minds of the public thereby cementing the further degradation of social
capital in these communities.*

I concluded the concept note by presenting the Safer Communities
project as an ideal platform for improving the responsiveness of
police and municipal authorities to public concerns:

*Citizen Security Forums (CSF) address this need for greater social cohe-
sion at the community level by creating 'linkages for developing sustainable changes in the living conditions and well-being of communities'.
When introduced to divided communities, these CSFs are also well positioned to have a significant impact on policies aimed at addressing the
social and economic integration of individuals at risk of marginaliza-
tion...Specifically, the SCP is designed to have a significant impact on
two forms of social capital: bridging social capital and linking social
capital...*[33]

The concept note was initially well received by the Project Manager
and the Community Policing Advisor who later incorporated some
of these ideas into a final project report. However, the concept

[33] The quoted material makes reference to the *The Ties That Bind* report. The
report describes 'bridging social capital' as 'horizontal relationships—connecting
people from different backgrounds' and 'linking social capital' as 'vertical
relationships—connecting people with dissimilar social standing and spanning
power differentials' (see UNDP 2009*b*: 27).

note prompted concern from the Project Manager who questioned whether abstract discursive elements of this narrative could actually be translated into a set of measurable indicators that could be used to monitor the team's progress when it came time to implement the project.[34] On the basis of the Project Manager's concerns, this early attempt to translate the Safer Communities concept into language that linked a thematic, capacity development issue with the European security interests in the Western Balkans was dismissed.

Taking the lead in developing this concept note made me aware of the significant degree of influence and discretion that relatively disempowered international development workers enjoy when it comes to articulating the discursive contours of police capacity building projects. Our options were very much limited by the institutional aims of UNDP and the structural environment in which we were operating but there was certainly scope for negotiation and creativity. On the other hand, the experience also made me aware of the fact that our attempts to reformulate the project's narrative so that it would fit with the strategic priorities of donors meant that we were working to position ourselves as agents of global liberal governmentality and that doing so had the potential to conflict with UNDP's capacity development ethos. Yet another realization was that the process of constructing a viable discourse for legitimating the project to donors amounted to a creative exercise rather than one that can be described as 'evidence-based'. In other words, the only evidence that we appeared to be genuinely concerned with at this stage was that which afforded us insight into the strategic aims of the European Commission or that which appeared to support our proposal. By comparison, evidence relating to what might work locally was of limited relevance with respect to the continuation of the project. Accordingly, this early attempt at developing a concept note showed less concern for what the Safer Communities model could realistically achieve in this context than with what we as policy translators thought the project would need to achieve in order to attract donor investment.

Subsequent attempts by the Safer Communities team to construct an attractive narrative for the project illustrate an important

---

[34] Conversation with the Safer Communities team's Project Manager on 14 February 2011.

shift of power within this contact zone. The possibility of linking this model to the issue of refugees and returnees[35] was briefly discussed but promptly dismissed once the Project Manager was informed by a senior UNDP manager based at the BiH country office that this was no longer an appealing issue for European donors.[36] The prospect of reducing crime through the work of the CSFs provided the Safer Communities team with perhaps the most obvious discursive marketing point but this too was problematic in practice because it meant that the Safer Communities team would have to actually demonstrate that these forums were reducing levels of crime and public insecurity within their respective municipalities. This implied that the team would have to predefine the anticipated outcomes of applying the Safer Communities model in municipalities throughout BiH for local CSFs in order to measure progress. Of course, this went against the team's capacity development ethos because it entailed restricting the possibility of allowing CSFs to subsequently develop their own performance indicators based on locally-defined priorities. Instead, the Project Manager felt that it was necessary to develop a single set of indicators that could be applied uniformly throughout BiH in order to convey the national significance of the project because donors would not be interested in local outcomes relating to the management of the country's stray dog population or improvements in local street lighting.[37]

On a pragmatic level, conveying the anticipated benefits of this project was also problematic given that the *Public Opinion Poll* (2010) had found that levels of crime and public insecurity were relatively low. As previously discussed, the Safer Communities team attributed these findings to the public's limited expectations of security governance within their respective communities so it was also anticipated that using these forums to boost public expectations of public service provision might initially contribute to an increase in reported crimes along with increased levels of subjective insecurity and greater dependency on formal providers

---

[35] 'Returnees' refers to individuals who were internally displaced by the war but have since returned to their homes.

[36] Conversation with the Safer Communities team's Project Manager on 14 March 2011.

[37] Conversation with the Safer Communities team's Project Manager on 2 February 2011.

which were already constrained by limited budgetary resources. The speculated increase in reported crime was based on our belief that functional CSFs would need to generate greater awareness of the public security issues that affected their respective communities before they could convince the public of their value as sites of governance.[38]

The possibility that functional CSFs might potentially contribute to increased levels of reported crime in the short term was recognized as being problematic because the envisioned extension for the Safer Communities project was only to last three years. This meant that within this three-year period, the Safer Communities team would have to evidence its progress towards achieving its predefined performance targets or risk termination and repayment at the discretion of the European Commission. While the team was optimistic that CSFs could eventually generate meaningful improvements in the local governance of security in BiH, it was not confident that these improvements could be readily expressed as statistical reductions in local levels of crime or insecurity. This concern was especially apparent from the Project Manager's suggestion that crime prevention would have to be designated as a primary function of the CSFs but that translating non-events into indicators is extremely problematic for reasons relating to causation and displacement.[39] Methodologically, demonstrating the project's success to donors was problematic because we lacked credible baseline data that would allow us to measure any progress. Official crime statistics in BiH appeared to represent the only available data source for longitudinal comparison but we assumed that auditors from the European Commission would inevitably question their reliability.

The issue of developing a single set of indicators to convey the impact of Safer Communities to prospective donors proved to be a stress inducing prospect for the entire Safer Communities team and it prompted the Project Manager to seek advice from a senior colleague that might help us to determine what kind of indicators might appeal to the European Commission. During a meeting between the Project Manager and this senior manager that I attended in March 2011, the Project Manager explained how

---

[38] Field notes, 2 February 2011.

[39] Conversation with the Safer Communities team's Project Manager on 2 February 2011.

we were struggling to develop a set of indicators because of the 'broad and flexible nature of this project'.[40] The senior colleague suggested that part of the problem was that 'we were missing the bigger picture'. In other words, supranational donors increasingly recognized the need for a project to be managed flexibly and so there is no expectation that a funding proposal would contain finite indicators. Rather, the senior colleague believed that the European Commission would support the project if it was seen as facilitating BiH's progress towards EU accession.

Based on this feedback, we momentarily dismissed the possibility of marketing Safer Communities as a strategy for reducing crime and improving the governance of security in local communities and we considered aligning the project's aims directly with this accession agenda. To this end we reviewed two key accession documents, the *Copenhagen Criteria* which lists three key benchmarks 'that a candidate country must have achieved' before it can become a member of the EU (EU 1993: 13) and BiH's *Stabilisation and Association Agreement* (2008) which outlines the specific obligations that the country must fulfil before it can be considered a candidate for EU membership.[41] Based on this review, we determined that the Safer Communities model could be linked with the *Copenhagen Criteria's* emphasis on the need for 'stable institutions that guarantee democracy, the rule of law, human rights, and respect for minorities' (EU 1993: 13) and Article 78 of BiH's *Stabilisation and Association Agreement* (2008: 47–8) which prioritized '[r]einforcement of [i]nstitutions and [r]ule of [l]aw' by '... developing adequate structures for the police, customs and other law enforcement bodies' and 'fighting corruption and organised crime'. The idea that emerged from our deliberations was that the Safer Communities model could represent a local extension of a vertically-integrated security model. In other words, CSFs might serve as an important source of local intelligence for state-level police organizations like the State Investigation and Protection Agency (SIPA) with its focus on combatting organized crime and terrorism and also for the BiH

[40] Paraphrasing a conversation between the Safer Communities team's Project Manager and a Senior Manager at UNDP BiH on 14 March 2011.

[41] As of March 2012, BiH remains a potential candidate country for EU accession as it has not ratified its *Stabilisation and Association Agreement* which it signed in June 2008.

Border Police.[42] This in turn would fit with the EU's interest in combatting serious and organized crime in the region. The prospective appeal of this proposal was enhanced by BiH's fragmented policing landscape which made coordinating intelligence sharing activities between different entity and cantonal police forces difficult.

The prospect of actually translating this idea into practice was problematic for two reasons. First we were sceptical that local community policing activities would actually generate meaningful intelligence on high profile criminal activities of regional significance.[43] Second, we determined that the nodular structures established by the Safer Communities project during the pilot phase lacked the hierarchical character necessary for channelling relevant information upwards to relevant state-level agencies. The possibility of facilitating such exchanges through the creation of cantonal and entity level steering boards was momentarily explored but ultimately dismissed by the Project Manager based on concerns that establishing another level of nodal governance would create 'too much bureaucracy' and merely add to an already crowded system of underperforming institutions.[44] Another concern was that establishing a new hierarchical structure for the Safer Communities model would in effect contradict the local orientation of the project and undermine the aim of capacity development.[45] While securitization for the purpose of supporting Europeanization ultimately failed to provide us with a viable selling point, our consideration of this possibility did prompt an important dialogue amongst the members of the Safer Communities team that led us to conclude that the conceptual and

---

[42] The State Border Police was renamed the BiH Border Police in July 2007.

[43] This scepticism was supported by Tilley's (2003: 3) doubts about the value of using 'problem-oriented policing' to support a National Intelligence Model in England and Wales. Interestingly, the OSCE has subsequently published a handbook titled *Preventing Terrorism and Countering Violent Extremism and Radicalization that Lead to Terrorism: A Community Policing Approach* which confidently states, 'Community-oriented approaches to countering terrorism aim to strengthen public confidence in, and support for, counterterrorism policies and measures, including police action, thereby contributing to their legitimacy in the eyes of the public at large and certain communities in particular'. (OSCE 2014: 72). The evidence cited by the handbook in support of these claims appears to be quite thin.

[44] Paraphrasing a conversation with the Safer Communities team's Project Manager on 25 March 2011.

[45] Conversation with the Safer Communities team's Project Associate on 24 March 2011.

programmatic contours of this project must continue to be oriented towards improving the local responsiveness of security governance rather than increasing security as defined by European donors.

Policy Translation and Exclusion

By March 2011, it was apparent that our concerted efforts to rebrand Safer Communities amounted to a significant distraction from the actual development and implementation of project activities that had fallen behind schedule. Following a meeting of the Safer Communities team about the issue of indicators, one colleague announced that 'we already lost the game'.[46] This observation denoted our recognition of a significant shift in the power politics of the Safer Communities project as a contact zone, one which served to prioritize the perceived interests of the EU. It further illustrates how the hierarchical structures associated with liberal state-building, Europeanization, and donor-driven development allow powerful supranational actors to steer security governance from a distance. The significant economic resources of the European Commission as a potential investor allowed it to play an influential albeit indirect role in temporarily shaping the conceptual and programmatic contours of the project through a series of deliberations and negotiations that were conducted by the Safer Communities team.

With reference to UNDP's capacity development ethos and the aim of contributing to the development of more democratically responsive structures for governing security in BiH, this structural dynamic was problematic because it restricted opportunities for democratically-elected domestic policymakers to participate in important decision-making processes. This restriction was problematic because it signified that the preferences of CSF members including local political elites, police practitioners, and members of the general public might ultimately fail to have a significant impact on meta-deliberations relating to the governance of security governance within this nodal setting. It also appeared to diverge from UNDP's goal of eventually generating local ownership for the Safer Communities project because the Safer Communities team did not

---

[46] Quoting an undisclosed member of the Safer Communities team during a conversation which took place on 24 March 2011.

include these local stakeholders in this translational process. Their exclusion can be accounted for on the basis of the limited economic resources of domestic policymakers and governing institutions in BiH which negated their relevance as potential investors for the project. The local policy makers and the practitioners who would ultimately be tasked with implementing the reform were also physically excluded from this translational process and indeed probably unaware of the fact that our meta-deliberations were even taking place. The inaccessibility of this contact zone is further illustrated by the fact that its deliberative boundaries overlapped with the physical boundaries of the Safer Communities office located in UNDP's BiH headquarters. The office featured a secure entry system and a strict visitor protocol that would have physically prevented any individual lacking an invitation from UNDP to access this nodal setting and take part.

By emphasizing the exclusion of these individuals from the contact zone, I do not wish to suggest that UNDP or the Safer Communities team consciously or intentionally acted to restrict participation in this deliberative sphere. Rather, we simply assumed that CSF members and other government officials would have little interest in participating in the planning process or, that lacking an understanding of the UN development system and donor interests, if they did participate they would have nothing to contribute. Elsewhere, Maglajlić and Rašidagić (2007: 156) have written that 'Bosnian social-sector professionals [find] themselves both unable to communicate with international aid agencies and incapable of adopting the style of work these agencies brought with them'. Accordingly, Maglajlić and Rašidagić suggest that it is 'local staff' of international organizations like UNDP, such as my colleagues, who must take on the role of policy translators due to their ability to access these contact zones which link international organizations like UNDP to local settings.

Salvaging 'Safer Communities'

In March 2011 the Safer Communities team concluded that in order for the project to have a meaningful impact on the local governance of security in BiH and for the CSFs to be rendered locally accountable and sustainable, the conceptual and programmatic prescriptions for this project would need to remain flexible. In other words, the team recognized that the governance of security should remain responsive to the diverse needs and expectations of the CSF partners rather than rigid interpretations of the interests of prospective supranational benefactors. Accordingly, the team determined that establishing and supporting the development of new municipal level CSFs throughout BiH must necessarily serve as the project's primary focus and projected output.[47] While the previous sub-section's account of the pressures for the Safer Communities team to align this project with the interests of prospective donors presents a fatalistic assessment of local participation in the nodal governance of security in BiH, subsequent developments indicate that the Safer Communities team may have identified an alternative solution to this funding dilemma that would allow it to reconcile its aims with local and global priorities.

Following a series of meetings between the Safer Communities Project Manager and a senior UNDP manager based in the BiH country office, the Safer Communities team developed a creative proposal to pursue the expansion of the Safer Communities project as a component of the UN's Armed Conflict and Violence Prevention Programme (AVPP).[48] It was hoped that this would enable the team to access additional core funding from UNDP's Crisis Prevention and Recovery budget and then work alongside other UN development agencies like the UN Population Fund (UNFPA) to develop a range of project activities that could be marketed to the CSFs. The idea was that CSFs would still be afforded the opportunity to choose which project activities they wished to pursue while the Safer Communities team could provide technical and administrative support to these forums and draw upon its position within the network to connect the forums directly to appropriate donors.[49] The benefit of this proposed solution with respect to UNDP's capacity development mandate was that it promised to reduce the pressures for the Safer Communities team to manage the project on the basis of anticipated results. Instead it enabled the Safer Communities team to develop a flexible list of objectives relating to the project and to include this list in the concept note that

[47] Field notes, 25 March 2011.
[48] Conversations with multiple members of the Safer Communities team on 12 April and 14 July 2011.
[49] Personal communications from an undisclosed member of the Safer Communities team in December 2011 and February 2012.

was eventually submitted as part of the team's bid for UNDP Crisis Prevention and Recovery core funding in early 2012.[50]

It is not clear if this bid was ultimately successful but the fact that my colleagues were able to conceive of this solution can be explained by UNDP's proximity to the Safer Communities project as an active contact zone and its habitual emphasis on managerial creativity as a means of achieving capacity development objectives amidst these financial pressures (Murphy 2006: 348). Creative problem-solving in this instance was made possible by the fact that the UN development system continues to offer limited pockets of core funding that allows projects like Safer Communities which are not particularly resource intensive to remain independent of non-core investment if they can be linked with designated funding areas (Browne 2011: 119). As of May 2014, there is no mention of 'Safer Communities' on the UNDP in BiH website. Rather, the main 'Justice and Security' project being implemented in BiH by UNDP is a follow-up to the SACBiH project called 'Project EXPLODE'. The project is funded by the European Union (€3,837,537 between 2013 and 2015) and its 'Project Plan' states:

The Project EXPLODE develops and implements military logistical operations. It supports the Ministry of Defense of Bosnia and Herzegovina's efforts to prevent uncontrolled explosion of old and unstable ammunition that may cause humanitarian crisis.

The Project EXPLODE destroys high hazardous ammunition and complex weapons system. It supports the Armed Forces of Bosnia and Herzegovina to decrease military ammunition stockpiles to the manageable quantities. The Project conducts training for the senior military officers and certifies ammunition specialists for ammunition inspection and demilitarization.

The Project EXPLODE implements construction engineering projects aiming to improve safety and storage conditions of the military weapons and ammunition storage depots.[51]

---

[50] This is a reference to a later version of the document that I provided feedback on in December 2011, once my internship had ended. In exchange for this feedback, I requested permission to use this document for my research but provided assurances to the team's Community Policing Advisor that I would not explicitly quote it or reference it for publication until the team received a decision on its application.

[51] 'Explosive Ordnance Destruction'. *Explosive Ordnance Destruction— EXPLODE.* UNDP, n.d. Web. 6 May 2014. Available: <http://undp.akvoapp.org/en/project/931/>.

Interestingly, a blog entry posted by a former intern with Project EXPLODE on the UNDP in Europe and Central Asia website in July of 2013 indicates that discursive elements of the Safer Communities project persist:

The task of the project is massive due to the shockingly large number of old, chemically unstable munitions sitting in storage facilities throughout Bosnia and Herzegovina. But it's worth it. The project will make life safer for not only those working with hazardous ammunition but for the many people living in (mostly rural) communities.

Eliminating the possibility of dangerous uncontrolled explosions will have a big impact, but it's just the beginning. Socio economic development needs to happen in safe communities, so the exciting part is what will happen after a town is free of its dangerous munitions depot (Bray 2013, emphasis added).

Exiting this contact zone has limited my ability to probe the discursive link between the Safer Communities project and Project EXPLODE but it does not appear to be the case that CSFs actively contribute to disarmament activities. What is clear is that UNDP continues to identify improvements in the safety of local communities as an important development priority. Whereas the Safer Communities team struggled to identify an upwardly-appealing-yet-flexible vision for the work of CSFs, the members of Project EXPLODE have articulated a vision for making communities safer that appears to resonate with the interests of international donors and local citizens alike. For international donors, the blog entry presents munitions destruction as a necessary prerequisite for economic development and foreign investment in BiH. It is also reasonable to assume that destroying munitions is viewed as desirable by local residents because it reduces the risk of uncontrolled explosions which represent a genuine security risk in certain rural parts of the country. Interestingly, discourses of crime and community policing appear to be entirely absent from Project EXPLODE which suggests that they were lost in translation.

Sustaining 'Safer Communities'

Returning to my ethnography of the Safer Communities project in 2011, it is important to note that sustainability represented an important priority for the Safer Communities team. It also served as a major source of confusion because it was not entirely clear what the Safer Communities team was actually meant to be sustaining. The official answer was the project's outputs, that is, the CSFs. Sustaining the CSFs meant that the team would need to develop strategic recommendations to enable CSF members and prospective local stakeholders to continue to operate these forums once the Safer Communities project had expired. Members of the Safer Communities team also recognized that the Safer Communities project played an important role as a central coordinating node for these CSFs so we questioned whether the forums would continue to operate without ongoing financial and technical support from an international organization or an NGO. Institutional motives also factored into this discussion. Notably, the team's concerted search for a source of non-core funding suggests that UNDP hoped to sustain its presence within this contact zone. Finally, individual motives factored into our deliberations about sustainability because members of the Safer Communities team realized that their jobs were dependent on their ability to prolong the project. Reflecting on the Safer Communities team's efforts to develop a sustainability report for the project between January and April 2011 provides a useful illustration of these competing pressures, their influence on the habitus of the Safer Communities team, and the extent to which policy translation is simultaneously responsive to competing interests within a contact zone.

Sustainability initially emerged as an important issue in January 2011 because the Safer Communities team had been invited by the SDC to contribute to the development of a new 'Book of Rules'[52] for community policing that was being developed for the Ministry of the Interior in RS.[53] As noted in Chapter 3, the SDC's

[52] A 'Book of Rules' is a set of by-laws which describe the specific roles and responsibilities for different types of police officers. It is maintained by the different Ministries of the Interior at the entity level in RS and at the canton level in FBIH and any changes must be proposed and approved by their relevant assemblies. Asked about the significance of the Book of Rules, the Safer Communities team's Community Policing Advisor responded that 'a vacancy must be defined in it in order for it to be budgeted and filled' (personal communication from the Safer Communities Team's Community Policing Advisor on 2 April 2012).

[53] The Project Manager issued this assignment to the Safer Communities team via email on 6 January 2011. I only became aware of the fact that our work on the sustainability report was linked to the SDC's plan in late March 2011 at a meeting with the Safer Communities Project Manager regarding a draft that I was developing with the Community Policing Advisor. The Project Manager informed me

community policing project was granted a one-year extension by the Swiss Government in 2011 based on the recommendations of the project's external review team (see Wisler and Traljic 2010). Its primary objective during this period was to work to facilitate the adoption of relevant by-laws within entity and canton-level ministries that would formally recognize community policing as a specialist function and provide specialist units with a guaranteed budget line. The SDC brought this proposal to the attention of the Safer Communities project because it considered CSFs[54] to be important mechanisms for sustaining the outputs that it generated through its community policing project and because the SDC believed that these forums were necessary for generating holistic solutions to a range of problems identified by specialist officers. Without functioning CSFs, the SDC anticipated that its problem-oriented prescriptions for community policing (discussed in the following chapter) would fail to materialize and the entire concept would lose credibility in the eyes of practitioners and the public alike. The prospect of sustaining a problem-oriented community policing strategy in BiH was therefore linked with the need to sustain local CSFs (Wisler and Traljic 2010: 10–11).

For the Safer Communities team, sustaining these CSFs was important because it was linked with UNDP's capacity development ethos. In other words, it was thought that if the forums were to cease their operations once UNDP withdrew its support, the project would fail to generate locally sustainable outputs that could independently contribute to improvements in the governance of security in BiH. The sustainability of these CSFs was therefore identified as an important measure of the project's success by the team's Community Policing Advisor and Project Associate who drafted multiple 'sustainability reports' designed to address this

that the impetus for us to produce a sustainability report at a fairly early stage in the project was linked to the SDC's imminent plans to introduce a revised strategy for community policing to the Ministry of the Interior in RS before its project expired at the end of 2011 (conversation with the Safer Communities Team's Project Manager on 26 March 2011). Follow-up correspondence sent by the Safer Communities project's Community Policing Advisor suggests that the SDC's plans never materialized (personal communication from the Safer Communities team's Community Policing Advisor on 2 April 2012). Nonetheless, the recommendations that we developed were included in the 'Concept Note' that the Safer Communities team submitted with its funding proposal the following year.

[54] The SDC refers to CSFs as 'citizen security boards'.

issue and ultimately supply the SDC with concrete recommendations to be included in the forthcoming proposal.

The first step towards developing these recommendations involved identifying various threats to the sustainability of these forums. This was achieved during a series of in-house deliberations. It was also informed by a series of meetings with members of the pilot CSFs that I attended with the team's Community Policing Advisor in early February 2011.[55] The Community Policing Advisor took the lead with this task and was influential in shaping our collective understanding of how this project could succeed in the long term. According to the team's Community Policing Advisor, the primary threat to the sustainability of these forums involved the question of how we could keep CSF participants motivated once UNDP withdrew its support for the Safer Communities project. The Community Policing Advisor attributed the initial wave of interest in this project to the fact that participating in these nodes afforded different municipal actors direct access to discretionary UNDP funds but expressed concerns that without this financial incentive, individuals would lack a tangible incentive to participate in this scheme.[56]

The Project Manager, Community Policing Advisor, and local CSF members were also conflicted over the question of whether CSF members should be financially compensated for performing their CSF roles. For example, the Project Manager was concerned that unless the Safer Communities team used its influence to compel local municipal assemblies to establish permanent salaried positions for CSF members, individuals would lack an incentive to effectively administer these forums. However, the team's Community Policing Advisor remained adamant that participation in CSFs must be voluntary because otherwise they would attract individuals who lacked an intrinsic motivation to develop holistic solutions for local problems but who were instead there to draw a salary. During our meeting with the CSF in Bratunac, a senior municipal official and 'permanent' member of the

---

[55] The CSFs we visited included Bratunac, Prijedor, Sanski Most, and Zenica. Also present at these meetings was a representative from Saferworld who was involved with community safety reform projects in Central Asia and Kosovo. Representatives from a local NGO known as the Centre for Security Studies also attended the meeting in Zenica.

[56] Conversation with the Safer Communities team's Community Policing Advisor on 31 January 2011.

municipality's CSF expressed similar concerns about the risks of compensating CSF members for their participation. He suggested that this would spawn jealousy amongst members of the public who would ask, 'why is he being paid to serve on the committee and not me'.[57] This individual's assessment suggests that compensating CSF members for participating in these nodes could undermine their legitimacy in the eyes of the public because it would essentially amount to paying municipal employees a second salary for carrying out their existing responsibilities.

During this series of meetings with the pilot CSFs, the need to institutionalize these forums was also addressed. For example, a senior member from one of the better established forums suggested that one of the difficulties that this CSF faced was a lack of support from the city's Mayor. This individual added that the CSF was not formally recognized by the city's municipal assembly with the effect that it lacked a mandate to generate compliance from its membership which frequently failed to attend scheduled meetings and deliver when it came time to implementing agreed-upon solutions.[58] These sentiments were thought to be particularly problematic by the Community Policing Advisor who was convinced that if the well-established forum in this municipality failed, the model would fail elsewhere.[59]

Following a series of deliberations amongst the members of the Safer Communities team, it was decided that institutionalization would be crucial for the sustainability of local CSFs. This meant that the Safer Communities team would subsequently work to provide support for the five pilot CSFs in order for them to achieve recognition by their municipal assemblies through 'Terms of Reference' documents that would also provide them with a small annual budget line. This budget line was determined to be especially important for sustaining CSF operations because it would afford these nodes a renewable stream of discretionary funding that could be spent on collaborative safety projects.[60] While fiscal

[57] Paraphrasing a conversation with a senior municipal official at a meeting in Bratunac on 8 February 2011.

[58] Meeting attended with CSF members in an undisclosed municipality on 10 February 2011.

[59] Conversation with the Safer Communities team's Community Policing Advisor on 31 January 2011.

[60] Field notes, 25 March 2011.

constraints meant that the municipal funds allocated to different CSFs would be extremely limited, the Project Manager and the Community Policing Advisor suggested that its very existence would help to legitimize these nodes in the eyes of local citizens. It was also hoped that, in the long run, the budget would prompt new member agencies to participate in the forum, recognize the value of partnership working, and contribute financially to collaborative activities from their own budgets.[61]

The nature of the working relationship between the Community Policing Advisor and representatives from four of the CSFs (Bratunac, Sanski Most, Višegrad, and Zenica)[62] when it came to developing rules and procedures for the forums raised further doubts about whether the forums could operate independently. These concerns were especially apparent at a meeting with CSF members in Zenica. One of the forum members noted that the local media was creating negative publicity about the forum by suggesting that it was not transparent or publicly accountable in its decisions. To address this problem, the forum member proposed that 'UNDP should step in to influence the media to do their job better'. This suggested that they viewed it as UNDP's responsibility to address this issue rather than that of the forum. Later in the meeting, the Community Policing Advisor raised the question of how this forum would survive once UNDP was no longer supporting the project. A senior police officer and CSF member responded that the forum's results and successes up to this point were directly attributable to UNDP's involvement. Another CSF member explained that UNDP involvement is so important because 'compared to local NGOs, UNDP is widely recognized as being neutral and not affiliated with any political parties'. [63] This suggests that local political elites in Zenica had been constructing the legitimate authority of the CSF on the basis of their affiliation with UNDP.

The Community Policing Advisor also believed that the use of measured coercion was necessary for managing these relationships

---

[61] Field notes, 22 February 2011.

[62] The exception was the CSF in Prijedor which the Community Policing Advisor felt regularly demonstrated initiative and managed to sustain itself once its initial benefactor, the UK Department for International Development, withdrew its support in 2009.

[63] Paraphrasing a senior CSF member during a meeting which was held in Zenica on 9 February 2011.

because 'top-down' authority structures were viewed as normal in BiH. In other words, CSF members who had previously worked for autocratic institutions in the SFRY and subsequently at the direction of international organizations like the OHR expected to be told what to do. On the basis of this cultural assumption, the Safer Communities team rationalized the practice of mobilizing domestic political elites to support its agenda through a utilitarian logic which held that some coercion was necessary for generating and ultimately sustaining policy outputs that truly reflected the public interest due to the limited governing capacities of domestic political institutions. This view also prompted the Safer Communities team to reflect on whether it was necessary to sustain this Safer Communities project as a contact zone in its own right so that it could continue to provide local CSFs with access to different sources of financial and technical support. For this reason, the capacity development goal of sustaining the project's outputs became confused with our aim of sustaining the project itself.

UNDP's capacity development ethos constituted a powerful source of influence on the habitus of the Safer Communities team who believed that UNDP was the only international organization in BiH which was capable of effectively administering this contact zone in accordance with local interests. This belief reflected a romanticized description of UNDP staff by Murphy (2006: ix) who writes:

The overwhelming majority of UNDP staff have been people who passionately believe in the goals of the organization, individuals who have overcome daunting obstacles—and often the conventional wisdom of the day—to develop hundreds of initiatives... Such creative results came about because UNDP has attracted people who not only believe in what they do, but who have been able to be creative in times of crisis, and been willing to put themselves on the line...

This indicates that UNDP's capacity development ethos can also be studied as an important source of institutional pride which is rooted in UNDP's ontological insecurity described earlier in this chapter. In other words, a capacity development mandate affords UNDP a significant degree of flexibility with regards to the types of projects that it seeks to initiate but this flexibility also implies that UNDP is replaceable. In order to survive, UNDP as a development organization must therefore encourage its staff to develop competitive project proposals designed to attract non-core funding. Once it receives this funding, its staff must manage for results.

I encountered evidence of this competitive culture in April 2011 when the Safer Communities team learned that another UN proposal for Safer Communities was currently being developed by a different UN agency in BiH. We were not provided with details of which agency was developing this bid, the nature of its proposal, or the sources of funding that it was targeting but my impression was that this news was not welcomed by my colleagues who had spent the past three months struggling to develop a viable proposal to extend the project. In the end, my understanding is that both of these proposals were subsequently amalgamated into the single multi-agency project bid for additional seed funding from UNDP's Crisis Prevention and Recovery core budget but the example illustrates that even the UN development system embodies a plurality of interests.

It is also important to consider that strong incentives exist for international development workers at UNDP to use RBM to extend their projects. Murphy (2006: 348) suggests that this is achieved through a creative problem-solving mentality which is encouraged by senior UNDP managers and achievable due to a limited donor presence 'on the ground'. The implication is that 'mission creep' is not only problematic for development agencies but, rather, it risks becoming an endemic feature of their operations. The lure of mission creep can be inferred from the individual motives of some members of the Safer Communities team who hoped to prolong their employment with UNDP. Strong disincentives existed for them to discontinue the project or concede their oversight of this contact zone to a competitor because this could effectively lead to the termination of their contracts. In the course of a private conversation that I had with a local project worker employed by an undisclosed international development agency in BiH, I asked this individual what they, as a BiH citizen, hoped to achieve through their work. This individual responded that given the seemingly insurmountable challenges facing BiH at the macro-political level, they were just 'happy to draw a pay cheque'.[64]

---

[64] Quoting a personal conversation which took place in January 2011.

Discussion

The perceived need for the Safer Communities project to appeal to the interests of the European Commission as a prospective donor and the extent to which this perception influenced our translational activities highlights some important issues about the responsiveness of this contact zone to hierarchical pressures for structural alignment. The prospect of securing additional non-core funding for the project served to passively introduce a powerful new supranational stakeholder into this contact zone and the European Commission's significant economic resources allowed it to indirectly influence the shaping of the project's conceptual and programmatic contours through the translational activities of local international development workers at UNDP. This analysis is illustrative of the processes of liberal governmentality (Ryan 2011) introduced in Chapter 2 and it provides further empirical support for the argument that powerful donors can use their substantial resources to indirectly align police reforms with their interests (Ellison and Pino 2012). It also illustrates how certain events and processes, in this case the prospective influx of non-core funding into an active contact zone, can have a momentarily profound effect on the habitus of international development workers and render their translational activities responsive to the 'security politics' (Loader and Walker 2003: 16) of global liberal governance. This possibility, and the frequency with which it is said to occur, forms the basis of Ellison and Pino's (2012) argument that international police development assistance projects are invariably tainted by the same structural inequalities that characterize the international development system. Aspects of this analysis are thus fatalistic.

While these critiques do not preclude the possibility that domestic stakeholders may ultimately benefit from the outputs generated by these policing reforms, they do suggest that important transnational governing structures are themselves inaccessible and ill-responsive to local interests. The experience of the Safer Communities project highlights the fact that the power politics which underpin the institutional work of multilateral international development organizations in weak and structurally dependent societies like BiH is inevitably skewed towards supranational and institutional interests rather than those of local citizens. This means that the nodal cartography for security governance in these contexts is characterized by democratic deficits. This holds significant implications for the prospect of ultimately establishing locally accountable and democratically responsive nodal assemblages that might independently govern security as a 'thick public good' (Loader and Walker 2001).

Beyond this fatalistic assessment, this chapter has also presented a nuanced account of the relationship between liberal state-building and policing reforms, one which highlights the added benefit of exploring these power relations and the habituses they generate through a nodular framework and in relation to the conceptual framework of policy translation. As Johnston and Shearing (2003: 146) suggest, governance cannot be reduced to 'the mere power of one agent over another' but, rather, it exists as 'a varying relationship between agents'. This implies that security governance in weak and structurally dependent societies like BiH cannot be reduced to purely hierarchical terms and that the presence of asymmetrical power structures, self-interested donors, and the myopic prescriptions of policy entrepreneurs need not translate into non-democratic or anti-democratic policing outputs.

Deconstructing the nodal politics that shaped Safer Communities has therefore highlighted the dynamic character of power and governance within this nodal assemblage and identified ways in which seemingly disempowered actors and institutions were able to capitalize on their unique positioning in networks of governance in order to structure the contours of emergent contact zones like Safer Communities in relation to their own habitus. The fact that members of the Safer Communities team were momentarily compelled to examine the prospects for aligning the project with what we considered to be the European Union's security agenda in the Western Balkans illustrates the significant role that hegemonic structures of global liberal governance play in shaping the local governance of policing. However, the Safer Communities team's reflexive activities allowed it to anticipate the long-term impact of policy alignment on local populations and this illustrates the meditational capacities of the international development worker. In this example, the international development worker initially used creativity and their limited knowledge of the international development system to establish a new 'space' for pursuing the project with limited interference from powerful donors. In the long run, it appears that staff at UNDP were able to redefine community safety so that it addressed the interests of donors and citizens alike.

As discussed at the beginning of this chapter, a local capacity development ethos plays an important role in structuring the habitus of the international development worker who in this case felt compelled to embrace concepts like 'grass-roots participation', 'local ownership', and 'empowerment' as desirable outcomes for their work. Incorporating these concepts into an RBM framework was difficult to achieve in practice but the concepts are at least compatible with Dryzek's (2002) prescription for deliberative governance which represents an impugnation to the inaccessible and impenetrable formal institutions of liberal governance.[65] While it is important to acknowledge the 'educative' and the community-generating potential of the Safer Communities model as a mechanism for supporting deliberative democracy, its value as a platform for supporting democratically responsive policing is evident in relation to the following statements by Cooke (2000: 950, 952, 954):

...the procedure of public deliberation improves the fairness of democratic outcomes...
...public deliberation contributes constructively to the practical rationality of democratic outcomes...
...deliberative democracy elucidates an ideal of democracy that is most congruent with 'who we are'...

This is to suggest that, in theory, the CSF model can improve the procedural fairness of security governance by rendering these decision making processes transparent and accessible to broader segments of the community. Procedural fairness represents an important means of legitimizing policing outcomes (Cohen 1997: 73 referenced by Cooke 2000: 950) in liberal democracies as well as an important mechanism for rationalizing them. The idea that CSFs as nodes of deliberative governance might also contribute to more rational policing outcomes therefore corresponds with the

---

[65] Bender and Knaus's (2007: 24) characterization of BiH as an 'international protectorate' suggests that its formal institutions of governance are primarily responsive to the interests of supranational powers whose presence constitutes an additional layer of transnational governance that is structured in relation to the transnational political economy of the EU. This implies that these domestic institutions have limited autonomy compared to those of advanced liberal democracies while their questionable functionality in relation to the established architecture of governance in BiH indicates that their prospective value as discursive mechanisms of governance is inherently limited.

second qualifier for democratically responsive policing that I have identified with Aitchison: 'efficiency', 'effectiveness', and 'delivery of service' (see Aitchison and Blaustein 2013: 500). It also fits with Marenin's (1998: 169) emphasis on 'congruence' as an important element of his prescription for democratic policing.

Cooke (2000: 953) further argues that deliberation provides a basis for compromise and action but acknowledges that the outcomes generated from such compromises will only be viewed as legitimate if they can be justified in relation to 'an epistemic standard of rationality' (Cooke 2000: 953; also Habermas 1996 and Rosenvallon 2011). The issue of congruence is particularly important in the context of weak and structurally dependent societies because powerful global actors play an important role in dictating this 'epistemic standard of rationality' so that it is congruent with the interests of global liberal governance. Insofar as CSFs might improve service delivery by supporting collaborations between the police and other municipal institutions in ways that reflect local security interests and needs, they can be said to foster congruence and promote governing outcomes that reflect 'who we are' (Cooke 2000: 954). However, if these forums are compelled to define their 'epistemic standard of rationality' in ways that conflict with or negate local interests and needs, both responsiveness and perhaps procedural fairness are sacrificed.[66] With respect to Beetham's (1991) three criteria for legitimate power which were noted in Chapter 2, it is also evident that mediatory organizations like UNDP may play an important role in promoting congruence between the global and the local by identifying or constructing common discursive platforms that may foster more legitimate forms of transnational security governance.

The capacity of the Safer Communities team to use policy translation to buffer this contact zone from the EU's security interests in the Western Balkans and ultimately identify common ground suggests that international development workers can actively foster discursive democracy despite having limited resources at their disposal. The discursive character of CSFs was apparent from the fact

---

[66] One must consider that the outcomes generated by governing processes that are not procedurally fair may still appear to be legitimate or rational to disempowered citizens if these citizens are disinterested in policymaking processes. They may also consider incongruent governing processes to be legitimate if they continue to derive benefits from these outcomes.

that the SACBiH project initiated the Safer Communities project in order to improve cooperation between community police officers and municipal authorities at the local level. CSFs constituted governing nodes at which different security actors could hold each other accountable for their role in delivering security (i.e. 'horizontal responsiveness'; see Kuper 2006). This collaborative platform was also determined by UNDP to be necessary for improving the capacity of these institutions to respond to the local security needs of local citizens (i.e. 'vertical responsiveness'; see Kuper 2006). UNDP's technical and financial support for these five CSFs therefore established or sustained these nodes of discursive governance and provided local politicians and practitioners with the opportunity to collectively address enduring public safety issues like stray dogs that were indeed congruent with public expectations of general order policing. In the following chapter, I build upon this assertion by exploring the ways that field operators utilize policy translation to selectively implement externally-defined prescriptions for community-based policing using dramaturgical translation.

6

Community Policing
from the 'Bottom-Up'

Policy translation affects police capacity building projects at multiple stages of their transmission. This chapter accounts for the capacity of local police officers to act as policy mediators who help to determine the nature of policy outputs generated by police development assistance projects in BiH. A multi-site, single case study is used to contrast the progress of two community policing units working to implement a Swiss-inspired community policing model from the 'bottom-up' in Sarajevo Canto in 2011. The chapter begins by describing the organizational structure of the Sarajevo Canton Police and the model of community policing that the SDC developed for implementation in BiH. A number of intra-organizational challenges that typically confront community policing initiatives are considered and the importance of agency for overcoming cultural resistance to change is discussed. Drawing on my ethnographic observation and follow-up interviews with local police officers and project workers from the SDC, the chapter then proceeds to examine the operational effectiveness and cultural resonance of this initiative in early 2011. It focuses on an apparent disconnect between the rhetoric underpinning these strategic prescriptions and the diverse range of associated practices that I encountered during my field work with the two community policing specialist units (henceforth 'RPZ1' and 'RPZ2').

Motivated police officers from RPZ1 were found to have used their agency to support the initiative by facilitating cultural validation of community policing in their sector. This involved the strategic use of impression management to link what Herbert (2001) has elsewhere identified as 'effeminate' aspects of community policing with entrenched 'masculine' definitions of police work. By rendering the SDC's model palatable to colleagues and supervisors, the officers from RPZ1 were able to retain their subcultural credibility as police officers and demonstrate the operational utility of a less adversarial approach to policing. This created practical benefits for the officers from RPZ1. Notably, it afforded them operational autonomy and discretion which allowed them to devote a significant portion of their time to partnership-building activities. The officers believed this autonomy was necessary for outwardly improving the perceived legitimacy and responsiveness of the Sarajevo Canton Police.

The demonstrated progress of RPZ1 is then contrasted with the challenges encountered by a second unit, RPZ2. Officers from RPZ2 struggled to implement the reform in their sector due to a combination of contextual obstacles and limited managerial support. Their progress was further constrained by the officers' personal hesitations about embracing a more 'feminized' policing role. Their primary concern was that doing so would jeopardize their perceived credibility as professional police officers. The second case study therefore highlights how the agency of rank-and-file officers might also act to limit the prospects for achieving 'bottom-up' reform.

Taken together, the case studies indicate that even in weak and structurally dependent countries like BiH, rank-and-file police officers may possess the capacity to act as agents of institutional change. If motivated and relatively unconstrained by institutional and environmental factors, they can use their agency to translate relevant elements of 'off-the-shelf' community policing models into culturally and contextually appropriate policing practices. The processes through which they attempt to legitimize the model throughout the community and within their organization can improve the resonance of certain community policing models with local cultural understandings of police work. They also have the potential to alter local mentalities about crime and its control so that they come to reflect aspects of dominant 'Western' discourses. Through a Foucaultian lens, this appears to support the argument that rank-and-file officers act as intermediaries for international development agencies working to promote police capacity building projects in developing and transitional countries. But the reality is, rank-and-file officers who assume the role of change agents must grapple with various obstacles that require them to exercise creativity and critical reflection for the model to be implemented in a sustainable manner. Accordingly, it is more accurate to describe these policy recipients of police capacity building projects as mediatory actors whose habitus is structured concurrently by 'Western' discourses and local understandings. Like international development workers, they find themselves negotiating the meaning attached to community policing in ways that may either support or inhibit the development of glocal policing.

Community Policing in Sarajevo Canton

The policing landscape in BiH is highly fragmented with the effect that each of the ten Cantons in FBiH has its own police force.[1] This implies that the accountability structure of policing in FBiH is decentralized and in Sarajevo Canton the police form part of the Canton's Ministry of Internal Affairs (MUP KS). The Minister of Internal Affairs serves as the head of the Sarajevo Canton Police and is responsible for overseeing the internal rules and policies for the provision of policing in the Canton. The MUP KS also maintains a document called the *Regulation of Job Classification* which officially recognizes and defines the specific duties and responsibilities of different roles within the Sarajevo Canton Police.[2] While the MUP KS is responsible for proposing any changes to the *Regulation of Job Classification* document, these changes must ultimately be approved by the Cantonal Assembly. At the time of my research, the role of community policing specialists was not formally recognized meaning that these officers lacked an official mandate to perform this role. This lack of formal recognition was identified by both the SDC and community police specialists as a major obstacle to the successful implementation of the SDC's prescriptions.[3]

Under the Minister of Internal Affairs, the Sarajevo Canton Police has its own Police Commissioner who is appointed by an

---

[1] This section does not discuss the status of plural or private forms of policing in Sarajevo. This is due to the fact that the public police remain the primary security provider for citizens in Sarajevo Canton despite recent growth of the city's private security sector which focuses primarily on the commercial and diplomatic sectors (see Kržalić 2009). At the time of this research, multi-agency policing initiatives such as citizen security forums (CSF) had also yet to be established in Sarajevo Canton.

[2] Listed in Appendix 2.

[3] Field notes, 7 March 2011 and an interview with an SDC Project Associate on 26 June 2011.

'Independent Board' comprised of 'two representatives of the Ministry of Internal Affairs and five members from amongst the citizens' to serve a four-year term 'with the possibility of extension for one more term of office' (OHR 2002). The Police Commissioner is responsible for overseeing operational aspects of policing and for ensuring that police work is performed in accordance with the *Regulation of Job Classification*. The organizational structure of the Sarajevo Canton Police features a central hierarchy that includes various administrators and managers who operate under the Police Commissioner and central units that provide coverage for specific policing functions for the entire Canton. These units include the 'Office of the Commissioner', 'Crime Police', 'Legal, Personnel and Logistics', and 'Uniformed Patrol'. Uniformed Patrol is responsible for coordinating patrol activities throughout the Canton but the day-to-day management of patrol work is devolved to five different sectors. Geographically, the composition of these sectors is diverse and this produces evident variation in terms of the different approaches to uniformed patrol that are conducted throughout the Canton. Sectors 2 and 3 correspond with two of Sarajevo's urban municipalities while Sector 1 incorporates two urban municipalities and Sectors 4 and 5 provide coverage for a number of outlying towns and villages (see Table 1: MUP KS Police Sectors).

Each sector has a chief and every station has a commander and two shift commanders. Under these senior managers is a cadre of mid-level managers and sergeants who are responsible for overseeing various administrative and supervisory functions. Finally, the 'rank-and-file' officers based at each station include a mix of uniformed patrol officers, traffic officers, criminal investigators who deal with low profile incidents, and support staff.[4] The majority of rank-and-file police officers at each station perform sector-based patrol work. Depending on the geography of the officer's beat and the station's resources these patrols may be conducted either by foot or car. Most patrol officers spend a significant proportion of their time out in the 'community' and have received some training on community policing either by international organizations like the IPTF or the US International Criminal Investigation Training Assistance Program (ICITAP), or at the Police Academy in Sarajevo. Despite this training, the consensus amongst reformers

---

[4] High profile criminal investigations are conducted by a central unit.

Table 1 Brief Descriptions of MUP KS Police Sectors*

Sector 1	Covers two neighbouring urban municipalities in the city centre including 'Old Town' (Stari Grad) and the city's commercial and government centre ('Centar'). Sector 1's headquarters is based in Centar with a satellite station based in Stari Grad.
Sector 2	'Novo Sarajevo', an urban municipality in the city centre that is mainly residential.
Sector 3	'Novi Grad' is the largest municipality in BiH by population. Many residents live in Yugoslav-era apartment complexes.
Sector 4	Includes outlying urban towns of Ilidža and Hadžići.
Sector 5	Includes rural towns of Ilijaš and Vogošća.

* I have randomized the numbers assigned to the RPZ units meaning that they do not necessarily correspond to those of the sectors described in this table. This is to help maintain the anonymity of individual officers.

and local researchers was that by 2011, sector-based patrol officers had either failed or neglected to incorporate the philosophy of community policing into their routines (see, for example, Deljkić and Lučić-Ćatić 2011: 180–1).

In recognition of the evident limitations of generating reforms through the philosophy-based approach which was advocated by DFID (see Chapter 3), the SDC supported the MUP KS in piloting two community policing specialist teams that would subsequently operate out of Sectors 3 and 1. This occurred in 2008. An informal position was also created within the central 'Crime Police' unit for a community policing coordinator (henceforth 'RPZ Coordinator') who was responsible for overseeing the work of these units, supporting their ongoing development and publicizing their role throughout the Canton. In 2009, the original RPZ Coordinator was replaced by a veteran officer who served with the Sarajevo Canton Police since before the Bosnian War. The officer also boasted of their 'international policing' experience having served on a UN Mission in sub-Saharan Africa.[5]

In 2010, the MUP KS expanded its community policing project throughout Sarajevo Canton and new RPZ units were established in each of the remaining sectors. One of the original units was split into two separate units that subsequently operated out of smaller municipal police stations. Individual officers were assigned to

[5] Personal communication with RPZ Coordinator on 4 March 2011.

the new units by their sector chiefs or station commanders who enjoyed a significant degree of discretion when it came to making staffing decisions.[6] Most of these senior officers acted on the advice of the SDC and selected young, enthusiastic, and, in a few cases, highly educated officers, to serve as RPZ specialists. By contrast, a minority of senior officers chose to capitalize on their discretion and staff the RPZ teams with veteran officers who were approaching retirement, poor performers, and officers who were difficult to manage.[7] The competing approaches to staffing these units were evident with the two community policing specialist teams that I observed. RPZ1 was comprised of two male graduates in their 30s with degrees in 'criminalistics' from a university in BiH, a female officer in her late 20s, and an experienced male officer who appeared to be in his 40s who had previously delivered lectures on community policing at the Police Academy in Sarajevo. By contrast, RPZ2 was staffed by a veteran male patrol officer in his late 50s, a female officer in her late 30s, and a male officer in his early 40s. All of the officers from RPZ2 had previously worked uniformed patrol and one of them claimed to have served with a tactical response unit prior to receiving the community policing assignment.

The practice of staffing community policing posts with veteran or out-of-favour officers is documented in the Anglo-American literature but no consensus exists amongst academics as to which staffing approach is most effective. Rather, the existing research indicates that enthusiasm is generally a key determinant of whether community policing initiatives will be operationally effective from a police standpoint. Greene's (2000: 341–2) research on community policing in Philadelphia (USA) suggests that 'rookie' officers are better equipped for problem-oriented community police work than veteran officers because they are open-minded. This sentiment was also expressed by members of the SDC and the officers from RPZ1 when discussing the suitability of their colleagues from RPZ2.[8] Alternatively, a justification for assigning veteran

---

[6] The sector chiefs enjoyed this discretion because the RPZ specialist role had yet to be officially recognized by the *Regulation of Job Classification* at this point.

[7] Personal communication with the Safer Communities team's Community Policing Advisor on 17 March 2011.

[8] Personal communication with an officer from RPZ1 on 21 March 2011.

officers to RPZ roles can also be found in relation to Skogan and Hartnett's (1997: 88) research which found that 'older officers' involved with the Chicago Alternative Policing Strategy were 'generally less aggressive in their policing style' and in fact willing to support the initiative, as were young, college-educated officers.

Despite these competing approaches to staffing the units, the SDC continued to provide training and support until the end of 2010. The Canton's RPZ Coordinator and the experienced RPZ units subsequently assumed responsibility for expanding the programme and supporting the ongoing development of the newly established RPZ units. They did this by organizing training activities designed to promote the best practices of community policing in the Canton and they assumed responsibility for promoting the merits of the SDC's model and the RPZ role within the police organization and to external audiences. By early 2011, the consensus amongst my colleagues at UNDP, representatives of MUP KS, and the Canton's RPZ Coordinator was that RPZ1 had been very successful in implementing the SDC's strategic prescriptions for community policing but that RPZ2 had struggled to match this success.

Community Policing: The Swiss Way

Unlike its predecessors, the SDC aspired to promote a micro-level community policing model that defined community police work as a specialist activity to be carried out by designated community policing officers assigned to dedicated RPZ units (see Chapter 2). Between 2008 and 2011, the SDC supported MUP KS in introducing RPZ units to different sectors. It provided the officers assigned to these units with training that was modelled on what the SDC identified as the 'best practices' of community policing in Switzerland. This training introduced the officers to four components of community policing: 'security marketing', 'intelligence sharing', 'transactional analysis', and inter-agency cooperation. The SDC describes these components in its 2010 *Manual for Community-Policing in Bosnia and Herzegovina* which was distributed to the officers (SDC 2010; henceforth '*Manual*'). The terminology employed by the SDC was ultimately adopted by local community police officers who referred to these concepts when discussing their work.

Security Marketing

'Security marketing' was introduced as a problem-solving methodology that is consistent with the idea of problem-oriented policing. Goldstein (1979: 236) describes problem-oriented policing as a process of:

> Identifying…problems in more precise terms, researching each problem, documenting the nature of the current police response, assessing its adequacy and the adequacy of existing authority and resources, engaging in a broad exploration of alternatives to present responses, weighing the merits of these alternatives and choosing among them.

Along these lines, the *Manual* proposes that the first step for 'achieving a Security Market[ing] process' involves identifying the 'causes of insecurity of the population' based on the perceptions of community police officers. Step two involves identifying local problems that affect 'a large number of citizens'. Third, the *Manual* states that community police officers should conduct a group analysis of the issues identified in steps one and two in order to develop 'an objective perspective on the problem'. Drawing from their analysis, the fourth step encourages the officers to 'realize that they cannot solve the problem alone' and to actively seek out local 'partners' who could contribute to addressing the problem 'in a sustainable way'. Step five advocates collaborating with these partners to develop and implement an appropriate solution to this problem and step six calls on the officers to evaluate 'the result of the actions taken' (SDC 2010: 66–7).

Aspects of the 'security marketing process' are quite similar to the 'SARA' methodology ('Scanning', 'Analysis', 'Response', and 'Assessment') that is commonly associated with community policing practice in Europe and North America. The difference between the two approaches, at least according to the *Manual,* is that 'security marketing' provides community policing specialists with a toolkit for addressing 'complex security problems' whereas SARA is to be used by the officers to '[solve] local problems of lower intensity' (SDC 2010: 81). The *Manual* does not actually distinguish between 'complex security problems' and 'problems of lower intensity' so it is safe to assume that this was left to the judgment of RPZ officers.

Intelligence Sharing

The second element of the SDC's model, 'intelligence sharing', appeared to reflect the idea that community policing represents a form of knowledge work that can be used to communicate risk to internal and external partners. To this effect, the *Manual* prescribes that RPZ teams should take the lead in presenting the local intelligence gathered via 'security marketing' to colleagues throughout the organization and to partners in the community (SDC 2010: 56). To perform this 'intelligence sharing' function within the police organization, the *Manual* states officers should maintain an 'affairs board' within their station that lists recent incidents and events and that the officers present their analyses of these findings to their colleagues during daily briefings (SDC 2010: 54). It also suggests that community policing specialists should work directly with station managers and supervisors to streamline communications and bypass hierarchical reporting procedures that restrict the flow of information within this organizational setting. To perform this intelligence sharing function with partners in the community, the *Manual* calls for RPZ specialists to 'know their area/sector of responsibility and the citizens living there' (SDC 2010: 39) so that they can establish a functional network of partners throughout the community. Specifically, the *Manual* states:

Community policing officers should contact all citizens, whatever their social status, origin, culture and lifestyle might be. They should also partner with other stakeholders, mainly from the social and educational areas which requires (sic) good knowledge of stakeholders...

Community policing officers will be asked various questions, which will not always be related to their scope of competences, but anyhow the attitude of service to the population should be a guide. [RPZ] officers will make efforts to find solutions, resorting to the partners' competences and services (SDC 2010: 46).

Theorizing the significance of partnership-based community policing in the Canadian context, Ericson and Haggerty (1997: 70–1, 73) reference the work of Stenson (1993) in arguing that community policing constitutes a particularly important 'institutional methodology for communicating risk management' that 'constitutes the police as professional experts... [who possess]... abstract knowledge about risk that is valuable to others'. This idea is implicit in the SDC's belief that appealing to community values and interests through positive, non-adversarial interactions is important for establishing police legitimacy and reaffirming the traditional role of the public police as an important institution for risk communication in the community. Establishing a network of contacts is also important in relation to this idea of policing as risk communication because it seeks to develop what Ericson and Haggerty (1997: 72) identify as '[improved] connections with the communications circuitry of other risk institutions'.

Transactional Analysis

The third element of the SDC's community policing model was derived from Canadian psychiatrist Eric Berne's (1959/1996; 1961) theory of 'transactional analysis'. In an article published in the *Indian Journal of Psychiatry* in 1959, Berne (1959/1996: 154–5) describes transactional analysis as follows:

> *The system is based on the observation that psychic functioning and social behavior are related to states of mind which may be called ego states. An ego state may be described phenomenologically as a coherent system of feelings, and operationally as a set of coherent behavior patterns; or pragmatically, as a system of feelings which motivates a related set of behaviour patterns. It can be further observed that there are three types of ego stages, each derived from a psychic organ: exteropsychic, neopsychic, and archaeopsychic...*
>
> *Colloquially, exteropsychic ego states are called collectively the Parent. These are replicas of the physiological and emotional attitudes and social behavior of parent figures. Neopsychic ego states are called collectively Adult. These are manifested by objective data processing and an alertness of the outside world of reality, including the psychological reality of other people. Archaeopsychic egostates are collectively called the Child. These are revivals of fixated ego states from earliest years... It should be noted that Parent, Adult and Child are not concepts, like Superego, Ego and Id, but phenomenological and social realities.*
>
> *After patients (or therapists) become somewhat adept at diagnosing between exteropsychic, neopsychic, and archaeopsychic ego states, they may proceed to simple transactional analysis. The problem here is to distinguish direct transactions from complex transactions. The latter are of two kinds: crossed and ulterior.*

Research on transactional analysis has evolved since the late 1950s but the fundamental idea is that it provides individuals with a schema and vocabulary that supports continuous reflection about how different psychological influences shape their social interactions. The 'theory' posits that individuals can use this reflective process to understand and improve the quality of their communication and relationships with others. It is beyond the scope of this chapter to consider the scholarly merits and limitations of transactional analysis but it is worth accounting for how the idea was interpreted by the SDC and why it was prescribed as a method for achieving a 'security marketing process' in Sarajevo Canton. To this effect, the *Manual* states:

Transactional Analysis starts from three fundamental ideas:
  Human being is basically good (OK);
  Everyone has an ability to think;
  Humans can influence their own fate and can, therefore, influence the outcome of events
  The goal of [transactional analysis] is to lead people to a direction enabling them to abandon negative or limited thinking schemes. Alone or in combination with other methods, [transactional analysis] provides an effective conflict solving tool in professional and personal life. It mainly helps mitigate conflicts by appealing to common sense (SDC 2010: 30).

The rationale for incorporating these ideas into a community policing model is also described in the *Manual*:

The person having [transactional analysis] training has an ability to determine, in a discussion:
  Whether the partner feels and acts like some other authoritarian person from his/her surrounding (e.g. parents).
  Whether the partners feels, thinks or acts in a way that he/she decided in full awareness, based on the analysis of the situation.
  Whether the partner feels or acts by a behavioural pattern adopted in childhood ...
  An ability to see clearly their own values and feelings will help the police officers create their own spaces of manoeuvre in interacting with other people (you are OK, the way you are, with all your deficiencies), thus increasing their professional capacities.

Essentially, the SDC viewed transactional analysis as a means of enabling and encouraging rank-and-file police officers to take the initiative of working to improve their relationship with different segments of the community as it was thought that this would improve the prospect of inter-agency cooperation. According to the SDC's website, 'more than 10,000 employees of police agencies' undertook training in transactional analysis which was delivered by '100 trainers' between 2006 and 2010 (see 'SDC Bosnia and Herzegovina ...'). I did not personally have the opportunity to observe or take part in the SDC's transactional analysis training so it is not clear from this research which specific elements of Berne's (1961) 'system' were being utilized by the officers. What was clear from my observation was that officers from RPZ1 frequently made reference to the rhetoric of 'transactional analysis' while performing community police work and they appeared to embrace it as a valuable resource for interpreting their efforts to nurture trust in the community. This was particularly evident in relation to their role in implementing a youth outreach programme developed by the SDC called 'Civilian Courage'.

Inter-agency Cooperation

A final element of the SDC's model is linked with the previous three: 'partnership-building'. The *Manual* states:

> *In this partnership model the police are one of the stakeholders in solving local problems, and do not have a professional problem-solving monopoly. Therefore, the police do not consider it has exclusive competence, it sees itself as a partner. All partners must assume their roles in their respective fields of competence. The correlation of various field of competence helps identify sustainable solutions* (SDC 2010: 29).

The discourse invoked in the *Manual* is very similar to that associated with community-based policing approaches throughout Western Europe, specifically, the cliché that 'the police can't do it alone'. In England and Wales, for example, Crawford (1999: 56) describes how, in the 1990s, '...a growing body of opinion both in academic and government circles...endorsed the need for greater multi-agency "co-operation" primarily at the local level, as providing the most effective means of policy formation and service delivery'. Citing the work of Jock Young (1991), Crawford (1999: 56–7, original emphasis) adds:

> *Social control in modern industrial societies, it is argued, is by its very nature multi-agency. Different agencies have a different 'purchase on a given crime problem' due to their particular expertise (Young 1991). The problem, however, is that this response is not co-ordinated, but disparate, with no overall rationale. It lacks 'systemization'. Agencies are more often in conflict with each other than mutually supportive...failings of criminal justice have come to be defined as arising out of a lack of co-ordination...In its place practitioners have been, and continue to be, urged to form* **horizontal** *'partnerships' which cut across* **vertical** *bureaucratic imperatives.*

Crawford's (1999) account of the appeal of partnership working draws primarily from England and Wales but it also describes how similar discourses began to present themselves internationally during the 1990s. To illustrate this point, Crawford quotes an excerpt from a resolution passed by the United Nations Congress on the Prevention of Crime and the Treatment of Offenders in August 1990 which describes how different public organizations 'with responsibility for planning and development, for family, health, employment and training, housing and social services, leisure activities, schools, the police, and the justice system' must work together 'in order to deal with the conditions that generate crime' (UN 1991 quoted by Crawford 1999: 56). From the SDC's perspective, the appeal of this discourse was linked with the agency's belief that many police officers in BiH continued to resist the idea of taking on a broadened mandate. Embracing new roles and responsibilities was considered by the SDC to be a prerequisite for addressing mundane yet complex public safety issues that fell beyond the traditional police remit. Visibly responding to issues like the city's stray dog population and poor street lighting was also thought to represent an important means by which the Sarajevo Canton Police could bolster its perceived legitimacy and establish a more collaborative approach to policing.

The idea that a functional network of partners might enhance the capacity of the police to generate intelligence and perform knowledge work is also indicative of a 'responsibilization strategy' which Garland (1996: 452) argues:

...involves the central government seeking to act upon crime not in a direct fashion through state agencies...but instead by acting indirectly, seeking to activate action on the part of non-state agencies and organisations. This is the essence of the new crime prevention approach developed by the UK government [since the mid-1980s]. Its key phrases are terms such as 'partnership', 'inter-agency cooperation', 'the multi-agency approach', 'activating communities', creating 'active citizens', 'help for self-help'. Its primary concern is to devolve responsibility for crime prevention on to agencies, organizations and individuals which are quite outside the state and to persuade them to act appropriately.

However, whereas Garland's (1996) articulation of this concept emphasizes the state's role in steering the actions of those who are activated, this case study accounts for a state institution (the police) with limited governmental capacities that was advised by an international organization (the SDC) to enrol local partners (different municipal agencies) to contribute to the governance and provision of policing by participating in intelligence sharing practices and contributing resources to multi-agency initiatives. Essentially, it was much more complex. This analysis is consistent with Ryan's (2011: 155) argument that promoting a partnership-based, community policing model in the context of a liberal state-building process is conducive to the establishment of a 'complex assemblage of thin blue lines' that are designed to activate an array of local institutions and actors to act as upwardly-responsive security providers. The SDC's embrace of the idea of responsibilization is further evident from its aforementioned enthusiasm for 'transactional analysis' which it introduced to encourage individuals to reflect on their own behavior so as to 'accept one's own person…to bring about a change for the better in every-day (sic) behaviour' (SDC 2010: 30).

Returning to the UK context, it is important to briefly account for the contested nature of what Crawford (1999: 299) describes as the 'language of responsibilization'. The contest in question is that between those who seek to advance the discourse to 'combat structural inequalities and imbalances of power' which are identified as 'a prerequisite for the performance and maximization of communal responsibility' and members of the New Right (e.g. Murray 1990) who deployed the concept of responsibility in support of a neo-liberal agenda which calls for the demise of the welfare state. The point is that there is no fixed meaning attached to the concept of 'responsibility' so despite its neo-liberal connotations in 'Western' crime control policy discourses, there is scope for actors to interpret, negotiate and reconstruct its meaning through policy and practice. By implication, the discourses underpinning a responsibilization strategy in one context may differ from those associated with it in another. I revisit this idea later in this chapter by questioning the degree to which partnership-building activities in Sarajevo Canton were structured by emergent global neo-liberal discourses described by Ellison and Pino (2012).

'Bottom-Up' Reform

Concepts like 'security marketing' and 'intelligence sharing' played an important role in structuring the mentalities of community policing specialists in Sarajevo Canton but it was ultimately left to local police officers to translate these prescriptions into practice.

The translational discretion accorded to these officers stands in contrast to what Marks and Sklansky (2012: 4) identify as 'technocratic' approaches to 'top-down' police reform throughout much of the developed world today. Along this vein, Bayley (2012: 19) adds that, in North America, community policing reforms were historically introduced from the 'top down' by organizational outsiders 'with no discernable input from the rank-and-file'. The 'general response', according to Bayley (2012: 19), has been one of 'active scepticism and resistance'.

An interview with a Project Associate from the SDC who was involved with the development of the model and later worked to oversee its implementation in BiH revealed that the SDC was aware of this risk and decided to leave the model vague so that local police officers would take ownership of it and adapt it to fit with local circumstances.[9] This approach was in part facilitated by the fact that the SDC subscribed to a capacity development ethos which was similar to that of UNDP. It is also important to consider that there were pragmatic reasons for the SDC to adopt what might perhaps be described as a 'bottom-up' approach to implementing the reform. Most notably, representatives from the SDC recognized that local knowledge was necessary for successfully adapting these prescriptions into a functional community policing strategy because there could be no 'one-size-fits-all' solution for making the model fit. The aim was thus to counteract perceptions amongst the rank-and-file that the model was being introduced to the Sarajevo Canton Police from the 'top down'.

A 'bottom-up approach to police reform' is described by Marks and Sklansky (2012: 5) as one which recognizes the importance of rank-and-file officers as 'change agents'. In other words, 'bottom-up' reform is about 'encouraging' members of the rank-and-file 'to be thoughtful and creative about their work' thereby embracing them as a resource for innovating enhanced policing practices. The SDC project team embraced the agency of a select group of rank-and-file officers from the Sarajevo Canton Police as a potential vehicle for overcoming the organizational resistance that had undermined previous community policing initiatives. The idea was that the specialists from the RPZ units would use the SDC's methods to demonstrate the utility of community policing to colleagues and

---

[9] Interview with an SDC Project Associate on 22 June 2011.

supervisors. This was thought to be necessary for promoting cultural acceptance of this role within the police organization.[10]

Police culture has been defined by Reiner (2010: 117) as 'the values, norms, perspectives and craft rules which inform police conduct'. According to Reiner (2010: 118), '[c]op culture offers a patterned set of understandings that helps officers cope with the pressures and tensions confronting the police'. In practice, the concept is somewhat misleading because as Reiner (2010: 132) observes, 'police culture is not monolithic'. Rather, he suggests that 'the organizational division of labour is related to a variation in distinct types of perspective around the core elements of the culture'. He adds:

There are particular variants—'subcultures'—that can be discerned within broader police culture, generated by distinct experiences associated with specific structural positions (ranks, specialisms, areas, etc.), or by special orientations that officers bring with them from their past biographies and problems of their environments, and the legacies of their histories (Reiner 2010: 116).

In other words, police organizations can be said to foster subcultural divisions that often correspond to different roles and functions within the organization. To this effect, Reuss-Ianni and Ianni (1983) identify a fundamental distinction between 'street cop culture' and 'management cop culture'. The former 'provides the values and so the ends toward which officers individually and in task groups strive' and the latter 'is concerned with the problem of crime on a system-wide or citywide rather than localized level' (Reuss-Ianni and Ianni 1983: 7–8). Historically, the division between the rank-and-file and police managers has represented an important site of tension within modern, bureaucratic police organizations. In the United States, for example, Reuss-Ianni and Ianni (1983) describe how attempts to professionalize the police and increase managerial oversight of street-level policing activities have been perceived by members of the rank-and-file as a threat to their operational autonomy. The implication is that changes which are introduced or supported by 'management cops' will not necessarily be embraced by 'street cops'. Rather, attempts by managers to structure the work of street-level officers may generate resistance if they are perceived as undermining the latter's ability to autonomously perform their duties, or if the

---

[10] Interview with an SDC project associate in July 2011.

changes in question appear to conflict with established subcultural definitions of police work.

In liberal democracies, subcultural resistance to community policing by the rank-and-file has been linked with the idea that the model is often perceived to conflict with a romanticized ethos of police work (Herbert 2001: 64). This ethos is shaped by institutional discourses that emphasize 'danger and authority' (Skolnick 1966), 'violence' (Loftus 2009: 96–9), and 'masculinity' (Herbert 2001: 57–9).[11] The activities and the values associated with community policing are often viewed by the rank-and-file as a threat to their authority because they aspire to establish 'a more conciliatory, nonaggressive style of policing' (Miller 1999: 197 quoted by Herbert 2001: 64). In other words, community policing challenges the assumption that the police possess a unique ability to administer coercion and control crime through its aspiration to reduce the social distance between the police and members of the public (Herbert 2001: 64). This implies the creation of a model of policing whereby 'everyday definitions of neighborhoods developed by residents' are no longer 'rendered subordinate to the demands of apprehending dangerous suspects' but, rather, accorded 'dominant' status in relation to the process of negotiating orders (Herbert 2001: 64).[12]

Manifestations of organizational resistance to community policing reforms will inevitably vary due to cultural differences

---

[11] A more expansive list of subcultural values that are commonly associated with the rank-and-file is provided by Fielding (1994: 47): '(i) aggressive, physical action; (ii) a strong sense of competitiveness and preoccupation with the imagery of conflict; (iii) exaggerated heterosexual orientations, often articulated in terms of misogynistic and patriarchal attitudes towards women; and (iv) the operation of rigid in-group/out-group distinctions whose consequences are strongly exclusionary in the case of out-groups and strongly assertive of loyalty and affinity in the case of in-groups'. This list is for the most part consistent with that provided by Reiner (2010) as well as the themes of 'danger and authority' and 'masculinity' which have been identified by Skolnick (1966) and Herbert (2001), respectively.

[12] The differences between 'street cop culture' and 'management cop culture' are well documented but it is important to consider that there may exist some important commonalities between the two. In other words, the subcultural values that are used by the rank-and-file officers to construct their role are familiar to management cops who, in the vast majority of police organizations, were once themselves rank-and-file officers. While their understanding of police work is likely to have changed due to the nature of their role, it must be acknowledged that police managers may also prove resistant to changes that are perceived to be a threat to the romanticized values.

between police organizations operating in different contexts and structural differences stemming from the socially defined functions of the police. Citing studies by Jones and Levi (1983) and Foster (1989), Reiner (2010: 136) acknowledges that significant cultural differences do exist between organizations within countries but argues that 'certain commonalities in cop culture...arise from the police role in liberal democracies'. These commonalities reflect the fact that all police organizations in liberal democratic societies share a 'fundamental remit to control crime and disorder in unequal, divided societies while adhering to principles of the rule of law' (Reiner 2010: 137). Accordingly, Bowling and Sheptycki (2012: 82) identify a set of universal 'parameters' that structure rank-and-file subculture in different jurisdictions. These include: 'the ability to use coercion to "get the job done" '; recognition that '[i]nformation is considered the "life-blood" of policing'; 'the role that law plays as part of the tools of the trade, and the double-edged qualities of counter-law'; 'modern police management'; 'the political framing of policing; 'masculinity'; 'racism'; and the 'danger-authority nexus'. Many of these parameters appear to be consistent with the hyper masculine values that are argued by Herbert (2001) to have underpinned subcultural resistance to community policing in the United States. The implication is that, regardless of context, the philosophical embrace of community policing by senior managers regularly fails to translate into concrete changes in terms of street-level policing activities or changes in how rank-and-file police officers construct their professional identity in established and aspiring democratic societies alike.

In Australia, this is evident from Chan's (1997) account of organizational resistance to former New South Wales Police Commissioner John Avery's attempts to introduce community-policing reforms from the 'top down' during the 1980s:

There was little doubt that, in spite of the depth of Avery's vision of community-based policing, he did not have a great deal of support within the organisation. He was considered an 'academic' and his swift and decisive assault on traditional policing values and institutionalised corruption created a great deal of discontent (Chan 1997: 154).

Chan adds:

My research suggests that community-based policing was interpreted [by the officers] in a superficial way and was mainly seen as a public relations exercise. Apart from the predominance of middle-class, respectable citizens in community consultative committees, there was some concern about the tokenistic use of minority community 'leaders' as representing the interests of minority groups, the exclusion of operational issues as appropriate for community consultation, and the tendency to see the setting up of committees as an achievement in itself... Consequently, many of the old definitions still prevailed, and ethnic stereotyping, for example, was still seen as a useful way of categorizing citizens at the street level of police work (Chan 1996: 129).

This excerpt describes how changes to formal rules and procedures may fail to translate into changes in the habitus of policing and the practices it generates.

In Israel, Weisburd et al. (2002: 93) describe how a majority of rank-and-file police officers surveyed expressed support for key tenants of community policing including the need to 'consider community needs when developing good police work but conclude 'the professional model of policing which emphasizes the primacy of police in defining the strategies of policing is still very salient among Israeli police officers'. In other words, even if rank-and-file police officers prove to be receptive to rhetorical elements of community policing, this is not deterministic of whether or not they will implement the reform. Additional factors that may impede upon the implementation process include a lack of resources, challenges associated with measuring the performance of community police officers and demonstrating its strategic value in a performance management regime, and, of course, obstacles that arise from exogenous factors. The issues of limited resources and measuring performance are associated with the obstacle of cultural resistance because police managers who do not appreciate the strategic utility of community policing are unlikely to resource it or staff it adequately. It is worth reiterating that these obstacles may present themselves differently in different contexts but it is reasonable to assume that challenges associated with limited resources and generating external support for partnership-based policing activities may be greater in developing and transitional countries (see Davis et al. 2003). To this effect, Frühling (2007) notes that international attempts to introduce community policing to Latin America since the 1980s have resulted in the popularization of discourses which advocate the need for greater community involvement with policing activities (i.e. 'responsibilization') but implementation continues to lag. Citing similar experiences around the world, MacKenzie and Henry (2009: 31) conclude that 'implementation failure is so common [with respect to community policing] as to largely neutralise the capacity of researchers to say whether CP would "work" if its concept(s) ever were to make a flawless transition into practice'.

Implementation challenges are pervasive but the policing literature does account for a few cases whereby community policing reforms have achieved a degree of institutional recognition and acceptance by members of police organizations, including the rank-and-file (see, for example, Skogan and Hartnett 1997; Wilson et al. 2011). The possibility of overcoming organizational resistance from the rank-and-file can be explained by the fact that police occupational culture is mutable and continuously shaped by a combination of individual, institutional, and structural factors. It is also the case that culture is not deterministic of individual actions. Rather, its cultural scripts play an important albeit limited role in structuring the habitus of police work which in turn plays an important albeit partial role in structuring practice. To this effect, Chan (1996: 111) writes, '[w]hile culture may be powerful, it is nevertheless up to individuals to accommodate or resist its influence'. To illustrate this point she quotes Fielding's (1988: 135) account of how new police recruits are assimilated within occupational culture in England:

One cannot read the recruit as a cipher for the occupational culture. The occupational culture has to make its pitch for support, just as the agencies of the formal organization exert their influence through control of resources. The stock stories of the occupational culture may be effective as a means of ordering perception which maximizes desirable outcomes. If they contradict the recruit's gathering experience they are likely to be dismissed.

According to Chan (1996: 112), this implies that 'a sound theory of police culture should recognize the interpretive and active role of officers in structuring their understanding of the organization and its environment'. For change to occur, members of the occupational culture must accept the proposed changes and use their agency to align them with existing subcultural values. This requires two things: the ability of officers to alter cultural and subcultural definitions of police work and their motivation to do so. The ability of rank-and-file police officers to act as 'agents of change' is linked with what Bayley (2012: 22) identifies as their 'craft knowledge', that is, their 'understanding of the tactics needed to achieve control, justice, amelioration, and legitimacy in daily encounters with the public'. It is also a product of their cultural knowledge and social capital within the organization. Together these provide rank-and-file police officers with 'a thorough, nuanced understanding of their fellow officers' which is necessary for developing creative strategies for promoting acceptance of non-traditional policing strategies and tactics (Marks and Sklansky 2012: 6). To this effect, Goldsmith (original emphasis 1990: 91) has argued that we can embrace police discretion as 'a potential *resource* in the formulation of rules governing police powers and practices'. Monique Marks's (2000; 2005) research on police reform in South Africa further builds on this idea by describing the possibility of generating institutional support for police reforms from the 'bottom up'. Marks (2000: 558) writes:

...internal resistance or challenge is one of the most effective and direct mechanisms for bringing about change in policing agencies, but that for this challenge to be successful, a commitment, on the part of the police agency itself, to a change in the formal rules of policing must be evident.

As evident from the experiences of RPZ1 and RPZ2, which I present in the following section, the agency of rank-and-file can at best be described as a *potential* resource for change because the motivation for officers to assume the role of change agents is not always present. Motivation may be intrinsic, extrinsic, or a combination of the two. In other words, individual officers may voluntarily embrace community policing because they believe in its purported benefits or they may feel compelled to do so by managers. In Sarajevo Canton, enthusiasm for community policing was inconsistent amongst RPZ specialists and police managers alike.

RPZ1

For nearly three years, the officers from RPZ1 had proactively worked to promote the SDC's model for community policing. They did so through regular, informal encounters with members of the public and local organizations in their sector. These interactions were used to generate publicity for their role and to attract support for the idea of partnership. The officers from RPZ1 were initially effective in using these relationships to identify local public safety issues that affected local citizens but they struggled to actually develop 'holistic' solutions for addressing complex problems like stray dogs or inadequate street lighting. The main problem according to the officers was that the municipal authorities responsible for addressing these issues frequently refused to recognize the authority of police officers to intervene in matters that had traditionally lay beyond the remit of police work.[13]

RPZ1's ongoing struggle to initiate a collaborative solution to the municipality's stray dog population illustrates the difficulties that the officers encountered while attempting to translate the SDC's prescriptions for 'security marketing' and 'partnership-building' into viable practices. These difficulties are documented in my field notes during an impromptu community meeting that I attended with two of the officers following an incident in which a child was attacked by a stray dog outside a local school. The meeting was held at the school in question one evening in March 2011. All of the conversations took place in Bosnian and my field notes account for my observations and the communications as they were presented to me by one of the English-speaking officers who acted as my translator.

We arrive at a local school for a community meeting regarding the stray dogs issue. At the meeting, most of the attendees are parents of local children, mostly women. [One of the officers] begins the meeting by noting that he sympathises with the parents' concerns but that the police are struggling to address the problem because they are still waiting for city officials to respond. At this point it is clear that this is a rather hostile room. The parents begin yelling at the officers and [according to the other officer] threatening to withhold their children from school if the problem is not addressed. My impression is that all of these parents are reasonably well-off as evident from the fact that many are wearing their work clothes.

The school director does most of the talking at this point and the two RPZ officers and I sit quietly and observe. The director encourages [the parents] to stop sending their kids to school until the problem is solved.

[One of the RPZ officers] responds by presenting a report that the officers had prepared and submitted to municipal officials about the issue. They note that despite their efforts, the issue was never acted on.

---

[13] Personal communication with an officer from RPZ1.

I am not receiving translation at this point but I sense that [the officer] is saying that 'we are doing all that we can'. The parents in attendance all share a laugh. They do not appear to take these assurances very seriously.

[The officer] continues to talk for a while as [their colleague] flips through the report. [The officer] reads out a response from the Cantonal Government regarding the stray dog issue. The officer appears to acknowledge the absurdity of the situation [with respect to the lack of responsiveness from the local government] and recognises that this is a hostile situation.

One visibly upset woman addresses the officers. She describes how she has presented the matter at a [local government meeting] and with other officials but nobody acts. A man speaks but is interrupted by the angry woman and it starts to get very heated. More parents are speaking and venting about the issue to the director [rather than to the police]. One parent suggests that [the problem is that] the kids try to play with stray dogs and this attracts them into the school. The school director now appears to be upset and is talking to the officers. [One of the officers] tries to respond but is interrupted [by the parents]. At this point, the meeting is out of control... By the end of the meeting the parents appear to have reached some kind of agreement and are nodding their heads.

We leave the meeting early once a decision has been made. [One of the officers] explains that the parents have decided to organise a protest. He then reflects on the meeting and presents to me his views about the challenges of implementing community policing in Sarajevo:

'We went to the meeting and heard their problems. Tomorrow we will meet with our chief. He will ask us about it and help us to deal with it. However, if this happened in another municipality, the chief or the commander would not make himself available for a meeting. The RPZ officer would make promises at the meeting but without support they would not be able to show results. This would ultimately mean that the community would not respect them or take them seriously'.[14]

The officer was effectively suggesting that their Sector Chief was receptive to the idea of community policing and willing to lend his support. According to the officer, the importance of establishing this direct link with senior police managers was that it provided the RPZ unit with a channel for bringing local public safety issues to the attention of senior municipal officials. Lacking this link, the officer believed that the unit would struggle to demonstrate to members of the public that they were actually making meaningful progress towards resolving the issue. Failure to demonstrate

[14] Field notes, 22 March 2011.

progress risked jeopardizing the credibility of the RPZ unit and, potentially, community policing altogether.

The main challenge which obstructed the officers' ability to resolve the stray dog issue was their inability to enlist the support of the municipal authorities. During a previous conversation with the same officer, it emerged that municipal authorities were often resistant to police involvement when it came to public safety issues. To this effect, the officer explained that members of the unit would regularly bring a problem like broken street lighting to the attention of the municipal authorities only to be asked, 'why is this your business?'.[15] This implies limited recognition of a broadened policing mandate by potential partner institutions and their reluctance to recognize the authority of the RPZ officers if it meant that they might be forced to account for their actions (or inaction) down the line. These difficulties are perhaps unsurprising given that bureaucratic inertia and institutional resistance to partnership-based community policing models are well-documented in the context of advanced liberal democracies including Britain (Crawford 1999), the United States (Greene 2004), and the Netherlands (Terpstra 2008), all of which enjoy better resources and broader recognition of the community policing model and mandate.

The officers from RPZ1 recognized that achieving public recognition for this expanded policing mandate and generating enthusiasm for the idea of inter-agency cooperation would take time. This sentiment was voiced by an officer from one of the newer RPZ units who I interviewed following my period of observation with RPZ1:

Me: 'Does this work in practice?'
Officer from RPZ3: 'It does but it takes time. We are working in a very big sector with only limited resources and the public's mentality of the police as an adversarial organisation persists. This is changing, but it takes time'.[16]

---

[15] Paraphrasing a conversation with an officer from RPZ1 on 9 March 2011.

[16] Paraphrasing an officer from RPZ3 during an interview conducted on 4 April 2011. The interview was conducted in Bosnian through an interpreter. Like RPZ1, this unit was comprised of young, enthusiastic officers who volunteered for the RPZ role. Members of this newly established unit shadowed the officers from RPZ1 as part of their training which explains why they exhibited similar attitudes about implementing the model.

This sentiment was echoed by an officer from RPZ1 who described community policing as 'a long-term project' and suggested, 'You can't just tell police officers that community policing is the best and then expect them to implement it'. Rather, the officer believed that they would have to come to realize this for themselves.[17]

Contextual Dissonance and Cultural Consonance

The officers from RPZ1 also recognized that important contextual differences existed between BiH and the project's donor state Switzerland. One of the officers commented that, from his perspective, '[community policing] is a very good idea in terms of relationships and partnerships and building high levels of trust but the way we get there is not the same'. [18] The officer went on to explain that:

...the SDC's contribution has been essential in terms of resources and training but their Swiss-model for everybody approach is problematic. The situation in [our sector] is not the same as the situation in Switzerland which is much more tranquil and less demanding for police due to lack of a recent history of conflict and better economic development. [This sector] requires a different management approach, a different methodology. In the past, the SDC was disappointed when they found that something was implemented differently than how the Swiss do it.

This statement demonstrates the officer's recognition of the need to adapt the model in order for it to work in Sarajevo Canton. It also suggests that the SDC may have been inconsistent with respect to its advocacy of the need for local RPZ officers to take ownership of the model and alter it as required.

Perhaps the SDC utilized the rhetoric of bottom-up reform for the purpose of legitimating the model and, by extension, their intervening role. This interpretation would fit with Goldsmith and Sheptycki's (2007: 15; see Chapter 2) argument that reformers actively work to distance themselves from imperialist motives in the spheres of transnational policing and police capacity building. The officer's account on its own is insufficient for establishing whether or not the SDC genuinely embraced the agency of these

---

[17] Quoting an officer from RPZ1 during a conversation which took place on 7 March 2011.

[18] Paraphrasing a personal communication with an officer from RPZ1 on 7 March 2011.

officers as an asset to the reform process but it does indicate that the officers were aware of the difficulties of translating the model into contextually relevant practices. It also highlights the fact that they possessed the ability to critically reflect on both their and the SDC's roles in relation to this translational process.

The fact that the RPZ officers were attuned to contextual differences was also apparent from an interview I conducted with an RPZ officer based in a different sector. Reflecting on a five-day visit to Switzerland which formed part of the RPZ training programme,[19] the officer described how he and another officer from BiH had witnessed two women snorting cocaine in a bus station in Switzerland. He then proceeded to suggest that 'drugs are a European problem' and explained that 'before the war, drugs were not a problem [in BiH] but now it is much more common to hear about young people dying from overdoses'.[20] By probing this claim, it is not my intention to overstate the severity of the 'drug problem' in Sarajevo in real terms.[21] Rather, I seek to briefly account for how a combination of global and local factors appears to have contributed to the construction of the 'drug problem' in Sarajevo. In this respect, the officer's comment is interesting because it demonstrates their presumption of the criminogenic consequences of BiH's ongoing relationship with EU/EEA countries since the Bosnian War.

Although the causal relationship between Europeanization and the prevalence of drug use in BiH was not made explicit by the officer, the sentiment could be interpreted in a manner reflective of Bowling's (2010) analysis of the consequences of international drug trafficking and transnational enforcement efforts in the Caribbean. For example, criminalization of certain psychotropic substances in donor countries has fuelled demand for illegal narcotics in the global North. This has rendered regions like the Caribbean and the Balkans important transit hubs for producer nations. In the Caribbean, the substance in question is cocaine and

[19] All of the RPZ officers had visited Switzerland to observe the 'best practices' of community policing in this context. The visits were paid for by MUP KS and the SDC.

[20] Paraphrasing an officer from RPZ4 during an interview on 5 March 2011.

[21] In fact, the 2011 European School Survey Project on Alcohol and Other Drugs (ESPAD) Report found a low prevalence of drug and alcohol use amongst fifteen to sixteen year old students in BiH compared to the European average. The survey found that only 4% of the sample reported having used cannabis (compared to 17% for the European average) and only 2% reported having used 'other illicit drugs' (compared to 6%; see Hibell et al. 2011: 103).

in the Balkans, it's heroin. Located on the periphery of donor countries, both of these regions have also been designated important strategic sites for combatting international narcotics trafficking through a combination of transnational policing and police development assistance projects (see, for example, EUROPOL 2013).

Constructing the 'drug problem' in BiH as a global problem speaks truth to the hegemonic influence of the European Union in shaping policies and discourse surrounding this issue but it is worth considering that the country's status as a transit nation predates the development of global liberal governance. For example, a *New York Times* article from 1984 describes how 'Yugoslavia... has long been an unwilling and unwitting channel for drug traffic to the profitable markets of Frankfurt, Amsterdam, Brussels and Paris' (Binder 1984). Similarly, an article published by Block (1989) in the *Journal of Social History* accounts for the fact that between the first and second World Wars, Yugoslavia was one of only three European countries[22] which actually produced opium for export to European markets. In 1928, for example, Block states that Yugoslavia produced approximately 205 tons of opium, over half that of Turkey which he describes as the leading European producer at the time. The implication is that BiH's relationship with certain psychotropic substances (namely opiates) long predates its relationship with the EU. It is reasonable to assume then that if citizens of the former Yugoslavia were involved with producing these substances, they were also likely to have consumed them.

Another important question relates to how the role of law enforcement has changed with respect to drug enforcement activities in recent decades. That is, to what extent have the attitudes and responsibilities of local BiH police officers changed as a result of the country's relationship with the EU when it comes to controlling illegal substances? The answer cannot be inferred from the officer's comments alone and it is worth briefly noting that an American Embassy Official quoted in the same *New York Times* article described how, during the 1980s, the United States Drug Enforcement Agency provided assistance to Yugoslav narcotics inspectors to assist them with their efforts to combat the drug trade (Binder 1984). The article does not clarify whether this

---

[22] Along with Turkey and Greece.

assistance was requested by Yugoslav officials or thrust upon them by the United States. It is therefore unclear if the origins of the country's law enforcement driven response to the 'drug problem' are in fact 'European' as described by the police officer, American as might be inferred from the Embassy Official's account and the scholarly literature on the global war on drugs (see Andreas and Nadelmann 2008), or local and rooted in the historical legacy of opium production and trafficking in the Balkan region and the policies of the SFRY. In all probability, the 'drug problem' in BiH has been constructed in relation to all three.

Perhaps then it is worth considering that the RPZ officer's description of the problem as 'European' reflected their perception of the growing cultural appeal of this illicit economy in BiH. In other words, it was not necessarily the availability of illicit substances which has changed[23] but, rather, the appeal of consuming the substances or participating in this illicit economy and attaining status within the criminal subcultures it fosters. To this effect, an RPZ officer assigned to one of the newly established units which operated on the outskirts of the city described how 'young people, especially teenagers, do not respect the police' because 'they have bad influences, people who got rich as criminals after the war, who are involved with organised crime and driving fancy cars'.[24]

The appeal of this subculture can also be accounted for in relation to underlying structural changes that have affected the country since the Bosnian War. Along these lines, an officer from RPZ1 suggested:

...for many of these kids, they lack family structure. The war destroyed many families and created single parents. We try to show these kids a normal life and the risks associated with criminal behaviour. It is a real challenge to convince them of the negatives of the criminal lifestyle because they see criminals driving around in Mercedes with girls while citizens are forced to work long hours and at the end of the month, their paycheque...[25]

This suggests that the appeal of 'criminal behaviour' stems from the absence of legitimate economic opportunities available to

---

[23] Although it is safe to assume that certain substances including cocaine are more widely available in BiH today than in the 1980s.

[24] Paraphrasing an interview with an officer from RPZ3 which was conducted in Bosnian through an interpreter.

[25] Paraphrasing an officer from RPZ1 during a conversation that took place on 21 March 2011.

young people in BiH. Referring back to the New *York Times* article from 1984, it is once again evident that this issue predates the effects of economic liberalization and the country's relationship with the European Union. In fact, the sources cited by the article attribute rising levels of drugs use amongst young professionals in the SFRY to a lack of work opportunities as well as their embrace of Western materialist values (Binder 1984). More recently, in 2013, World Bank reported that 57% of those aged fifteen to twenty-nine were unemployed and less than 50% of those below the age of twenty-nine who were employed 'work in a field in which they were educated' (World Bank 2013). The point the officer was making is that schoolchildren become aware of the fact that their opportunities are limited at an early age and this in turn strengthens the appeal of the 'criminal lifestyle'.

Materialism predates economic liberalization in BiH but the latter might be said to have intensified the population's embrace of and resistance to 'Western' cultural appetites. Similarly, the prolonged presence of a large ex-pat community in Sarajevo has fundamentally transformed the city's landscape by fuelling demand (or perhaps more accurately, the perception of demand) for spaces of consumption. At the time of my fieldwork in 2011, the city featured three major shopping centres that hosted European shops (for example, the fashion retailers Mango and New Yorker and restaurant chains including Vapiano: see Figure 6.1).[26] A fourth shopping centre which promised to eclipse the others in size was also being constructed. These shopping centres were considered too expensive by many local residents and they catered primarily to the city's ex-pat community and local professionals. Their existence alongside a growing number of 'European-style' cafes and shops on the high streets nevertheless reinforced the normalization of these materialist values and represented an important symbolic reminder of the population's cultural and structural exclusion. The cumulative effect of all this was that young people in Sarajevo were being raised to think glocally and embrace consumerism but their means of constructing a European identity

[26] In July 2011, McDonald's also opened its first restaurant in Sarajevo, thus signifying the company's perception of the city's growing Western cultural appetites. Interestingly, the first McDonald's restaurant in the former Yugoslavia was opened in Belgrade back in 1988. This supports the idea that these cultural appetites actually predate the Bosnian War.

Figure 6.1 ALTA Shopping Centre in Centre, Sarajevo (2011)

through legitimate channels were for the most part restricted due to their status as BiH citizens. In other words, their identity as defined by the architects of global liberal governance limited their prospects for actually deriving their economic livelihood by participation in the European economy.

Based on their concerns about the vulnerability of young people in BiH, the officers from RPZ1 designated youth work as their main operational priority. They constructed the issue as a local problem which had its roots in the War but, as evident from the preceding analysis, the purported appeal of the criminal lifestyle to young people must also be understood as a glocal phenomenon. It was beyond their capacities to address the underlying sources of structural inequality and exclusion that rendered this subculture attractive so they attempted to use their transactional analysis training as a means of altering the mentalities and expectations of local schoolchildren. Specifically, the officers engaged with local schools to instil in children an appreciation of the values of citizenship and personal responsibility at a young age. One of the officers from RPZ1 explained:

...youth issues are one of the most significant problems in Sarajevo because parents continue to subscribe to this mentality that denies their

own responsibility ... they continue to tell their kids to ignore social problems because they do not feel it is their responsibility but the state's.[27]

While young people in BiH appear to be confronted with a particularly virulent strain of what Jock Young (2007) has elsewhere labelled the 'vertigo of late modernity', the officer's comment indicates that older generations exhibited resistance to liberal, or perhaps more accurately, neo-liberal, discourses which emphasized notions of individual responsibility in the sphere of governance. This resistance can be attributed to a combination of widespread nostalgia for the communitarian and authoritarian values of the Yugoslav era and disaffection towards the BiH state and its governing institutions. The intergenerational dialogue described by the officer accounts for a local confluence of different sources of disaffection to the project of global liberal governmentality in the sphere of security governance. The officers took it upon themselves to adjust these attitudes because they believed that the viability of the entire political system was dependent on greater participation and cultural acceptance of the need for active citizenship; they had no intention of using their influence to align the mentalities of future generations of BiH citizens with an overarching agenda for liberal or neo-liberal globalization. Nor would it be accurate to suggest that the approach they adopted to altering these mentalities was altogether effective.

Civilian Courage

One of the means by which the officers from RPZ1 worked to promote civic values through their interactions with young people was by implementing the SDC's Civilian Courage programme. Civilian Courage was developed by the SDC to promote the core philosophical values of transactional analysis throughout BiH. It consisted of a series of games and trust building exercises that the officers were supposed to lead with the support of teachers and school administrators. In March 2011, I observed the officers

---

[27] The conversation took place in English and is paraphrased in my field notes. The officer did repeatedly mention the concept of 'responsibility' in our discussion and at one point suggested that assuming responsibility was essential in a democracy. It is not clear the extent to which the officer's views were influenced by exogenous sources like the SDC or nostalgia for the Yugoslav era and, unfortunately, it did not occur to me at the time to probe this theme.

from RPZ1 as they attempted to implement these activities at a local primary school. The officers began the session by greeting approximately twenty students who were between the ages of ten and twelve years old. The officers then proceeded to distribute promotional hats and t-shirts emblazoned with the 'Civilian Courage' logo which were paid for by the SDC. After conducting two 'ice breaker' exercises that provided the officers with a chance to introduce themselves as friendly and approachable, they ran a third activity which required the children to critically reflect on the harmfulness of different behaviours. The exercise is described in my field notes:

A scale '0', '25', '50', '75' and '100' is laid out on the floor in the centre of the room in order of increasing severity. All the groups are given a [behaviour] (theft, rape, etc) and they are told to indicate using the scale on the floor how severe it is. The first group to go has 'rape'. A boy proceeds to place his paper on '50' and this stirs up some debate [in Bosnian]. I turn to [one of the officers] and tell him that I think this exercise is a bit problematic because these kids are very young and probably do not understand what rape really means. He nods and shrugs his shoulders . . . As the kids each place their card with a violent action on the floor, [another officer] stands in the middle and leads a discussion about the activity and challenges [the students] when they don't rate [an issue] highly enough. By the end of the exercise every option is being ranked at 100 . . . The only issue which provokes any real debate between the kids is 'boxing' with many of the girls arguing that it is violent while the boys feel that it is a sport.[28]

The officers demonstrated initiative by coordinating these exercises and using the occasion to promote positive interactions with children. However, the observations led me to question the suitability of the curriculum for primary school-aged children. Specifically, the officers' approach to correcting the students which resulted in all of the harms receiving a score of '100' appeared to negate the purpose of the actual lesson which was to promote critical reflection and dialogue. After the session, one of the officers was willing to acknowledge the difficulties that the team had faced in its attempts to implement the Civilian Courage curriculum in schools but the team remained adamant about the importance of engaging with local schools. A previous conversation with

[28] Field notes, 9 March 2011.

this officer provides additional insight into why they viewed youth outreach as an important operational priority. To paraphrase the officer:

...young people lack trust in Bosnian institutions but, at the same time, they must be made aware of the rules and follow them before they can complain otherwise it is a double standard...nobody else deals with this problem so we have to. Otherwise in five to ten years, they will be an ever bigger problem.

He added,

High school kids [in particular] don't often realize or care that getting a criminal record for smoking pot or other small crimes now will affect their chances later so we try to make them aware of this at an early age.[29]

In addition to their involvement with the Civilian Courage programme, the officers demonstrated their commitment to working with young people through their efforts to develop relationships with local school administrators throughout the sector.[30] They frequently visited schools and met with these individuals in order to develop a better sense of the problems that young people were experiencing. They provided these 'partners' with their personal contact details and told them to call them at any time. While the officers may not have possessed the capacity to address many of the issues which were brought to their attention, establishing this direct communication link helped to signify their interest in this particular issue and, thus, their responsiveness. The officers also made it known to their partners that they were able and willing to relay information directly to the Sector Chief if their input was required. Asked about the unit's relationship with high school students throughout the sector, one of the officers commented:

...trust is generally good because every class has a president and all the presidents are invited to a monthly meeting that we attend. During

---

[29] Paraphrasing an officer from RPZ1 during a conversation which took place on 7 March 2011.

[30] During my period of observation with the officers from RPZ1, I visited five different schools. The purpose of these visits included implementing the Civilian Courage programme, holding informal chats with school directors, investigating a case of suspected parental abuse, and speaking to two primary school aged children who had been in a fight.

breaks, we casually chat to them about problems like smoking, drugs and drinking.[31]

It is impossible to establish from the officer's response the degree of trust between the unit and young people in this particular sector but it does demonstrate that the officers made an effort to engage with students as well as school administrators.

While the officers from RPZ1 had the support of their Sector Chief when it came to devoting a significant portion of their time to working on youth-related issues, they recognized that doing so was potentially problematic because these activities did not initially resonate with established subcultural definitions of police work. To this effect, the officers from RPZ1 acknowledged that they had developed a reputation as 'school police' amongst rank-and-file colleagues in their sector as well as in the eyes of certain other RPZ officers based in other sectors where youth work was not a priority. Despite this reputation, their role was tolerated because the officers were able to reassert their credibility as 'real' police officers within their sector. This can be attributed to two factors. First, they had been authorized by their Sector Chief to implement the community policing plan as they saw fit. Second, the officers were able to make effective use of impression management techniques which enabled them to foster an appreciation for their role within their sector. They did this by emphasizing one particular aspect of their role through their interactions with colleagues and supervisors: intelligence sharing.

Impression Management

To crudely summarize Goffman (1956), impression management involves the purposive manipulation of others' perceptions for the purpose of sustaining or advancing a projected definition of oneself. Simply stated, a social being alters their behaviour and personality in relation to those they are interacting with. The 'performer' must segment their audience because different groups have different expectations regarding what constitutes a legitimate representation of a mutually recognized role. Audience segregation is achieved by adopting different fronts which will resonate with

[31] Paraphrasing an officer from RPZ1 during a conversation which took place on 7 March 2011.

the diverse expectations of the intended audiences. By implication, failure to adapt one's front may potentially undermine the credibility of a 'performance' as well as the performer.

Referring back to Bottoms and Tankebe's (2012) work on 'dialogic legitimacy' which was discussed in Chapter 2, it is worth considering that the interactions described by Goffman (1956) constitute a legitimation process through which power holders seek to generate consent from those they seek to subordinate. For legitimation to occur, the power holder/performer must be able to justify their actions and their decisions to their audiences. Actors (or groups of actors) who utilize impression management techniques to manipulate the perceptions of others, be it for the purpose of legitimation or self-aggrandizement, can be said to exercise power over their audience. Insofar as the interactions constitute a dialogue, it must also be recognized that the audience is empowered by its ability to choose to either accept or reject the performance. Accepting a performance means conferring acceptance of the performance and, by extension, the presenter whereas rejecting it means discrediting the performance and, in some cases, the performer.

Police officers regularly utilize impression management techniques in the course of their interactions with colleagues (internal audiences) and members of the public and partner agencies (external audiences). In *Police Work*, Manning (1977: 17) writes, '[t]he police are dramatic actors and they must wrestle collectively and individually with the salient dramatic dilemmas of their role and occupation'. To external audiences, managing impressions represents a fundamental strategy for legitimating their coercive authority. To internal audiences, police officers must utilize impression management to demonstrate cultural fit. Manning (1977: 127–38) writes that the presentational strategies utilized by Anglo-American police organizations generally focus on the 'mandate and mission of the organization' which includes: 'the professionalism rhetoric' and 'the utilisation of scientific management systems'; 'the bureaucratic ideal'; 'technology'; and 'crime statistics'. It is also worth adding 'community policing' to this list.

The officers from RPZ1 made effective use of impression management to alleviate scepticism amongst fellow officers about the strategic value of community policing. As previously noted, the officers from RPZ1 recognized that community policing would take time to implement but that their lack of demonstrable short-term 'results' risked jeopardizing the long-term sustainability of this specialist role. Sustaining the role was necessary for sustaining their focus on youth. To this effect, one of the officers from RPZ1 described how the unit's early inability to achieve results using the 'security marketing' methodology fuelled cynicism from patrol-based colleagues who appeared to be resentful of the unstructured and improvisational nature of their work in the community.[32] This problem was particularly evident in relation to what the officers determined to be an important partnership-building ritual: drinking coffee with local residents. The officer observed, 'when we go and drink coffee at a shopping centre, we are also doing work, gathering intelligence, meeting with the public... the other officers don't see this'.

It was even more crucial that the officers retained the support of senior managers, specifically their Sector Chief who, as one of the RPZ officers noted, 'makes all the station's strategic decisions so if he doesn't care about [community policing] or know about [community policing], it won't work'.[33] Without the support of this individual, the officers recognized that they would be denied the privilege of defining their own operational priorities which enabled them to attend community meetings at which local residents would voice their concerns about various public safety issues. One of the officers described the importance of maintaining their flexible working schedule.

...meetings take place between 18:00 and 19:00...Normally we work from 7:30 to 16:00 however there are 27 [local community centres] in [the sector] and 6–7 meetings take place each month. We try to go to all of them because attendance is part of the trust building exercise. If they see you are interested when there is not a problem, this will build trust. You must always go though, not just when you need something.[34]

The officer added that 'if the Chief is made to recognise the benefits of [community policing] as a problem-solving tool, he will facilitate it'.[35] Unable to initially present their colleagues and supervisors

---

[32] Conversation with an officer from RPZ1 in March 2011.

[33] Paraphrasing a conversation with an officer from RPZ1 on 9 March 2011.

[34] Paraphrasing an officer from RPZ1 during a conversation on 7 March 2011. Elsewhere Pino (2001: 202–3) describes the emphasis on trust-building in community policing as 'social capital building'.

[35] Research by Wycoff and Skogan (1994) supports the idea that participatory management and operational autonomy can have a significant positive impact

with an immediate sense of the tangible benefits of security marketing or partnership-building, the officers recognized that their
intelligence sharing role afforded them a means of asserting their
credibility to fellow officers. This was achieved by constructing
an image of their role that would fit with established subcultural
definitions of police work, at least as it was meant to be performed
by male officers in Sarajevo Canton.

Before I proceed to account for these subcultural translations,
it is worth acknowledging that the gendered status of police work
in Sarajevo Canton did not necessarily detract from the professional credibility of female police officers. Rather, as a carry-over
from the Yugoslav era, female officers performed unique, albeit
gendered roles such as dealing with female residents or administrative matters. In fact, one of the station supervisors made a point
of saying that female officers were valued by their male colleagues
because of their ability to deal with elderly women who continued to model their expectations of policing on the Yugoslav era
and, thus, felt uncomfortable dealing with male officers.[36] This is
not to suggest that females were accorded equal status within the
organization or that they were encouraged or indeed allowed to
perform certain roles reserved for their male counterparts. Rather,
the point is that the seemingly unique relationship between male
and female officers in Sarajevo Canton was a product of police
culture (and societal culture in a broader sense) which was shaped,
at least in part, by the historical legacy of policing in this context.
On more than one occasion, I noticed female RPZ officers wearing
strong perfume on the job. At one point, I observed a senior officer
proclaim, 'Scent of a Woman', in the presence of one of the female
RPZ officers.[37] The female officer smiled and did not appear to
take offence. Again, this suggests different expectations regarding gender relations within the organization, notably, the fact that
female officers within the Sarajevo Canton police did not appear
to feel a need to hide their femininity in order to assert their professional credentials.[38]

on the receptiveness of community police officers themselves to change and the
extent to which they perceive the significance of their work.

[36] Paraphrasing one of RPZ1's Station Supervisors during a conversation on
7 March 2011.

[37] Quoting the RPZ Coordinator for Sarajevo Canton on 4 March 2011.

[38] Field notes, 4 March 2011.

Because three of the officers from RPZ1 were male, there was a need for them to present a masculinized version of community policing to colleagues. One of the ways that they did this was by assuming responsibility for managing the sector's crime map. They drew from their growing network of 'partners' in order to generate intelligence on criminal activity in the sector and this allowed the unit to demonstrate that it was working towards recognized goals of crime fighting and prevention.

One of the officers described how the unit combined intelligence sharing with security marketing to address a recent wave of bet shop[39] robberies in the sector. The officers determined that bet shops represented attractive targets because they regularly held up to 30,000 KM[40] in cash on site and the owners refused to hire security guards or invest in preventative technologies because the money was insured. Previously, lottery shops served as ideal targets for armed robberies but the officers noted that the Canton had recently introduced legislation requiring the owners to employ armed security guards as a condition of their licence, after which the sector had only experienced one recorded incident. Part of the problem appeared to stem from displacement but the officers recognized that the bet shop owners had political connections in the Canton which negated the prospect of reducing the opportunities by drafting similar legislation. What they did then was use their intelligence sharing role to identify high risk locations and feed this information back to their Shift Commanders who would strategically assign uniformed and plain clothes officers to 'problem areas'.

This illustrates that the unit's ability to translate its work into culturally acceptable practices clearly benefitted from the social capital that the officers had accumulated in the community through their ongoing partnership building activities. They also drew on these connections to support criminal investigations. This was observed in the aftermath of an aborted bank robbery that occurred approximately 200 metres from the police station where I sat drinking coffee with the officers during my second day of observation with RPZ1. The experience is documented in my field notes:

Our discussion is then interrupted by a call over the radio... An armed bank robbery is in progress a few blocks away. The room becomes very

---

[39] Elsewhere referred to as 'betting shops' in the UK.
[40] Approximately €15,000.

tense. We wait for a while as the officers listen to the call. After a few minutes of listening they decide to respond. 'Come on they say'. [Two RPZ officers] run ahead while I follow about 20 paces behind with [a third]. We are on the hunt for an armed robbery suspect... We reach the team's car and drive a few blocks, get out and walk over to the scene of the incident, all the time the officers are scanning for possible suspicious individuals. The mood is tense but their guns are not drawn so I assume this means that they do not think the suspect is a threat if confronted. We stand around for a while [and two of the RPZ officers] talk with other [patrol] officers who arrive at the scene before [we return] to the car and drive around in search of the nondescript subject. This seems pointless to me given that we are looking for a masked male suspect in the middle of winter (everybody has beanies and hoods on). [One of the officers] notes that if the suspect isn't found the police will go around and ask for information. We give up the search and we head back to the station and my assumption is that this will now be the focus for the rest of the day (field notes, 7 March 2011).

The officers' decision to respond to the call enabled them to express their solidarity with their colleagues on patrol and the investigators called to the scene. It served to reaffirm their professional identity as police officers by outwardly emphasizing the masculine attributes of their interpretation of community police work. The investigation of the incident also provided the officers with an opportunity to show off their unique intelligence sharing abilities and to express the utility of what was perceived by their colleagues to represent a more feminized approach to policing as an adjunct to traditional response-based policing activities.

Throughout the day, the officers placed calls to various contacts in an attempt to solicit information about the incident. Hours later, one of the officers received a phone call on their personal mobile phone from a local shopkeeper who confirmed the identity of the suspect.

We sit around drinking coffee for a while when all of a sudden all three officers start getting a bunch of phone calls. Then they start calling people. About 10 minutes later, without much sense of enthusiasm or achievement [one of the officers] announces, 'that was a local shop owner calling who knows [the fourth RPZ officer who was not present]. [The informant] called me because now [they] trust all of us. [They] know that we will not reveal [their] identity in our report and keep the tip anonymous. [They] gave us intelligence on the attempted bank robber from earlier. We know who [they are] now'. I ask [the officer if the informant] would have given this information to any patrol officer. 'No, because [the individual] doesn't trust that [the patrol officers] will keep [the informant's] identity secret.[41]

Implicit in this response is the officer's belief that members of the public also viewed the officers from RPZ1 as being distinct from their 'traditional' rank-and-file counterparts and, thus, more approachable.

The next morning, a different officer from RPZ1 explained that, upon receiving this tip, the unit filed an anonymous report with the criminal investigation unit and an arrest was imminent. While it is impossible to establish whether the interaction which led to the arrest was genuine,[42] a follow-up interview with a shift supervisor confirmed that members of the public, at least those who were familiar with community policing, were more willing to come forward with information to RPZ officers than patrol officers because they trusted them to protect their identity.[43] This implies that the feminized scripts for community policing may have actually enhanced the appeal of the officers from RPZ1 to members of the public and, by extension, their legitimate authority. Furthermore, while the officer's comment does not alone provide a sufficient empirical basis for determining whether or not the public actually 'trusted' the officers from RPZ1, it does highlight the fact that the officers were comfortable with dissociating themselves from their colleagues in order to demonstrate the advantages of community policing.

By translating the SDC's scripts for community policing into culturally accepted roles and practices, the officers from RPZ1 made important progress towards validating the model. I encountered further evidence of this during a follow-up interview with RPZ1's station commander and a shift supervisor. The commander reflected that 'for the last 10-15 years, the police station has been working to find a way to implement similar strategies, aimed at improving public trust in the police' but previous initiatives had failed because they emphasized the idea that 'every officer should be a [community police] officer'. This sentiment was echoed by the shift supervisor who noted that '... in theory, every officer should be a [community police] officer but the reality is that patrol officers

---

[41] Field notes, 7 March 2011.
[42] As opposed to having been staged for my benefit.
[43] Interview with RPZ1's shift commander on 4 April 2011.

have too many other responsibilities'. The shift supervisor added that this model of community policing 'is excellent because it contributes to improved communication with the public that serves to enhance trust with the police'.[44]

RPZ1's concerns about the long-term sustainability of their progress highlights the significance of their individual contributions to the implementation process. Responding to my question, 'what happens when you get promoted or when [one of the officers] leaves the department', a member of the unit replied, 'this is a big concern... we have discussed it with our chief and he agrees that the success of [community policing in this sector]... is down to [us] and the trust [we] have established'.[45] This response indicates that the social capital accumulated by the officers from RPZ1 enhanced their agentive capacity and, in turn, allowed them to make progress towards rendering community police work legitimate in the eyes of their colleagues and supervisors. Equally, it suggests that the absence of a wider mechanism for collective action such as, for example, a police union that embraced the initiative or even formal recognition of the RPZ role within the Canton meant that this progress was not necessarily sustainable. If the officers were promoted as a result of their success or assigned to perform a different role, the legacy of community policing in their sector would depend at least in part on the ability and the willingness of their replacements to use their agency to advance a similar agenda. As the experience of their counterparts from RPZ2 indicates, this was far from inevitable.

RPZ2

Whereas the officers from RPZ1 were highly successful in using impression management techniques to demonstrate the utility of their role to colleagues and supervisors, other units failed to replicate their success. Part of the problem was that the unit's operational routines were defined primarily by their Sector Chief and Station Commander rather than by the RPZ officers themselves. RPZ2's Sector Chief tolerated community policing but did not embrace it like his counterpart in RPZ1's sector. In other words,

---

[44] Quoting RPZ1's shift supervisor during an interview which took place on 4 April 2011.

[45] Paraphrasing a conversation with an officer from RPZ1 on 7 March 2011.

the Chief did not view the RPZ role as a priority for the sector due to the station's limited budget and personnel shortage. This view was also influenced by important contextual differences between the two sectors, mainly the fact that RPZ1 operated in what was a largely residential sector while the officers from RPZ2 were based in what the Canton's RPZ Coordinator described as 'the most demanding sector' in the city centre.[46] The challenge of policing this sector was linked with the fact that it was home to numerous international organizations, government agencies, and commercial premises which meant that the job was by its very nature unpredictable. Strikes and protests were common occurrences and the Chief was also frequently required to contribute officers for diplomatic protection activities. Faced with the options of diverting patrol officers to perform these tasks or using the RPZ officers, the Sector Chief regularly chose the latter.

Limited Autonomy

The Sector Chief justified the decision to assign RPZ officers to take on this public order policing role by suggesting that it was part of community policing. He explained:

[the officers] are used as go-betweens between the patrol officers and the citizens [and] they are not involved with repressive activities ... these officers are supposed to talk with people and reduce tensions.[47]

Was this a case of managerial resistance to change or an honest attempt by the Sector Chief to adapt the model to fit the needs of the sector? Skogan (2008: 24) argues that middle and senior police managers may be resistant to community policing and problem-oriented policing models because they afford a significant degree of discretion to rank-and-file officers and this is seen to erode the ability of senior officers to exercise hierarchical control over their subordinates in the field. The officers from RPZ2 were permitted to schedule their community policing activities around their public order policing duties but the arrangement rendered them hesitant to schedule meetings with established or prospective 'partners' because of the risk that they might be forced to cancel at the last

---

[46] Quoting the RPZ Coordinator during a conversation on 4 March 2011.

[47] Paraphrasing RPZ2's Sector Chief during an interview conducted on 5 April 2011.

minute.[48] To this effect, one of the officers from RPZ2 described how 'protests are not predictable which means that on days when we are assigned to work [them], [we] cannot make other plans because [we] will not know how long [we] are there'.[49] On the other hand, it is worth considering that the Sector Chief was probably in a better position to define the strategic priorities for policing in this sector than the RPZ officers, the SDC, or I. The point is that, regardless of the motives, this manager played an important role in translating the RPZ role in a manner he thought would render it better suited to the needs of the sector.

The consequence of limited autonomy was that the officers from RPZ2 struggled to establish a network of partners throughout the community. This restricted their ability to utilize their security marketing toolkit and make use of intelligence sharing as a means of demonstrating their worth to colleagues and supervisors. This dynamic was evident from a series of encounters between the officers and individuals whom the officers described as 'partners'. During an impromptu 'patrol', my interpreter Adnan and I accompanied one of the officers from RPZ2 at a series of unscheduled meetings with: a secretary for a neighbourhood community centre (known as a 'mesne zajednice'); a bet shop owner; a school director; and the chief psychiatrist at a methadone clinic. None of these 'partners' revealed any 'problems' for the officer to address and nor did the officer appear to be following up on previous issues. Rather, the 'partners' repeatedly assured us that 'everything is ok' and their relationship with the officers from RPZ2 was 'good'. Adnan and I concluded that these meetings were likely staged for our benefit, albeit without the prior knowledge of the 'partners' who appeared surprised and inconvenienced by our appearance.

We also determined that these individuals exhibited little interest in presenting their problems to this officer, perhaps because they did not believe that the officer possessed the authority or the influence to address the underlying issues. For example, the secretary from the community centre informed the officer that diplomats at a nearby embassy were illegally parking their cars on a side street and that this was creating traffic problems for local residents. They commented that when she previously brought this matter to the

---

[48] Conversation with the RPZ Coordinator on 4 March 2011.
[49] Paraphrasing a personal communication with an officer from RPZ2 on 15 March 2011.

attention of the traffic police, the response she received was that the police were unable to intervene because the vehicles had diplomatic plates. The secretary then explained that there had been some issues with drug dealing in the neighbourhood but assured us that it was 'not really a problem' because 'everybody knows who is responsible and parents tell their kids to avoid them'.[50] On the basis of this assurance, the officer from RPZ2 did not appear to press the matter further.

The following day, Adnan and I observed another impromptu meeting that took place between all three officers from RPZ2 and a secretary from another community centre. This encounter gave us further cause to question the genuineness of the 'partnerships'. At the beginning of this meeting, the officers introduced me as a representative from UNDP and instructed the secretary to discuss their relationship with the unit. The individual replied, 'the partnership between the [community centre] and the police is ok, but it could be better'. When asked to elaborate on why the 'partnership' was lacking and how it could be improved, the individual responded, '[RPZ2] could visit more often' but refused to elaborate further in the presence of the officers. The comment prompted a heated exchange (in Bosnian) between the secretary and the officers which, as Adnan subsequently informed me, involved a complaint filed by the secretary that the officers from RPZ2 had not dealt with. Apparently, a number of local residents had complained to the secretary about underage drinking and loud music from a local café. The secretary brought this matter to the attention of one of the officers from RPZ2 during a previous meeting but the officer neglected to intervene. Following Adnan's debrief, I asked one of the male officers from RPZ2 for his take on the matter. His response was that 'this is not our job but the job of environmental police'.[51] This indicates a degree of resistance to the RPZ role from the officers themselves.

Constructing the 'Community'

My observation of partnership working as it was performed by the officers from RPZ2 stands in stark contrast to my account

---

[50] Paraphrasing a conversation with a Secretary from a local community centre on 14 March 2011.

[51] Paraphrasing a conversation with an officer from RPZ2 on 15 May 2011.

of partnership working as it was performed by the officers from RPZ1. In other words, the officers from RPZ1 unit contacted their 'partners' in advance to inform them of the purpose of the visit and the fact that I would be present. In cases where we arrived without prior notice, the officers from RPZ1 and I were warmly received and the 'partners' spoke openly in front of the officers about the issues they were facing. For example, I attended a series of meetings between the officers from RPZ1 and representatives from a local charity that provided day care services for residents of the municipality with mental health issues.[52] At one of the meetings, the officers even stopped to purchase flowers for the charity's director to mark the occasion of International Women's Day which is widely celebrated in BiH. The flowers were well-received by the charity director who hugged both of the officers present and invited them to stay for coffee. As previously stated, drinking coffee with partners represented an important intelligence sharing ritual in Sarajevo Canton because it provided the officers with an informal opportunity to learn about their partners' problems.

According to the charity's director, the organization was struggling financially and its income was limited to the profits it generated from the sale of handmade crafts and foreign donations. The officers from RPZ1 were candid about the fact that they lacked the influence to persuade the Cantonal government or donors to step in and fund the organization but they had previously supported the charity in other ways. For example, they would on occasion requisition police vehicles (with the Sector Chief's permission) to pick up supplies or take the charity's users to picnics in the mountains and, at one point, the unit even organized a charity concert to raise money for the organization and promote its work to senior police officers and Cantonal officials. The interactions that I observed between the officers and the staff and users of this day centre indicated that this partnership was genuine and well-established. It also demonstrated that these officers were willing to actively promote non-adversarial relations and partnership with segments of the population that experienced high levels of social exclusion and were traditionally ignored by the police. In other words, they used their role to promote an inclusive definition of the community.

---

[52] This included individuals who were thought to be suffering severe post-traumatic stress as a result of their experiences during the war.

The officers from RPZ2 appeared to be less interested in working to develop partnerships with vulnerable and excluded populations in their sector. This was particularly evident from their aversion to the prospect of developing partnerships with members of the sizeable Roma population which resided in their sector. To paraphrase one of the officers from RPZ2:

> ... they have their own system and culture which the police do not understand and that whenever there is a problem they prefer to handle it themselves . . . [we] are called to deal with a problem but when they get there the people pretend like nothing happened making the police look like idiots.[53]

This suggests that the officers from RPZ2 were highly selective in terms of how they defined the boundaries of the 'community' they were responsible for policing. Clearly, the local Roma population was not included in this definition because they were viewed as different and self-contained.

While this dismissive attitude is unsettling from a liberal standpoint, it was also problematic for strategic reasons because it restricted the unit's ability to form links with a population which was widely regarded by non-Roma citizens of BiH as 'deviant'. I frequently encountered this prejudicial view during my time in BiH but it was expressed most explicitly by the Canton's RPZ Coordinator in an interview. The RPZ Coordinator commented:

> young [Roma] kids start as beggars, then they become thieves, then they get involved with drug smuggling or prostitution and then maybe they become murderers.[54]

---

[53] Paraphrasing a personal communication with an officer from RPZ2 on 14 March 2011.

[54] Paraphrasing my interview with the RPZ Coordinator on 14 April 2011. I had previously encountered similar views when speaking with friends about the location of the apartment I was renting. My friends would frequently mock me for living in a 'gypsy neighbourhood' and told me that it was not safe for me to walk home at night. All of the non-Roma residents of the neighbourhood appeared to have bars on their windows and gated driveways. I experienced further anecdotal evidence of this attitude during a meeting I attended between a community secretary and one of the officers from RPZ2. The secretary explained that a local resident recently went to the police to report the theft of a newly purchased shower unit from his home and the officer laughed and casually explained that 'gypsies steal strange stuff which they try to sell off at the local markets' (paraphrasing a conversation with an officer from RPZ2 and the Secretary from a local community centre on 14 March 2011).

If for arguments sake we momentarily accept that Roma are responsible for a disproportionate amount of criminal activity in Sarajevo (note that I am not suggesting this is an empirical fact), the lack of engagement by the officers was problematic because it restricted their ability to gather intelligence about the incidents and prolific offenders. The absence of any evident partnership also restricted their ability to identify underlying social issues that are thought to affect Roma communities in the Balkans, notably poverty and social exclusion. If one adopts a left realist perspective, it is important to consider that the populations and groups which are most commonly associated with criminal behaviour are often the same as those most likely to experience victimization. Research on victimization of Roma in BiH is limited; anecdotal accounts describe the problems of gender-based violence against Romani women[55] and the economic and sexual exploitation of Romani children.[56]

To this effect, a Romani journalist named Hedina Sijercic who grew up in Sarajevo writes:

Along with all this society's discrimination, our women suffer from domestic discrimination in their families as well. They work at home, rear the children, beg, and work for the men who are mostly alcoholic (sic). Our women also have cleaned other houses, and worked, and their husbands take this money to buy first alcohol and then food for the family. Men often beat the women and kids. Kids beat their mothers too, and often some of the men (sic) family members beat the women too (Sijercic 2007).

As one might expect, I did not personally encounter any evidence of gender-based violence against Roma women during my time in Sarajevo but it was not uncommon to see unsupervised and visibly malnourished children, some as young as infants, begging in the city centre. In the evenings, I was told by friends that the children would hand their money over to their guardians. I believe that I witnessed this on more than one occasion. These sights, along with the frequent experience of being confronted by aggressive

---

[55] See, for example: 'Roma Women Turning the Tide of Violence and Discrimination', UN Women, 22 Nov. 2011. Web. 29 May 2014. Available: <http://www.unwomen.org/en/news/stories/2011/11/roma-women-turning-the-tide-of-violence-and-discrimination> [Accessed: 29 May 2014].

[56] See, for example, BiH's Country Narrative in the 2011 Trafficking in Persons Report which was produced by the US State Department (US State Department 2011: 93–4).

female beggars who are generally thought to be Roma, serve to reinforce prejudicial attitudes towards this group.

It is further worth noting that the Roma in BiH are not a homogenous population. In fact, Sijercic (2007) describes how there are two distinct Roma populations in BiH, both of which have historically co-existed with non-Roma citizens in the former Yugoslavia. According to Sijercic (2007), the Gureti-Chergash leave their homes during the summer months while the Thanesko Gurbeti maintain permanent residences. An interview with an RPZ officer based in the 'Old Town', which was popular with tourists and therefore beggars, revealed that the majority of the beggars were Gureti-Chergash, not Thanesko Gurberti. This implies that many of these individuals did not permanently reside in Sarajevo but instead they commuted to the city (or perhaps in some cases were trafficked) from Tuzla (northeast BiH) and neighbouring countries including Serbia. According to the officer, their mobility made it very difficult for police officers to take coercive action against the traffickers of exploited women and children and it also restricted their ability to provide support for their victims.[57]

The prospect of developing a partnership-based approach to policing these transnational communities was also undermined by the assumption that many of the beggars were not even BiH citizens. The implication was that they were not entitled to receive state benefits so there was nothing social services could contribute to an intervention.[58] If we accept that a proportion of this beggar population in Sarajevo were residents of neighbouring countries and potentially stateless,[59] the only means of addressing their victimization and affording them access to basic social services was through a transnational, multi-agency partnership that would link local organizations like the police and social services with their counterparts in neighbouring countries and to national and international organizations including UN Women and the Council of Europe. Even today, no such framework exists and the prospect of developing a viable, transnational arrangement for policing this vulnerable community is limited. The officers from RPZ2 understood the nature of these problems and acknowledged the distinction between the Gureti-Chergash and the Thanesko Gurbeti. They

---

[57] Interview with an officer from RPZ3 on 5 April 2011.
[58] Interview with an officer from RPZ3 on 5 April 2011.
[59] See Council of Europe (2012: 24).

knew that the majority of Roma in their sector belonged to the latter group and had permanently resided in the city since before the Bosnian War but they did not appear to accept them as part of the 'community'. This gives us cause to briefly question what the concept of 'community' actually meant in this particular context.

Elsewhere Herbert (2006: 12) writes:

> [C]ommunity policing, when put into practice, makes a conflation between community and neighborhood. There is an implicit presumption that urban neighbors share common problems of crime and disorder. They should therefore organize at the scale of the neighborhood to address their problems through productive relations with the police.

The conflation of 'community' and 'neighbourhood' was evident from the SDC's model which assumed that highly trained police officers would play an important role in helping local citizens and organizations recognize their mutual interests. It is also evident from late modern, 'Western' political projects that aspire to activate 'communities' as sites of political and criminological action that will act as a remedy to the destabilizing effects of mass consumerism, value pluralism, and the diminishing capacity of the state to exercise formal social control (see, for example, Crawford 1999: 44–54; also Stenson 1993).

Herbert's (2006: 14–15) research on community policing in Seattle led him to conclude that 'community should not typically be seen as an effective carrier for our hopes for localized democracy' because 'constraints on communal efficacy fall more heavily on poorer communities'. The implication, he argues, is that 'efforts to devolve powers to local communities might reinforce existing class-based difference' (Herbert 2006: 15). The practices of the officers from RPZ2 add to this point by suggesting that even well-intentioned efforts to devolve responsibility for governing security at the local level to police officers may serve to reinforce existing social divisions. In other words, their attitudes and inaction when it came to building links with the settled Roma community demonstrates a selective interpretation of the SDC's belief that '[t]he main goal of community policing is to improve the quality of life' by 'solving problems in a sustainable manner' (SDC 2010: 24). Nevertheless, the influence of these officers when it came to designating who should and should not be constituted as members of the community is a testament to both their agency and their translational capacity. It further speaks to the idea that policy inputs play but a limited role in structuring outcomes. In fact, it was the input of the officers which arguably rendered the SDC's model iatrogenic rather than the SDC's prescriptions. Thus, it must be considered that the agency of the actors tasked with implementing off-the-shelf reforms may be responsible for potentially harmful or exclusionary translations rather than development agencies as the so-called functionaries of global liberal governance.

Discussion

From the perspective of the transnational policy actors who contribute to the global dissemination of Western models of policing, local police officers represent the 'end users' of police capacity building projects. This implies that the primary goal of many reformers is to enhance the abilities of local police practitioners to exercise social control in a manner conducive to glocal ordering. The aspiration of improving the local governance and provision of security as a public good is of secondary consequence although it is commonly evoked by reformers who are keen to legitimate their support for these projects. As suggested by the previous case study, it also resonates with members of development organizations who subscribe to the ethos of capacity development. Other reformers such as entrepreneurial consultants are not necessarily indifferent when it comes to the consequences of their work and issues such as political disempowerment but are often constrained and preoccupied by the need to design and implement their models in accordance with RBM regimes.

The case study presented in this chapter supports the argument that the architects of police capacity development projects play an important, albeit limited, role in structuring the mentalities of police officers. By implication, it further suggests that reformers play a limited role in structuring the practices that their projects will generate and, indeed, the societal outcomes that these practices will contribute to. Only one of the units demonstrated evident progress in terms of validating the Swiss community policing model and translating it into institutionally accepted practices but the experiences of both units demonstrates that local police officers play an important role in mediating the 'outputs' of police capacity building projects.

Although a case study is of limited value for assessing the democratic credentials of community policing in developing and transitional countries, it is worth considering that community policing might in theory support enhanced deliberation and may be permissive to the realization of democratically responsive policing outcomes. Elsewhere, for example, Aitchison and I (2013) have argued that there is a degree of overlap between democratically responsive policing and certain philosophical articulations of community policing, particularly in terms of their aspiration to stimulate local input into policing priorities and requiring police to take account of these. In other words, if community policing is defined as a mode of policing that aspires to exercise control through consent and consultation, it is arguably preferable to what Walker (1994:39) has identified as a 'crime attack model' of policing that relies primarily on coercive authority. It is undeniable that policing as an institution must always embody a certain degree of coercion but police practitioners enjoy significant discretion when it comes to determining how and when this coercion is exercised. If the philosophy of community policing shapes the habitus of these officers in a way that renders them less aggressive and more responsive to the needs of citizens, it can be said to improve the vertical responsiveness of the institution.

Cultural and subcultural validation represented an important component of this adaptive process for the officers from RPZ1. This finding is largely consistent with the literature on 'bottom-up reform' (Marks 2000, 2005; Marks and Sklanskey 2012) and the argument that police culture is malleable (Chan 1997; Loftus 2009). It was in relation to the unit's efforts to reconcile its interpretation of the SDC's model with subculturally entrenched definitions of police work that the policy translation process was evident. Local knowledge and social capital represented important translational resources that enabled the officers from RPZ1 to perform this transformational role and this improved the vertical responsiveness of their work. Representatives of international development agencies including the SDC lack the cultural knowledge and social capital to improve the vertical responsiveness of the police without the support of police officers who they rely on as change agents. The officers from RPZ1 clearly recognized their importance in this respect and embraced the challenge.

The officers from RPZ2 did not capitalize on their agency and therefore struggled to foster improvements in the vertical responsiveness of policing in their sector. This implies that weak or failed translations may inhibit the development of democratically responsive policing models in developing and transitional countries. Describing the difficulties faced by the officers from RPZ2, one of the officers from RPZ1 commented, 'successes are down to the people and their approach to work [but] the quality of the people is the most important thing'. The officer added, '[they] must fight for this if they really want community policing to succeed'.[60] This officer was not suggesting that the officers from RPZ2 were incapable of doing community police work. Rather, they were suggesting that they failed to exhibit the intrinsic motivation necessary for creatively addressing institutional and structural obstacles. One implication of this finding is that reformers should seek to enlist the support of motivated personnel when pursing an 'early-riser' approach to community policing reforms in developing and transitional societies. Other translational processes which were evident from the example of RPZ2 included the Sector Chief's decision to incorporate public order duties into the RPZ role and the officers' role in interpreting the concept of 'community' selectively and reproducing existing fault lines of exclusion through practice.

While there is some evidence of the capacity of the RPZ officers in Sarajevo Canton to foster improvements in the vertical responsiveness of local policing, horizontal responsiveness appeared to be weak. Part of the problem was the absence of established accountability mechanisms that the RPZ officers might use to hold their municipal counterparts responsible for delivering on their commitments. While the 'partnership' model has been criticized for its 'instabilities' (Hughes and Rowe 2007), specifically in terms of the perceived risk that centrally defined performance targets might serve as the primary drivers of security governance rather than 'community-oriented work', it is necessary to consider that in the context of Sarajevo Canton, these CSFs might also have helped to ensure that the work of RPZ officers remained congruent with local expectations of general order policing. In other words, CSFs could have constituted an important mechanism for structuring the habitus of RPZ officers and for rendering them accountable to transparent, deliberative processes.

---

[60] Quoting a conversation with an officer from RPZ1 on 21 March 2011.

7

Conclusions

Out of respect for both the complexity and the diversity of transnational policing as a field of study, policy, and practice, I do not intend to conclude this book by drawing from these case studies to articulate a new theory of global, transnational, or glocal policing. Admittedly, this book has focused on narrow and contextually specific manifestations of transnational policing power that are not representative of these fields in their entirety. Nor was it my intention to interpret my analysis in relation to a single discursive or theoretical tradition.[1] Indeed, my analysis combined elements of multiple discursive and theoretical traditions and my interpretation has undoubtedly overlooked others which have eluded me as a Northern researcher with a limited, ethnocentric understanding of this field of study. That said, neither was it my intention to conclude by debunking existing theoretical perspectives on global policing and police capacity building. Although they cannot provide fully comprehensive or definitive frameworks for interpreting these developments, the arguments put forth by Bowling and Sheptycki (2012), Duffield (2007), Ellison and Pino (2012), Hills (2012a; 2012b), and Ryan (2011) are essential for developing a critical understanding of transnational policing power and the potential consequences of its global expansion via police development aid networks.

Accordingly, I will conclude by briefly reiterating my findings in response to the questions I posed in the introduction. I will then elaborate on the idea of 'speaking truths to power' by briefly outlining the preliminary contours of a future programme for

[1] I have adopted this approach following a conversation with my colleague Richard Ireland who is a well-respected legal historian. Richard described to me how a colleague had recently asked him if he viewed his work as 'Foucaultian'. Richard responded, 'I don't know whether or not it's "Foucaultian" but it is definitely Irelandian'.

achieving ethical and impactful criminological research within transnational policy communities. My rationale for doing so stems from my belief that Northern criminologists conducting research 'abroad' have an obligation to ensure that their work fosters a better global politics of crime and security governance, especially in weak and structurally dependent societies.

How and why do international development workers and rank-and-file police officers in developing and transitional states mediate the global convergence of discourse, policies, and practice relating to crime control and security?

Established theoretical perspectives on global policing (Bowling and Sheptycki 2012), police capacity building (Ellison and Pino 2012), and the so-called 'punitive turn' (Wacquant 2009) assume that these phenomena constitute responses to the destabilizing effects of the global proliferation of liberal or neo-liberal policies and discourses. My analysis of two micro-level community policing initiatives in BiH illustrates the limited influence of such policies and discourses in the context of a developing democracy. It further demonstrates that convergence and the global structures which foster it play a partial role in influencing the mentalities and actions of international development workers and local rank-and-file police practitioners from a distance (see Duffield 2007; Ryan 2011). Absent from my analysis, however, was any evidence of a 'subculture of transnational policing' (Bowling and Sheptycki 2012). To reiterate, this is not surprising given that the case studies focused on seemingly disempowered actors involved with the crafting and implementation of low policing. Thus, the absence of evidence does not amount to an outright rejection of its posited existence. Rather, it suggests that a Manichean world view and securitization discourse are not a definitive feature of the transnational policy communities through which glocal policing is crafted. This implies that cultural composition of this field (or collection of fields) is more complex and diverse than has previously been argued.

The main finding of this research is that cultural and structural factors are not deterministic of glocal policing outputs, be they mentalities, structures, or practices. Rather, as argued in Chapter 2, my analysis of the case studies speaks to the idea that glocal policing is crafted through continuous dialogues between the global and the local. Thus, while it is accurate to describe the global structures that give rise to police capacity development projects as asymmetrical or ideologically-rooted, the institutional composition of the policy translation networks that facilitate policy convergence is also diverse. This means that the efforts of the so-called architects of global liberal governance to 'globalize' policing in weak states are mediated by the actions and interpretations of a diverse array of participants who activate key nodes within these networks. The institutions they represent are also diverse and foster distinct organizational habituses meaning that the reasons for individual members to involve themselves with police capacity building projects cannot be reduced to an overarching project of governing security globally. This is not to deny the structuring influence of global liberal governance, regional security complexes, or neo-liberal policy regimes. Instead, it amounts to an argument that these factors and the discourses they generate are forced to compete with institutionalized and localized understandings of concepts like crime and security. Simply, they are not deterministic of policy outputs or outcomes in recipient contexts. By extension, it is logical to conclude that the decision-making processes that take place within these networks cannot be reduced to a Foucaultian analysis which presents international development workers and local police officers as intermediaries of global liberal governmentality. This argument is consistent with Hills's (2009a; 2009b) findings which led her to question the existence and reach of a globalized security culture.

The first case study of the Safer Communities project found that international development workers may feel compelled to align their work with what they perceive to be the interests of powerful donors. It also accounted for their attempts to modify policy meaning and content in ways that were thought might resonate with the interests and the understandings of this international audience. Despite the evident effects of this governmentality, the habitus of my colleagues from the Safer Communities project remained primarily responsive to an institutionalized ethos for capacity development. Furthermore, the habitus was interpreted differently by members of the Safer Communities team meaning that their individual backgrounds and experiences shaped their actions and interactions within this contact zone. The cumulative effect of their contributions to the policy translation process was to mitigate the effects of securitization by identifying creative solutions for retaining a local focus for the project. Their reflexive awareness supported them to this effect and it also allowed them to limit the risk that the project would contribute to harmful or contextually inappropriate outputs.

The second case study which focused on the implementation of a Swiss community policing model in Sarajevo further highlights the fact that the RPZ role was initially developed by a Swiss organization and modelled on the 'best practices' of community policing in Western Europe and the United States. The organization's interests informed the role and concepts like 'problem solving', 'partnership working' and 'responsibilization' were either explicit or implicit in the model. It was evident from the experience of the officers from RPZ1 that these concepts clearly influenced how they performed their work but that the relative weighting of their four key 'scripts' was determined by the officers on the basis of their local knowledge and the need for them to validate their work in the eyes of colleagues and supervisors. Equally, the agency of rank-and-file officers and their ability to influence the policy translation process as 'end users' was also apparent from the problems encountered by the officers from RPZ2. Their failure or inability to translate these scripts into contextually meaningful practices nonetheless illustrated their mediatory function.

The very idea of policy translation challenges deterministic representations of transnational policing power but it is also necessary to recognize that translational activities may prove harmful in their own right. In other words, the fact that policy outputs do not mirror policy inputs does not imply that they will have a positive impact on their recipients. Indeed, it is worth considering that weak translations or mistranslations may actually render policy outputs more harmful than a perfect transplant. For example, the Community Policing Advisor's initial plan to incorporate self defence training as part of a programme for addressing the issue of domestic violence in Zenica might have increased the vulnerability of its participants as well as their perpetrators. With the second case study, the unwillingness of the officers from RPZ2 to engage with the sector's Roma population illustrates the potentially iatrogenic effects of weak translations. Specifically, the officers' unwillingness to accept the Roma as members of the community ensured that this population would continue to be treated as a part of the problem rather than a population which included legitimate victims and valued participants in the 'security marketing' process.

Can the translational abilities of international development workers and rank-and-file police officers support democratically responsive policing in countries like BiH?

The book further suggests that the concept of policy translation and nodal analysis of police reform processes provide alternative frameworks for exploring the ways in which localized human agency can potentially contribute to more democratically responsive policing in weak and structurally dependent countries like BiH. My first case study demonstrated that the capacity development ethos of the international development worker can be oriented towards the goal of establishing structures and institutions that foster what Dryzek (2002) labels 'discursive democratic' governance. This translational inclination was particularly evident in relation to the Safer Communities team's periodic use of participatory policy analysis and policy sharing to manage the project during its pilot phase and in investing its resources in establishing locally governed policy outputs in the form of its CSFs.

The deliberative character of these outputs was also evident from the fact that CSFs constituted governing nodes at which different security actors could hold each other accountable for their role in delivering security (i.e. horizontal responsiveness). The Safer Communities team also anticipated that these forums would improve the capacity of local security providers to collaborate and better respond to the needs of local citizens (i.e. vertical responsiveness). Of course, as evident from the second case study, policy outputs do not determine policy outcomes. This means that the democratic credentials of these CSFs will ultimately be determined by the manner in which they are used. For this reason, the most that can be said about the contribution of international development workers (and reformers in general) to the development of democratically responsive policing in developing and transitional countries is that they may help to establish a permissive framework and play a limited role in structuring the mentalities and practices of those responsible for the local governance and provision of security.

In terms of the contribution of rank-and-file police officers to the actualization of democratically responsive policing, the key issue relates to how they exercise their coercive power. Modern policing is coercive by its very nature but the discretion of individual officers plays an important role in determining when and how this coercion is exercised. Too much discretion risks jeopardizing the objective and professional identify of police officers but as Goldsmith (1990: 91) argues, discretion is also a 'potential resource' for promoting positive change. Community policing as a model for achieving democratically responsive policing may be advantageous if it maximizes opportunities for motivated, educated, and reflexive officers to define their own priorities and cultivate mutually beneficial relationships with diverse stakeholders throughout the community. The emphasis on motivation is consistent with arguments previously put forth by Marks (2000; 2005). The officers from RPZ1 used their discretion and operational autonomy to do just that and this enabled them to contribute to the improved vertical responsiveness of policing in their sector. Their contribution to improving the horizontal responsiveness of policing was largely negated by the absence of a formal framework for partnership working in their sector. By comparison, the officers from RPZ2 did not appear to contribute to improvements in either the vertical or horizontal responsiveness of policing in their sector.

It is evident that international development workers and police practitioners can use their agency to support democratically responsive policing in countries like BiH but one must not ignore the elite characterization of the policy translation processes that structure the contours of glocal policing in these contexts. In other words, the transnational contact zones at which policies and models are developed remain, for the most part, inaccessible to policy recipients. Members of the Safer Communities team and representatives from the SDC relied primarily upon the knowledge and expertise of international experts including Northern consultants and academics when it came to identifying policy inputs but their consultations with local stakeholders, including policymakers and practitioners, were used primarily to refine the models and improve their fit with respect to local circumstances and resources. This suggests that the 'expert' knowledge of local stakeholders had limited influence over the discursive identification of the problems confronting BiH citizens and the solutions for addressing them. It is this lack of input from local stakeholders when it comes to the process of constructing and interpreting issues related to crime and security in transnational policy communities that reinforces their political disempowerment and perpetuates discursive imbalances between the global and the local (see Connell 2007).

How might future Northern criminological engagement with transnational policy communities contribute to a better glocal politics of crime and security?

Speaking truths to power describes an agenda for promoting discursive empowerment and representation through criminological research and engagement. It rejects the idea that the power politics of contact zones can or should be reduced to a single truth, be it empiricist or critical. It recognizes that it is impossible to simultaneously reduce these fields to structural or post-structural narratives of control and disempowerment while also ensuring that one's analyses and interpretations remain representative of the nuanced views and experiences of those affected by transnational policing power. It means using one's research and participation in a contact zone to activate a plurality of voices and perspectives that share a stake in the glocal construction of crime and security. As argued in Chapter 2, this agenda fits with previous articulations of civic criminology, notably the role of the 'democratic under-labourer' which was developed by Loader and Sparks (2010). Democratic under-labouring is a 'sensibility' for prompting critical reflection by initiating constructive dialogues with those who govern and are governed alike. It can be embraced as a subtle form of counterpower and a means of resisting the domineering governmentalities associated with global liberal governance in the fields of transnational criminology. The question is, how might Northern criminologists translate this sensibility into practice?

An ethnographic approach readily lends itself to this mode of criminological engagement because it compels the researcher to continuously reflect on their positioning in their field of study (see Blaustein 2014a). It refutes the idea that knowledge can be objective and, by extension, the possibility that a single truth is waiting to be discovered. Rather, it accepts that truths are constructed through experiences and interactions between the researcher and the field. These interactions are important not just because they allow the researcher to develop understanding, but because they provide opportunities for mutual reflection and open dialogue between the researcher and their participants. As evident from my participatory policy ethnography of the Safer Communities project, these dialogues may help to illuminate potentially harmful mentalities or activities and reduce their potential damage. The policy ethnographer thus assumes the role of the critical friend and can seek to promote democratic under-labouring through the habitus of the setting. It must be acknowledged that democratic under-labouring is itself grounded in a liberal discursive tradition and thus features its own hegemonizing tendencies. However, despite this ideological baggage, the sensibility provides a promising starting point for pursuing Connell's (2007: 213–14) advocacy of a 're-working [of] the relations between the periphery and the metropole' insofar as it demands humility, reflexive awareness, and transparency with respect to the formative intentions and influences of researchers (Loader and Sparks 2010).

A more ambitious prescription for speaking truths to power might involve researchers drawing on their ethnographic fieldwork and collaborating with international organizations, policymakers, and practitioners to develop and utilize innovative policy sharing methods that allow for the 'expert' knowledge and policy preferences of local actors to be factored into otherwise inaccessible decision-making processes. One method which looks to be particularly promising for the purpose of initially structuring discursively responsive deliberations that bring together Northern/Southern understandings, both of a theoretical and a practical nature, is the policy Delphi which Edwards, Hughes, and Lord (2013: 264) argue can be used to 'better validate criminological constructs and support the kind of dialogue implied by public criminologists'. The method is described by Edwards, Hughes, and Lord (2013: 265) in the excerpt below:

The essence of the method is that key informants with established experience of and expertise about the policy problem in question are recruited onto panels; dialogue between panellists is structured by questionnaires that individual panellists complete on their own and return to the coordinators of the panel. Coordinators must summarize and report the responses of individual respondents back to all members of the panel and issue a further questionnaire (Q2) inviting individual panellists to concur or disagree both with arguments arising out of the initial questionnaire (Q1) and with the interpretation placed on these in the coordinator's reports. Through further iterations of questionnaire-report-questionnaire (Q2...Qn), the subjective accounts of the panellists are transformed into the objective opinion of the panel, whether this objective opinion reveals a high consensus of agreement or disagreement. This iterative method of deliberation across various questionnaires or 'rounds' facilitates both respondent and construct validation of the problems in question (Ziglio, 1996). As such, the method is particularly apposite for establishing common referents in arguments across different cultural contexts that might otherwise be lost in translation and through other research methods that do not admit collective respondent and construct validation of criminological problems.

For international development workers who subscribe to a capacity development ethos, 'collective respondent and construct validation' is important for ensuring that their work is simultaneously responsive to global and local discourse and needs. A key advantage of the method might be the anonymity that it affords its participants. This ensures that all of the participants can freely articulate their viewpoints and critically respond to each other without being situationally constrained by pre-existing power inequalities that might otherwise influence their responses. The information generated from this method could be used by reformers to develop a better idea of how their prospective policy recipients understand often taken-for-granted concepts like 'crime' or 'security', to identify and prioritize the problems they are experiencing, and to articulate responses to these issues that reflect a meaningful dialogue between global and local discourses. All of this is consistent with the idea of discursive representation and facilitating glocal dialogues through the use of participatory methods may improve the perceived legitimacy of the interventions prescribed by reformers (Dryzek 2010; see Chapter 2). This may in turn improve the sustainability of the outputs that they generate by encouraging local ownership.

Transnational criminology is an emerging area of study and our ability as Northern criminologists to actively contribute to a better global politics of crime and security governance demands the development of innovative research methods that combine the aim of understanding with that of discursive and political empowerment.

Appendix 1: Research Overview

Table A1.1 Phases of Fieldwork

Phase	Dates	Description
1	April/May 2010	Preliminary visit to BiH. Meetings with CSS, SDC, and UNDP. Access strategy identified.
2	January–April 2011	Internship with UNDP Safer Communities project. Organizational ethnography based on personal involvement with the project and attendance at various meetings. Also conducted the five-week qualitative study of community policing in Sarajevo Canton. Authored two UNDP project reports based on an evaluation of community policing in Sarajevo Canton and a policy brief for introducing the Safer Communities model to the City of Sarajevo.
3	June/July 2011	Follow-up visit to BiH. Interviews with SDC and former Cluster Coordinator at DFID.
4	July 2011–May 2012	Ongoing collaboration with UNDP Safer Communities project via Skype and email. Regular updates from colleagues on project developments and provided with copies of emerging project documents in exchange for feedback.

Table A1.2 Timeline: Safer Communities Project, January 2009–July 2012

Date	Event
January 2009	Safer Communities project established as a component of the SACBiH Project.
December 2009	Safer Communities project receives seed funding.
February 2010	SACBiH team hires **Community Policing Advisor**.
April–June 2010	**Community Policing Advisor**, **Project Manager**, and **Cluster Coordinator** carry out *Baseline Assessment* (published in June).
October–December 2010	Access negotiations with Safer Communities **Project Manager**; Delays with SACBiH Project creates distraction from Safer Communities project.

(continued)

Table A1.2 *(Continued)*

Date	Event
17 January 2011	Start of internship; **Community Policing Advisor** on personal leave.
31 January 2011	Meeting with **Deputy Mayor** for Grad Sarajevo, assigned the policy brief.
7 February 2011	Meeting with **Representative** from Council of Ministers. Safer Communities team works to generate governmental support for CSP model.
7–11 February 2011	**Community Policing Advisor** meets with five different CSFs about Operational Handbooks and project activities.
23 February 2011	UNDP hosts Igmam summit on youth justice.
February–March 2011	**Community Policing Advisor, Project Manager**, and I develop various concept notes and sustainability reports for Safer Communities project.
March 2011	**Project Manager** attends meetings with UNDP senior management to discuss future of the Safer Communities project.
July 2011	**Project Manager** submits policy brief to City of Sarajevo.
13–18 December 2011	I provide feedback to **Community Policing Advisor** on 'Concept Note' to link Safer Communities Project with AVPP.
19 December 2011	**Community Policing Advisor** submits 'Concept Note' to UNDP Cluster Coordinator for review.
January–February 2012	**Community Policing Advisor** and **Cluster Coordinator** map AVPP activities; work to coordinate 'Concept Note'/project proposal with other UN development agencies.
March 2012	'Concept Note'/project proposal submitted to AVPP.
May 2012	AVPP evaluators visit UNDP BiH to discuss 'Concept Note'.

Table A1.3 Timeline: Fieldwork with RPZ Officers in Sarajevo Canton

Date	Event(s)
23 February 2011	Access initiated via conversation with **RPZ1** officers and **RPZ Coordinator** at Igmam summit.
24 February–3 March 2011	UNDP submits formal access request to **Minister of Internal Affairs** for MUP KS who accepts the proposal and passes it on to **Police Commissioner** for compliance. **Police Commissioner** offers his support and designates **RPZ Coordinator** as my official organizational contact.
4 March 2011	Meeting to discuss access and research plan with **RPZ Coordinator**, initial introductions to RPZ1 and RPZ2, research schedule agreed upon.
7 March 2011	*Day One* observation with **RPZ1**. Key events included morning briefing, response to bank robbery, ethnographic interviews with members, visit to local charity, and coffee at a shopping centre.
8 March 2011	*Day Two* observation with **RPZ1**. Key events included ethnographic interviews with team members, coffee with station supervisor, visits to local schools, coffee with patrol-based colleague, response to vehicle accident, second meeting at local charity, RPZ officers pull over a young driver and issue him a warning, more school visits.
9 March 2011	*Day Three* observation with **RPZ1**. Key events included meeting with station commander, ethnographic interviews with **RPZ1** officers, visit to local schools, implementation of 'Civilian Courage' training, lunch with RPZ1 officers.
10–11 March 2011	*Days Four and Five.* Observation cancelled with **RPZ1** as their schedule consisted of 'Civilian Courage' training.
14 March 2011	*Day One* observation with **RPZ2**. Key events included ethnographic group interview, 'patrol' of sector and meetings with different 'partners' including MZ secretary, bet shop owner, school secretary, and Chief Psychiatrist at methadone clinic.
15 March 2011	*Day Two* observation with **RPZ2**. Ethnographic interviews with officers, brief encounter with **RPZ Coordinator**, meeting with second MZ secretary, lunch with officers.
16 March 2011	*Day Three* observation with **RPZ2**. Key events included ethnographic group interview, implementation of 'Civilian Courage', informal meeting with **RPZ Coordinator**.

(continued)

Table A1.3 *(Continued)*

Date	Event(s)
17 March 2011	RPZ Meeting attended by all of the RPZ units in Canton Sarajevo. Presentation by **RPZ Coordinator** followed by presentation by an officer from **RPZ2**, interrupted and concluded by **RPZ Coordinator**.
21 March 2011	*Day Four* observation with **RPZ1**. Key events included ethnographic interview, meeting with **Sector Chief**, meetings with local schools, lunch, and administrative work.
22 March 2011	*Day Five* observation with **RPZ1**. Key events included ethnographic interviews with officers from **RPZ1** and attendance at community meeting about the stray dog problem.
23 March 2011	*Day Six* observation with **RPZ1**. Attended EUPM sponsored SWAT team open day with community police officers and local schoolchildren.
4–13 April 2011	Interviews with other **RPZ** units, station commanders, and RPZ Coordinator (*see* Table A1.1).
Mid-April 2011	Submitted final evaluation report to **RPZ Coordinator**.

Appendix 2: Unpublished Drafts, Documents, and Primary Sources

Table A2.1 List of Unpublished Drafts, Project Reports, and Primary Sources

Referenced as	Title (Doc. Type)	Date	Author	Org.	Description
UNDP 2010	*Baseline Assessment in the Selection of Prospective Communities for the Safer Communities Project* (project report)	Aug. 2010	Safer Communities **Project Manager** and **RPZ Coordinator**	UNDP BiH	Preliminary assessment of policing and community safety in BiH designed to inform the selection of pilot municipalities for Safer Communities project.
UK Policing Services 2010a	*Community Policing Strategy Bosnia Herzegovina (BiH) Evaluation Report* (consultant report)	Nov. 2010	UK Policing Services	UNDP BiH	'On 27th September 2010 the United Nations Development Programme (UNDP), Small Arms Control Programme BiH (SACBiH) engaged UK Policing Services, a UK based consultancy specializing in the Evaluation of Policing, to undertake an evaluation of the level of implementation and outcomes of the BiH Community Policing Strategy published and rolled out for implementation in March 2007' (UK Policing Services 2010a: 2).
UK Policing Services 2010b	*Community Safety Partnership Development Strategic Framework* (consultant report)	Nov. 2010	UK Policing Services	UNDP BiH	Framework for transplanting CSP model to BiH.
DRAFT 'Safer Communities 2012–2015...', February 2011	*Concept Note Safer Communities Project 2012–2015: Security Governance as Social Capital* (project document, DRAFT)	18 Feb. 2011	**Jarrett Blaustein**	UNDP BiH	Draft of a concept note intended to link the Safer Communities project to the issue of social capital which was identified as a priority for BiH by UNDP BiH Human Development Report 2009.

	Title	Date	Author	Organization	Description
DRAFT 'Policy Brief: Community Safety Partnership in Sarajevo'	Policy Brief: Community Safety Partnership in Sarajevo (policy brief, DRAFT)	31 Mar. 2011	**Jarrett Blaustein**	UNDP BiH	Near final draft of the policy brief for the Deputy Mayor. This draft is referenced because it included specific recommendations for piloting the CSP model in the municipality of RPZ1.
Public Opinion Poll 2010	Public Opinion Poll in Bosnia and Herzegovina: Security in the Community ('DRAFT report')	Dec. 2010	Undisclosed research consultancy firm based in BiH.	UNDP BiH	'a quantitative research aimed at the collection of data on the views experiences and attitudes of the general population concerning security in Bosnia and Herzegovina and related issues'. Commissioned by the Safer Communities project.
	Regulation of Job Classification for MUP KS (institutional by-laws)	N/A	N/A	MUP KS, Cantonal Assembly for Sarajevo	A set of by-laws that defines the role of police officers in Sarajevo Canton Police.
	Sustainability Plan of Safer Communities Project in Bosnia and Herzegovina (project document, DRAFT)	Mar. 2011	**Community Policing Advisor** for Safer Communities project, **Jarrett Blaustein**	UNDP BiH	Early draft of sustainability plan for the Safer Communities project. This draft was rejected by the **Project Manager.** The **Community Policing Advisor** continued to develop a plan over the next twelve months, however, no final version of the document was ever agreed upon.

Bibliography

Aas, K. (2011) 'Visions of Global Control' in Bosworth, M. and Hoyle, C. (eds) *What is Criminology?* Oxford: Oxford University Press.

Aas, K. (2012) 'The Earth is One but the World is Not': Criminological Theory and Geopolitical Divisions', *Theoretical Criminology*, 16(5): 5–20.

Aas, K. (2013) *Globalization & Crime*. London: Sage.

Adorno, T. (2007) *History and Freedom: Lectures 1964–1965*. Cambridge: Polity Press.

Aitchison, A. (2007) 'Police Reform in Bosnia and Herzegovina', *Policing and Society*, 17: 321–43.

Aitchison, A. (2011) *Making the Transition*. Cambridge: Intersentia.

Aitchison, A. and Blaustein, J. (2013) 'Policing for Democracy or Democratically Responsive Policing? Examining the Limits of Externally Driven Police Reform', *European Journal of Criminology*, 10(4): 496–511.

Alderson, J. (1979) *Policing Freedom*. Plymouth: Macdonald and Evans.

Alvesson, M. and Sköldberg, K. (2009) *Reflexive Methodology*, London: Sage.

Andreas, P. and Nadelmann, E. (2008) *Policing the Globe: Criminalization and Crime Control in International Relations*. New York: Oxford University Press.

Anzic, A. (1992) 'Policija Kot Stredstvo Oblasti in Varnostni Mehanizem v Jugoslaviji', Revija za kriminalistiko'. *Kriminologio*, 43(1): 13–24.

Arendt, H. (2000) 'What is Freedom?' in Baehr, P. (ed) *The Portable Hannah Arendt* (pp. 438–61). London: Penguin.

Atkinson, S. and Hammersley, M. (2007) *Ethnography: Principles and Practice*. London: Routledge.

AtosKPMG.(2003)*Bosnia and Herzegovina: Community-based Policing and Community Safety: Technical Proposal/Project Memorandum*. DFID. UK Government Balkans Conflict Prevention Pool. [Internal Document, see Appendix 2].

Bauman, Z. (2013) 'Glocalization and Hybridity' *Glocalism: Journal of Culture, Politics and Innovation*, 1–5. Available: <file:///C:/Users/jab107/Downloads/bauman_gjcpi_2013_1%20(2).pdf> [Accessed: 24 April 2014].

Bayley, D. (1992) 'Comparative Organisation of the Police in English-speaking Countries', *Crime and Justice*, 15: 509–45.

Bayley, D. (2001) *Democratizing the Police Abroad: What to Do and How to Do It*. Washington DC: National Institute of Justice.

Bayley, D. (2006) *Changing the Guard: Developing Democratic Policing Abroad.* Oxford: Oxford University Press.

Bayley, D. (2012) 'Police reform: Who done it?' in Marks, M. and Sklansky, D. (eds) *Police Reform from the Bottom Up.* London: Routledge.

Bayley, D. and Mendelsohn, H. (1969) *Minorities and the Police.* New York: Free Press.

Beetham, D. (1991) *The Legitimation of Power.* London: MacMillan.

Belloni, R. (2001) 'Civil Society and Peacebuilding in Bosnia and Herzegovina', *Journal of Peace Research*, 38(2): 163–80.

Bender, K. and Knaus, G. (2007) 'The Worst in Class: How the International Protectorate Hurts the European Future of Bosnia and Herzegovina', *Journal of Intervention and State Building*, 1 (Special Supplement 1). Available: <http://www.davidchandler.org/pdf/journal_statebuilding/JISB%20BOS%205%205%20Bender%20Knaus.pdf> [Accessed: 27 July 2012].

Bennett, C. (1991) 'What is Policy Convergence and What Causes It?', *British Journal of Political Science*, 21(2): 215–33.

Berne, E. (1959/1996) 'Principles of Transactional Analysis', *Indian Journal of Psychiatry* 38(3): 154–9.

Berne, E. (1961) *Transactional Analysis in Psychotherapy.* New York: Grove Press.

Bieber, F. (2010) 'Policing the Peace after Yugoslavia: Police Reform between External Imposition and Domestic Reform'. Paper presented at the GRIPS State-Building Workshop 2010: Organizing Police Forces in Post-Conflict Peace-Support Operations, Tokyo. Available: <http://www3.grips.ac.jp/~pinc/data/10–07.pdf> [Accessed: 25 June 2012].

Binder, D. (1984) 'Drugs Dulling Golden Youth in Yugoslavia', *The New York Times*, 11 January. Available: <http://www.nytimes.com/1984/01/12/world/drugs-dulling-golden-youth-in-yugoslavia.html> [Accessed: 22 May 2014].

Blaustein, J. (2014a) 'Reflexivity and Participatory Policy Ethnography: Situating the Self in a Transnational Criminology of Harm Production' in Lumsden, K. and Winter, A. (eds) *Reflexivity and Criminological Research.* Basingstoke: Palgrave.

Blaustein, J. (2014b) 'The Space Between: Negotiating the Contours of Security Governance via 'Safer Communities' in Bosnia and Herzegovina', *Policing & Society*, 24(1): 44–62.

Blaustein, J. (2014c) 'Community Policing from the 'Bottom-Up' in Sarajevo Canton', *Policing & Society*, Online First: 1–22.

Block, A. (1989) 'European Drug Traffic and Traffickers between the Wars: The Policy of Suppression and its Consequences', *Journal of Social History*, 23(2): 315–37.

Bose, S. (2002) *Bosnia After Dayton: Nationalist Partition and International Intervention.* Oxford: Oxford University Press.

BiH Council of Ministers. (2010) *Operational Handbook on Police-Community Co-operation*. Sarajevo: Saferworld. Available: <http://www.saferworld.org.uk/BiH%20handbook%20English.pdf> [Accessed: 5 January 2015].

BiH Ministry of Security. (2007) *Strategy for Community-Based Policing in Bosnia and Herzegovina*. Sarajevo: CPU.

Bottoms, A. and Tankebe, J. (2012) 'Beyond Procedural Justice: A Dialogic Approach to Legitimacy in Criminal Justice', *Journal of Criminal Law & Criminology*, 102: 119–70.

Bourdieu, P. (1968) 'Systems of Education and Systems of Thought', *International Social Science Journal*, 19: 338–58.

Bourdieu, P. (1977) *Outline of a Theory of Practice*. New York: Cambridge University Press.

Bourdieu, P. and Wacquant, L. (1992) *An Invitation to Reflexive Sociology*. Chicago: University of Chicago Press.

Bowling, B. (2010) *Policing the Caribbean*. Oxford: Oxford University Press.

Bowling, B. (2011) 'Transnational Criminology and the Globalization of Harm Production', in Hoyle, C. and Bosworth, M. (eds), *What is Criminology?* Oxford: Oxford University Press.

Bowling, B. and Sheptycki, J. (2012) *Global Policing*. London: Sage.

Bray, C. (2013) 'Project Explode: Disarmament for a Safer Bosnia and Herzegovina'. Voices from Eurasia. UNDP in Europe and Central Asia, 24 July 2013. Web. 6 May 2014. Available: <http://europeandcis.undp.org/blog/2013/07/24/project-explode-disarmament-for-a-safer-bosnia-and-herzegovina/>.

Bringa, T. (1995) *Being Muslim the Bosnian Way: Identity and Community in a Central Bosnian Village*. Princeton: Princeton University Press.

Brodeur, J.P. (1983) 'High Policing and Low Policing: Remarks about the Policing of Political Activities', *Social Problems*, 30(5): 507–20.

Brodeur, J.P. (2010) *The Policing Web*. Oxford: Oxford University Press.

Brogden, M. (1999) 'Community Policing as Cherry Pie' in Mawby, R. (ed) *Policing Across the World: Issues for the Twenty-First Century*. London: Routledge.

Brogden, M. (2002) 'Implanting Community Policing in South Africa: A Failure of History, of Context, and Theory', *Liverpool Law Review*, 24: 157–79.

Brogden, M. (2005) ' "Horses for Courses" and "Thin Blue Lines": Community Policing in Transitional Society', *Police Quarterly*, 8: 64.

Brogden, M. and Nijhar, P. (2005) *Community Policing: International Concepts and Practice*. Cullompton: Willan.

Brogden, M. and Shearing, C. (1993) *Policing for a New South Africa*. London: Routledge.

Browne, S. (2011) *The UN Development Programme and System*. London: Routledge.

Bulmer, S., Dolowitz, D., Humphreys, P., and Padgett, S. (2007) *Policy Transfer in the European Union*. London: Routledge.

Buzan, B., Wæver. O., and de Wilde, J. (1998) *Security: A New Framework for Analysis*. Boulder: Lynne Rienner.

Buzan, B. and Wæver, O. (2003) *Regions and Powers: The Structure of International Security*. Cambridge: Cambridge University Press.

Cain, M. (2000) 'Orientalism, Occidentalism and the Sociology of Crime', *British Journal of Criminology*, 40(2): 239–60.

Caplan, R. (2004) 'International Authority and State Building: The Case of Bosnia and Herzegovina', *Global Governance*, 10: 53–65.

Centre for European Perspective (2008) 'Seminar on Police Reform in Bosnia and Herzegovina: Security Sector Reform and the Stabilisation and Association Process Report'. Sarajevo. 4–6 June. Available: <http://www.eupm.org/FCKeditor/Images/File/CEP%20brosura%20EN. pdf> [Accessed: 1 December 2012].

Chan, J. (1996) 'Changing Police Culture', *The British Journal of Criminology*, 36(1): 109–34.

Chan, J. (1997) *Changing Police Culture: Policing in a Multicultural Society*. Cambridge: Cambridge University Press.

Chandler, D. (1999) *Bosnia: Faking Democracy After Dayton*. London: Pluto Press.

Chandler, D. (2002) *From Kosovo to Kabul: Human Rights and International Intervention*. London: Pluto Press.

Chandler, D. (2006) *Empire in Denial: the Politics of State-building*. London: Pluto.

Chandler, D. (2010) *International Statebuilding: The Rise of Post-Liberal Governance*. London: Routledge.

Cohen, J. (1997) 'Deliberation and Democratic Legitimacy' in Bohman, J. and Rehg, W. (eds) *Deliberative Democracy*. Cambridge: MIT Press.

Cohen, S. (1988a). 'Western Crime-Control Models' in Cohen, S. (ed) *Against Criminology*. New Brunswick: Transaction Books.

Cohen, S. (1988b) 'The Last Seminar' in Cohen, S. (ed) *Against Criminology*. New Brunswick: Transaction Books.

Collantes-Celador, G. (2005) 'Police Reform: Peacebuilding through "Democratic Policing"?', *International Peacekeeping*, 12(3): 364–76.

Collantes-Celador, G. (2007) 'The European Union Police Mission: The Beginning of a New Future for Bosnia and Herzegovina?' (Vol. Working Paper no. 9). Barcelona: Barcelona Institute.

Collantes-Celador, G. (2009) 'Becoming "European" through Police Reform: A Successful Strategy in Bosnia and Herzegovina?', *Crime, Law and Social Change*, 51(2): 231–42.

Connell, R. (2007) *Southern Theory*. Cambridge: Polity Press.

Cooke, M. (2000) 'Five Arguments for Deliberative Democracy', *Political Studies*, 48: 947–69.

Council of Europe (2012) *Human Rights of Roma and Travellers in Europe*. Paris: Council of Europe Publishing.

Crawford, A. (1999) *The Local Governance of Crime: Appeals to Community and Partnerships*. Oxford: Oxford University Press.

Crawford, A. (2009) *Crime Prevention Policies in Comparative Perspective*. Cullompton: Willan.

Davis, R., Henderson, N., and Merrick, C. (2003) 'Community Policing: Variations on the Western Model in the Developing World', *Police Practice and Research*, 4(3): 285–300.

DeBlieck, S. (2007) *The Critical Link: Community Policing Practices in South East Europe*. UNDP Albania/SSSR Programme. Available: <http://www.ssrnetwork.net/uploaded_files/3578.pdf> [Accessed: 2 December 2012].

deLeon, P. (1992) 'The Democratization of the Policy Sciences', *Public Administration Review*, 52(2): 125–9.

Deljkić, I. and Lučić-Ćatić, M. (2011) 'Implementing Community Policing in Bosnia and Herzegovina', *Police Practice and Research*, 12(2): 172–84.

Deosaran, R. (2002) 'Community Policing in the Caribbean: Context, Community and Police Capability', *Policing: An International Journal of Police Strategies and Management*, 25(1): 125–46.

DFID (2005) 'Community-Based Policing and Community Safety: A Best Practice Toolkit', Balkan Safety, Security and Access to Justice Programme. *Internal Document*.

Dolowitz, D. and Marsh, D. (1996) 'Who Learns What from Whom: a Review of the Policy Transfer Literature', *Political Studies*, XLIV: 343–57.

Dolowitz, D. and Marsh, D. (2000) 'Learning from Abroad: The Role of Policy Transfer in Contemporary Policy-making', *Governance*, 13(1): 5–24.

Doyle, M. (1983) 'Kant, Liberal Legacies, and Foreign Affairs', *Philosophy & Public Affairs*, 12(3): 205–35.

Doyle, M. (2011) *Liberal Peace: Selected Essays*. London: Taylor and Francis.

Dryzek, J. (2002) *Deliberative Democracy and Beyond: Liberals, Critics, Contestations*. Oxford: Oxford University Press.

Dryzek, J. (2006) *Deliberative Global Politics: Discourse and Democracy in a Divided World*. Cambridge: Polity Press.

Dryzek, J. (2010) *Foundations and Frontiers of Deliberative Governance*. Oxford: Oxford University Press.

Duffield, M. (1999) *Global Governance and the New Wars: The Merging of Development and Security*. London: Zed Books.

Duffield, M. (2007) *Development, Security and Unending War: Governing the World of Peoples*. Cambridge, England: Polity.

Dziedzic, M. and Bair, A. (1998) 'Bosnia and the International Police Task Force' in Oakley, R., Dziedzic, M., and Goldberg, E. (eds) *Policing the New World Disorder: Peace Operations and Public Security*. Washington: National Defence University Press.

Eck, J.E. and Rosenbaum, D.P. (1994) 'The New Police Order: Effectiveness, Equity, Efficiency in Community Policing' in Rosenbaum, D. (ed) *The Challenge of Community Policing: Testing the Promises*. Thousand Oaks: Sage.

Edwards, A. and Hughes, G. (2009). 'The Preventative Turn and the Promotion of Safer Communities in England and Wales' in Crawford, A. (ed) *Crime Prevention Policies in Comparative Perspectives*. Cullompton: Willan.

Edwards, A., Hughes, G., and Lord, N. (2013) 'Urban Security in Europe: Translating a Concept in Public Criminology', *European Journal of Criminology*, 10(3), 260–83.

Elias, N. (2000) *The Civilizing Process*. London: Blackwell.

Ellison, G. (2007) 'Fostering a Dependency Culture: The Commodification of Community Policing in a Global Marketplace' in Goldsmith, A. and Sheptycki, J. (eds) *Crafting Transnational Policing: Police Capacity-building and Global Policing Reform*. Oxford: Hart.

Ellison, G. and Pino, N. (2012) *Globalization, Police Reform and Development*. London: Palgrave MacMillan.

Ellison, G. and Sinclair, G. (2013) 'Entrepreneurial Policing? International Policing Challenges', *Open Democracy*. Available: <http://oro.open.ac.uk/38329/3/Sinclair_Ellison_OD_July_2–13_R2.pdf> [Accessed: 24 April 2014].

Ericson, R. (1982) *Reproducing Order: A Study of Police Patrol Work*. Toronto: University of Toronto Press.

Ericson, R. and Haggerty, K. (1997) *Policing the Risk Society*. Toronto: University of Toronto Press.

EU (1993) *European Council in Copenhagen 21–22 June 1993: Conclusions of the Presidency*. SN 180/1/93 REV 1. Brussels. Available: <http://ec.europa.eu/bulgaria/documents/abc/72921_en.pdf> [Accessed: 28 June 2012].

European Forum for Urban Security. 2010. *Charter for a democratic use of video-surveillance*. Available: <http://www.cctvcharter.eu/fileadmin/efus/CCTV_minisite_fichier/Charta/CCTV_Charter_EN.pdf> [Accessed: 27 June 2012].

European Union Police Mission (2011) 'Mandate' [Online]. Available: <http://www.eupm.org/OurMandate.aspx> [Accessed: 25 June 2012].

EUROPOL (2013) *EU Drug Markets Report: A Strategic Analysis*. Lisbon: European Monitoring Centre for Drugs and Drug Addiction. Available:

<https://www.europol.europa.eu/sites/default/files/publications/att-194336-en-td3112366enc-final2.pdf> [Accessed: 29 Ma 2014].

Evans, M. (2004) *Policy Transfer in Global Perspective*. Aldershot: Ashgate.

Evans, M. (2009) 'Policy Transfer in Critical Perspective', *Policy Studies*, 30(3): 243–68.

Evans, M. and Davies, J. (1999) 'Understanding Policy Transfer: A Multi-level, Multi-disciplinary Perspective', *Public Administration*, 77(2): 361–85.

Foucault, M. (1991) 'Governmentality' in Burchell, G., Gordon C., and Miller, P. (eds), *The Foucault Effect: Studies in Governmentality*. London: Harvester Wheatsheaf.

Freeman, R. (2009) 'What is "Translation"?', *Evidence & Policy*, 5(4): 429–47.

Fielding, N. (1988) *Joining Forces: Police Training, Socialization, and Occupational Competence*. London: Routledge.

Fielding, N. (1994) *Community Policing*. Oxford: Oxford University Press.

Foster, J. (1989) 'Two Stations: An Ethnographic Study of Policing in the Inner City' in Downes, D. (ed) *Crime and the City*. London: Macmillan.

Frühling, H. (2007) 'The Impact of International Models of Policing in Latin America: The Case of Community Policing', *Police: Practice and Research*, 8(2): 125–44.

Fukuyama, F. (1992) *The End of History and the Last Man*. London: Penguin.

Garland, D. (1996) 'The Limits of the Sovereign State', *British Journal of Criminology*, 36(4): 445–71.

Garland, D. (2001) *The Culture of Control: Crime and Social Order in Contemporary Society*. Oxford: Oxford University Press.

Giddens, A. (1984) *The Constitution of Society: Outline of the Theory of Structuration*. Cambridge: Polity Press.

Giddens, A. (1990) *The Consequences of Modernity*. Stanford: Stanford University Press.

Goffman, E. (1956) *The Presentation of Self in Everyday Life*. Edinburgh: University of Edinburgh, Social Sciences Research Centre.

Goldsmith, A. (1990) 'Taking Police Culture Seriously: Police Discretion and the Limits of Law', *Policing and Society*, 1(2): 91–114.

Goldsmith, A. and Sheptycki, J. (2007) *Crafting Transnational Policing: Police Capacity-building and Global Policing Reform*. Oxford: Hart.

Goldstein, H. (1979) 'Improving Policing: A Problem-Oriented Approach', *Crime & Delinquency*, 25(2): 236–58.

Greene, J. (2000) 'Community Policing in America: Changing the Nature, Structure, and Function of the Police', *Criminal Justice*, 3: 299–370. Available: <https://www.ncjrs.gov/criminal_justice2000/

vol_3/03g.pdf?q=understanding-community-policing> [Accessed: 29 May 2014].

Greene, J. (2004) 'Community Policing and Organisation Change' in Skogan, W. (ed) *Community Policing: Can It Work?* Belmont, Ca: Wadsworth.

Habermas, J. (1994) 'Three Normative Models of Democracy', *Constellations*, 1(1): 1–10.

Habermas, J. (1996) *Between Facts and Norms.* Cambridge: MIT Press.

Haggerty, K.D. (2013) 'Ben Bowling and James Sheptycki *Global Policing* Sage 2012', *The British Journal of Sociology*, 64: 365–6.

Hammersley, M. (1992) *What's Wrong With Ethnography?* London: Routledge.

Hansen, A. (2008) 'Strengthening the Police in Divided Societies: Empowerment and Accountability in Bosnia and Herzegovina', *Policing and Society*, 18: 339–61.

Harper, R. (1998) *Inside the IMF: An Ethnography of Documents, Technology and Organisational Action.* London: Routledge.

Henry, A. (2009) 'The Development of Community Safety in Scotland: A Different path?' in Crawford, A. (ed) *Crime Prevention Policies in Comparative Perspective.* Cullompton: Willan

Herbert, S. (2001) ' "Hard Charger" or "Station Queen"? Policing and the Masculinist State', *Gender, Place & Culture: A Journal of Feminist Geography*, 8(1): 55–71.

Herbert, S. (2006) *Citizens, Cops, and Power.* Chicago: University of Chicago Press.

Hibell, B. et al. (2011) *The EPSAD Report: Substance Use Among Students in 36 Countries.* Stockholm: The Swedish Council for Information on Alcohol and Drugs. Available: <http://www.espad. org/Uploads/ESPAD_reports/2011/The_2011_ESPAD_Report_FULL_2012_10_29.pdf> [Accessed: 29 May 2014].

Hills, A. (2009) *Policing Post-Conflict Cities.* London: Zed Books.

Hills, A. (2012a) 'Globalising Security Culture and Knowledge in Practice: Nigeria's Hybrid Model', *Globalizations*, 9(1): 19–34.

Hills, A. (2012b) 'Lost in Translation: Why Nigeria's Police don't Implement Democratic Reforms', *International Affairs*, 88(4): 739–55.

Hobbes, T. (1947) 'Of Commonwealth' in Commins, S. and Linscott, R. (eds) *Man and the State: The Political Philosophers.* New York: Random House. [This is the edition referenced by Ryan 2011].

Hughes, G. and Rowe, M. (2007) 'Neighbourhood Policing and Community Safety: Researching the Instabilities of the Local Governance of Crime, Disorder and Security in Contemporary UK', *Criminology & Criminal Justice*, 7(4): 317–46.

Hulme, D. and Edwards, M. 1997. *NGOs, States and Donors: Too Close for Comfort?* Basingstoke: St. Martin's Press.

Hvidemose, D. and Mellon, J. (2009) *Monitoring and Evaluation Arrangements for the Implementation of Community Policing in Bosnia and Herzegovina: A Case Study.* London: Saferworld.

ICG (2002) *Policing the Police in Bosnia: A Further Reform Agenda.* Sarajevo/Brussels. Available: <http://www.crisisgroup.org/~/media/Files/europe/Bosnia%2046> [Accessed: 25 June 2012].

ICG (2005) *Bosnia's Stalled Police Reform: No Progress, No EU.* Sarajevo/Brussels. Available: <http://www.ecoi.net/file_upload/2107_1306244646_neu.pdf> [Accessed: 25 June 2012].

Ignatieff, M. (2003) *Empire Lite: Nation-building in Bosnia, Kosovo and Afghanistan.* London: Vintage.

Illich, I. (1977a) *Disabling Professions.* London: Marion Boyars.

Illich, I. (1977b) *Limits to Medicine: Medical Nemesis—the Expropriation of Health.* Harmondsworth: Penguin.

Ivanova, V. and Evans, M. (2004) 'Policy Transfer in a Transition State: The Case of Local Government Reform in the Ukraine' in Evans, M. (ed) *Policy Transfer in Global Perspective.* Aldershot: Ashgate.

Johnston, L. and Shearing, C. (2003) *Governing Security: Explorations in Policing and Justice.* London: Routledge.

Jones, S. and Levi, M. (1983) 'The Police and the Majority: The Neglect of the Obvious', *Police Journal,* 56(4): 351–64.

Jones, T. and Newburn, T. (2007) *Policy Transfer and Criminal Justice: Exploring US Influence over British Crime Control Policy.* Maidenhead: Open University Press.

Juncos, A. (2007) 'Police Mission in Bosnia and Herzegovina', in Emerson, M. and Gross, E. (eds) *Evaluating the EU's Crisis Missions in the Balkans,* Brussels: Centre for European Policy Studies.

Kaldor, M. (2007) *Human Security: Reflections on Globalization and Intervention.* Cambridge: Polity Press.

Karstedt, S. (2004) 'Durkheim, Tarde and Beyond: The Global Travel of Crime Policies' in Newburn, T. and Sparks, R. (eds) *Criminal Justice and Political Cultures.* Cullompton: Willan.

Knaus, G. and Martin, F. (2003) 'Travails of the European Raj', *Journal of Democracy,* 14(3): 58–67.

Kržalić, A. (2009) 'Private Security in Bosnia and Herzegovina'. Sarajevo: Centre for Security Studies. Available: <http://www.css.ba/wp-content/uploads/2011/06/images_docs_pscistrazivanjefinaeng.pdf> [Accessed: 13 May 2014].

Kuper, A. (2006) *Democracy Beyond Borders: Justice and Representation in Global Institutions.* Oxford: Oxford University Press.

Kvale, S. (1996) *Interviews: An Introduction to Qualitative Research Interviewing.* London: Sage.

Latour, B. (2005) *Reassembling the Social: An Introduction to Actor-network-theory.* Oxford: Oxford University Press.

Latour, B. (2007) 'How to Think Like a State'. Available: <http://www.brunolatour.fr/poparticles/P-133-LA%20HAYE-QUEEN.pdf> [Accessed: 28 April 2014].

Legrand, P. (2001) 'What "Legal Transplants" ' in D. Nelken and J. Feest (eds) *Adapting Legal Cultures*. Oxford: Hart Publishing.

Lendvai, N. and Stubbs, P. (2006) *Translation, Intermediaries and Welfare Reform in South Eastern Europe*. Paper presented at the 4th ESPANET Conference, Bristol. Available: <http://paulstubbs.pbworks.com/f/Lendvai%20Stubbs%20Bremen.pdf> [Accessed: 25 June 2012].

Lendvai, N. and Stubbs, P. (2007) 'Policies as Translation: Situating Trans-national Social Policies', in Hodgson, S. and Irving, Z. (eds) *Policy Reconsidered: Meanings, Politics and Practice*. Bristol: Policy Press.

Lendvai, N. and Stubbs, P. (2009) 'Assemblages, Translation and Intermediaries in South East Europe', *European Societies*, 11(5): 673–95.

Loader, I. and Sparks, R. (2010) *Public Criminology?* Abingdon: Routledge.

Loader, I. and Walker, N. (2001) 'Policing as a Public Good', *Theoretical Criminology*, 5(1): 9–35.

Loader, I. and Walker, N. (2003) *Civilising Security*. Cambridge: Cambridge University Press.

Loftus, B. (2009) *Police Culture in a Changing World*. Oxford: Oxford University Press.

Mackenzie, S. and Henry, A. (2009) *Community Policing: A Review of the Evidence*. Edinburgh: The Scottish Government.

Maglajlić, R. and Rašidagić, E. (2007) 'Bosnia and Herzegovina' in Deacon, B. and Stubbs, P. (eds) *Social Policy and International Interventions in South East Europe*. Cheltenham: Edward Elgar Publishing Limited.

Manning, P. (1977) *Police Work*. Cambridge, MA: MIT Press.

Manning, P. (2010) *Democratic Policing in a Changing World*. Boulder: Paradigm Publishers.

Maras, I. (2009) 'Exploring European Union-assisted Police Reform in Bosnia-Herzegovina: A Preliminary Assessment of the European Union Police Mission to Date'. Annual Convention of the International Studies Association. New York. 15–18 February 2009. Available: <http://www.ifsh.de/pdf/aktuelles/ISAPaper2009Maras.pdf> [Accessed: 1 December 2012].

Marenin, O. (1982) 'Policing African States: Toward a Critique', *Comparative Politics*, 14(4): 379–96.

Marenin, O. (1998) 'The Goal of Democracy in International Police Programs', *Policing*, 21: 159–77.

Marenin, O. (2007) 'Implementing Police Reforms: The Role of the Transnational Policy Community' in Goldsmith, A. and Sheptycki, J. (eds) *Crafting Transnational Policing*. Oxford: Hart Publishing.

Marks, M. (2000) 'Transforming Police Organizations from Within', *British Journal of Criminology*, 40(4), 557–73.

Marks, M. (2005) *Transforming the Robocops: Changing Police in South Africa*. Durban: University of KwaZulu-Natal Press.

Marks, M. and Sklansky, D. (2012) *Police Reform from the Bottom Up*. London: Routledge.

McMahon, P. and Western, J. (2009) 'The Death of Dayton'. *Foreign Affairs*. Available: <http://www.foreignaffairs.com/articles/65352/patrice-c-mcmahon-and-jon-western/the-death-of-dayton> [Accessed: 31 July 2012].

Melossi, D. and Selmini, R. (2009) ' "Modernisation" of Institutions of Social and Penal Control in Italy/Europe: The "New" Crime Prevention' in Crawford, A. (ed) *Crime Prevention Policies in Comparative Perspective*. Cullompton: Willan.

Melossi, D., Sozzo, M., and Sparks, R. (2011) *Travels of the Criminal Question: Cultural Embeddedness and Diffusion*. Oxford: Hart.

Merlingen, M. and Ostrauskaite, R. (2005) 'Power/Knowledge in International Peacebuilding: The Case of the EU Police Mission in Bosnia', *Alternatives*, 30: 297–323.

Miller, S. (1999) *Gender and Community Policing: Walking the Talk*. Boston: Northeastern University Press.

Miller, S.M. (2001) 'The Participant Observer and "Over-Rapport" ' in Bryman, A. (ed) *Ethnography* (Vol. I). London: Sage.

Mosse, D. (2005) *Cultivating Development: An Ethnography of Aid Policy and Practice*. London: Pluto Press.

Muehlmann, T. (2008) 'Police Restructuring in Bosnia-Herzegovina: Problems of Internationally-led Security Sector Reform', *Journal of Intervention and Statebuilding*, 2(1): 1–22.

Murphy, C. (2006) *The United Nations Development Programme: A Better Way?* Cambridge: Cambridge University Press.

Murray, C. (1990) *The Emerging British Underclass*. London: Institute for Economic Affairs.

Murray, C. (1996) *Charles Murray and the Underclass: The Developing Debate*. Lancing: IEA Health and Welfare Unit.

Nelken, D. (2010) *Comparative Criminal Justice: Making Sense of Difference*. London: Sage.

Newburn, T. and Sparks, R. (2004) *Criminal Justice and Political Cultures: National and International Dimensions of Crime Control*. Cullompton: Willan.

Neyland, D. (2008) *Organizational Ethnography*. London: Sage.

Neyroud, P. and Wain, N. (2013) 'Police Training and Reform in India: Bringing Knowledge-based Learning to the Indian Police Service' in Stainslas, P. (ed) *International Perspectives on Police Education and Training*. Abingdon: Routledge.

Nutley, S. and Webb, J. (2000) 'Evidence and the Policy Process' in Davies, H., Nutley, S., and Smith, P. (eds) *What Works? Evidence-based Policy and Practice*. Bristol: The Policy Press.

OECD and World Bank (2006) *Emerging Good Practice in Managing for Development Results Source Book*. 1st ed. Available: <http://www.mfdr.org/Sourcebook/1stEdition/MfDRSourcebook-Feb-16-2006.pdf> [Accessed: 25 June 2012].

OHR (1995) The General Framework Agreement for Peace in Bosnia and Herzegovina. Sarajevo. Available: <http://www.ohr.int/dpa/default.asp?content_id=380> [Accessed: 25 June 2012].

OHR (2002) *Law on Amendments to the Law on Internal Affairs of Sarajevo Canton*. Available: <http://www.ohr.int/ohr-dept/legal/oth-legist/default.asp?content_id=9192> [Accessed: 29 June 2012].

OSCE (2014) *Preventing Terrorism and Countering Violent Extremism and Radicalization that Lead to Terrorism: A Community-Policing Approach*. Vienna.

Osland, K. (2004) 'The EU Police Mission in Bosnia and Herzegovina', *International Peacekeeping*, 11(3): 544–60.

Paris, R. (2002) 'International Peacebuilding and the "Mission Civilisatrice"', *Review of International Studies*, 28(4): 637–56.

Peace Implementation Council (1997) *Conclusions of the Peace Implementation Conference Held at Lancaster House London*. Sarajevo: Office of the High Representative.

Perito, R. (2007) *U.S. Police in Peace and Stability Operations*. Washington DC: United States Institute of Peace.

Petrovic, Z. (2007) 'Lessons Learned'. Swiss Agency for Development and Cooperation. [Internal Document].

Pino, N. (2001) 'Community Policing and Social Capital', *Policing: An International Journal of Police Strategies and Management*, 24(2): 200–15.

PRC (2004) Final Report of the Work of the Police Restructuring Commission of Bosnia and Herzegovina. Sarajevo. Available: <http://www.ohr.int/ohr-dept/presso/pressr/doc/final-prc-report-7feb05.pdf> [Accessed: 25 June 2012].

Pratt, M.L. (1991) 'Arts of the Contact Zone', *Profession*, 91: 33–40.

Pratt, M.L. (1992) *Imperial Eyes: Travel Writing and Transculturation*. London: Routledge.

Rawls, J. (1997) 'The Idea of Public Reason' in Bohman, J. and Rehg, W. (eds) *Deliberative Democracy*. Cambridge: MIT Press.

Reiner, R. (2010) *The Politics of the Police*. Oxford: Oxford University Press.

Rose, N. (1996) 'The Death of the Social? Re-figuring the Territory of Government', *Economy and Society*, 25: 327–56.

Rose, N. (2000) 'Government and Control', *British Journal of Criminology*, 40: 321–39.

Rose, R. (1991) 'What is Lesson Drawing?', *Journal of Public Policy*, 11(1): 3–30.

Rosenvallon, P. (2011) *Democratic Legitimacy: Impartiality, Reflexivity and Proximity*. Princeton: Princeton University Press.

Reuss-Ianni, E. and Ianni, F. (1983) *Two Cultures of Policing: Street Cops and Management Cops*. New York: Transaction Publishers.

Rummel, R.J. (1997) *Death by Government*. New York: Transaction.

Ruteere, M. and Pommerolle M. (2003) 'Democratizing Security or Decentralizing Repression? The Case of Community Policing in Kenya', *African Affairs*, 102: 587–604.

Ryan, B. (2007). 'What the Police are Supposed to Do: Contrasting Expectations of Community Policing in Serbia', *Policing and Society*, 17(1): 1–20.

Ryan, B. (2011) *Statebuilding and Police Reform: The Freedom of Security*. Abingdon: Routledge.

Sartre, J. 2003. *Being and Nothingness*. London: Routledge.

Scraton, P. (2011) 'Defining "Power" and Challenging "Knowledge": Critical Analysis as Resistance in the UK', in Carrington, K. and Hogg, R. (eds) *Critical Criminology*. Abingdon: Routledge.

Schorer, P. (2007) *Community Policing Project in Bosnia and Herzegovina: Connection with the Strategy for Community Based Policing in Bosnia and Herzegovina*. Swiss Agency for Development and Cooperation. [Internal Document].

SDC (2010) *Manual for Community-Policing in Bosnia and Herzegovina*. Sarajevo.

'SDC Bosnia and Herzegovina—Community Policing'. SDC Bosnia and Herzegovina. Swiss Agency for Development and Cooperation, n.d. Web. 12 May 2014. Available: <http://www.swiss-cooperation.admin.ch/bosniaandherzegovina/en/Home/Domains_and_Projects/Rule_of_Law_and_Democracy/Community_Policing>.

Serber, D. (2001) 'The Masking of Social Reality: Ethnographic Fieldwork in the Bureaucracy' in Bryman, A. (eds) *Ethnography* (Vol. II). London: Sage.

Sheptycki, J. and Wardak, A. (2005) *Transnational and Comparative Criminology*. London: Cavandish.

Sherman, L. (2012) *Developing and Evaluating Citizen Security Programs in Latin America: A Protocol for Evidence-Based Crime Prevention*. Inter-American Development Bank. Technical Note No. IDB-TN-436. Available: <http://idbdocs.iadb.org/WSDocs/getDocument.aspx?DOCNUM=37080762> [Accessed: 28 April 2014].

Shore, C. and Wright, S. (1997) *Anthropology of Policy: Critical Perspectives on Governance and Power*. Abingdon: Routledge.

Sijercic, H. (2007) 'Roma Women in Bosnia and Herzegovina and Bosnian Roma Women in Western Europe'. Presented at the Romani Yag Gypsy Festival. Montreal, Canada. 14 October 2007. Available:

<http://kopachi.com/articles/roma-women-in-bosnia-and-herzego-vina-and-by-hedina-sijercic/> [Accessed: 29 June 2012].

Skogan, W. (2008) 'Why Reforms Fail', *Policing & Society*, 18(1): 23–34.

Skogan, W. and Hartnett, S. (1997) *Community Policing, Chicago Style*. Oxford: Oxford University Press.

Skolnick, J. (1966) *Justice Without Trial*. New York: Wiley.

Skolnick, J. and Bayley, D. (1988) *Community Policing: Issues and Practices Around the World*. Rockville: National Institute of Justice.

Soper, K. (2007) 'Yugoslavia (Former)'. Library of Congress. Available: <http://memory.loc.gov/frd/cs/yutoc.html> [Accessed: 26 July 2009].

Solana, J. (2003) *A Secure Europe in a Better World—European Security Strategy*. Brussels: The European Union Institute for Security Studies.

Spradley, J. (1979) *The Ethnographic Interview*. Austin: Holt, Rinehart and Winston.

Stabilisation and Association Agreement between the European Communities and their Member States, of the One Part, and Bosnia and Herzegovina, of the Other Part. 2008. Available: <http://www.official-documents.gov.uk/document/cm77/7743/7743.pdf> [Accessed: 28 June 2012].

Stenson, K. (1993) 'Community Policing as a Governmental Technology', *Economy and Society*, 22(3): 373–89.

Stojanovic, S. and Downes, M. (2009) 'Policing in Serbia: Negotiating the Transition between Rhetoric and Reform' in Hinton, M. and Newburn, T. (eds) *Policing Developing Democracies*. London: Routledge.

Terpstra, J. (2008) 'Police, Local Government, and Citizens as Participants in Local Security Networks', *Police Practice and Research: An International Journal*, 9: 213–25.

Tilley, N. (2003) 'Problem-Oriented Policing, Intelligence-Led Policing and the National Intelligence Model'. Available: <http://www.dgai.mai.gov.pt/cms/files/biblioteca/id117.pdf> [Accessed: 28 June 2012].

Tizot, J. (2001) 'The Issues of Translation, Transferability and Transfer of Social Policies: French and British "urban social policy": Finding Common Ground for Comparison?', *International Journal of Social Research Methodology*, 4(4): 301–17.

Topping, J.R. (2008a) 'Community Policing in Northern Ireland: A Resistance Narrative', *Policing and Society*, 18(4): 377–96.

Topping, J.R. (2008b) 'Diversifying from Within: Community Policing and the Governance of Security in Northern Ireland', *British Journal of Criminology*, 48(6): 778–97.

ul Haq, M. (1990) *Human Development Report 1990*. New York: Oxford University Press.

UN (1991) *Eighth United Nations Conference on the Prevention of Crime and the Treatment of Offenders*. Havana, 27 August–7 September 1990. New York: United Nations Secretariat.

UNDP (2007) *Evaluation of Results-Based Management at UNDP: Achieving Results*. Available: <http://web.undp.org/evaluation/documents/thematic/RBM/RBM_Evaluation.pdf> [Accessed: 25 June 2012].

UNDP (2009a) *SACBiH Project Document*. Available: <http://www.undp.ba/upload/projects/SACBIH%20Project%20Document%20ENG.pdf> [Accessed: 5 March 2012].

UNDP (2009b) *The Ties That Bind: Social Capital in Bosnia and Herzegovina*, National Human Development Report, Sarajevo.

UNDP (2010) *Baseline Assessment in the Selection of Prospective Communities for the Safer Communities Project*. Sarajevo. Available: <http://www.undp.ba/download.aspx?id=2497> [Accessed: 5 March 2012].

UN-HABITAT (2007) *Safer Cities Programme: A Safer and Just City for All*. Rio de Janeiro. Available: <http://www.unhabitat.org/pmss/images/buttons/pdf.gif> [Accessed: 20 June 2012].

UNSC (1995) *Resolution 1031*. Available: <http://daccess-ods.un.org/TMP/5271601.67694092.html> [Accessed: 25 June 2012].

UNSC (1997a) *Resolution 1107*. Available: <http://daccess-dds-ny.un.org/doc/UNDOC/GEN/N97/128/99/PDF/N9712899.pdf?OpenElement> [Accessed: 25 June 2012].

UNSC (1997b) *Resolution 1144*. Available: <http://daccess-dds-ny.un.org/doc/UNDOC/GEN/N97/375/23/PDF/N9737523.pdf?OpenElement?> [Accessed: 25 June 2012].

UNSC (1998) *Resolution 1184*. Available: <http://daccess-dds-ny.un.org/doc/UNDOC/GEN/N98/207/87/PDF/N9820787.pdf?OpenElement> [Accessed: 25 June 2012].

UNSG (2000) *Report of the Secretary-General on the United Nations Mission in Bosnia and Herzegovina*. S/2000/529. Available: <http://www.unhcr.org/refworld/docid/3ae6af880.html> [Accessed: 25 June 2012].

UNSG (2001) *Report of the Secretary-General on the United Nations Mission in Bosnia-Herzegovina*. S/2001/571. Available: <http://daccess-dds-ny.un.org/doc/UNDOC/GEN/N01/403/88/IMG/N0140388.pdf?OpenElement> [Accessed: 25 June 2012].

US State Department (2011) *Trafficking in Persons Report. Country Narratives: A-C*. Available: <http://www.state.gov/documents/organization/164453.pdf> [Accessed 29 May 2014].

Uster, H. (2007) 'External Evaluation of Phase 10 of the Regional Programme "Supporting Police Reforms in South Eastern Europe"'. Baar: Swiss Agency for Development and Cooperation. [Internal Document].

Vejnovic, D. and Lalic, V. (2005) 'Community Policing in a Changing World: A Case Study of Bosnia and Herzegovina', *Police Practice and Research*, 6(4): 363–73.

Venneri, G. (2010) *'Conquered' vs. 'Octroyée' Ownership: Police Reform, Conditionality and the EU's Member-Statebuilding in Bosnia-Herzegovina*. University of Westminster. Available: <http://www.westminster.ac.uk/__data/assets/pdf_file/0011/81596/Venneri.pdf> [Accessed: 25 June 2012].

Wacquant, L. (2009) *Punishing the Poor: The Neoliberal Government of Social Insecurity*. Durham: Duke University Press.

Wacquant, L. (2011) 'Habitus as Topic and Tool: Reflections on Becoming a Prizefighter', *Qualitative Research in Psychology*, 8: 81–92.

Waddington, P.A.J. (1998) *Policing Citizens: Authority and Rights*. London: UCL Press.

Walker, N. (1994). 'European Integration and European Policing: A Complex Relationship'. In Anderson, M. and Den Boer, M. (eds), *Policing Across National Boundaries*. London: Pinter.

Watson, A. (1974) *Legal Transplants*. Edinburgh: Scottish Academic Press.

Weisburd, D., Shalev, O., and Amir, M. (2002) 'Community Policing in Israel: Resistance and Change', *Policing*, 25(1): 80–109.

Wendt, A. (1987) 'The Agency-structure Problem in International Relations', *International Organisation*, 41: 335–70.

Wendt, A. (1999) *Social Theory of International Politics*. Cambridge: Cambridge University Press.

Wilson, D., Parks, R., and Mastrofski, S. (2011) 'The Impact of Police Reform on Communities of Trinidad and Tobago', *Journal of Experimental Criminology*, 7(4): 375–405.

Wilson, J. and Kelling, G. (1982) 'Broken Windows', *Atlantic Monthly*, March. Available: <http://www.theatlantic.com/magazine/archive/1982/03/broken-windows/304465/> [Accessed: 1 December 2012].

Wisler, D. (2005) 'The Police Reform in Bosnia and Herzegovina' in Ebnother, A. and Flurri, P. (eds), *After Intervention: Public Security Management in Post-Conflict Societies—From Intervention to Sustainable Local Ownership*. Vienna: Bureau for Security Policy.

Wisler, D. and Onwudiwe, I. (2008) 'Community Policing in Comparison', *Police Quarterly*, 11(4): 427–46.

Wisler, D. and Traljic, S. (2010) *External Review of the Community Policing Project of the Swiss Agency for Development and Cooperation: Final Report*. Geneva.

Wood, J. and Shearing, C. (2006) *Imagining Security*. Cullompton: Willan.

World Bank (2013) 'Improving Opportunities for Young People in Bosnia and Herzegovina'. 14 Feb. 2013. Web. Available: <http://www.worldbank.org/en/news/feature/2013/02/14/improving-opportunities-young-people-Bosnia-Herzegovina> [Accessed: 29 May 2014].

Wycoff, M. and Skogan, W. (1994) 'The Effect of a Community Policing Management Style on Officers' Attitudes', *Crime and Delinquency*, 40(3): 371–83.

Yanow, D. (1997) *How Does a Policy Mean? Interpreting Policy and Organizational Actions*. Washington DC: Georgetown University Press.

Young, J. (1991) 'Left Realism and the Priorities of Crime Control' in Stenson, K. and Cowell, D. (eds) *The Politics of Crime Control*. London: Sage.

Young, J. (2007) *The Vertigo of Late Modernity*. London: Sage.

Index